Living Vocationally

Living Vocationally

The Journey of the Called Life

PAUL J. WADELL
& CHARLES R. PINCHES

CASCADE *Books* · Eugene, Oregon

LIVING VOCATIONALLY
The Journey of the Called Life

Cascade Books
An Imprint of Wipf and Stock Publishers
199 W. 8th Ave., Suite 3
Eugene, OR 97401

www.wipfandstock.com

PAPERBACK ISBN: 978-1-7252-7339-9
HARDCOVER ISBN: 978-1-7252-7340-5
EBOOK ISBN: 978-1-7252-7341-2

Cataloguing-in-Publication data:

Names: Wadell, Paul J., author. | Pinches, Charles R., author.

Title: Living vocationally : the journey of the called life / Paul J. Wadell and Charles R. Pinches.

Description: Eugene, OR: Cascade Books, 2021 | Includes bibliographical references and index.

Identifiers: ISBN 978-1-7252-7339-9 (paperback) | ISBN 978-1-7252-7340-5 (hardcover) | ISBN 978-1-7252-7341-2 (ebook)

Subjects: LCSH: Vocation—Christianity. | Life cycle, Human—Religious aspects—Christianity.

Classification: BV4740 .L65 2021 (print) | BV4740 (ebook)

JANUARY 19, 2021

To Stanley Hauerwas
Teacher, Mentor, and Friend

Contents

Introduction | 1

PART I: PREPARING FOR THE JOURNEY

CHAPTER 1
An Invitation to the Called Life | 13

CHAPTER 2
Vocation—Exploring the Traditions | 36

CHAPTER 3
Stories of Call | 62

PART II: THE JOURNEY OF THE CALLED LIFE

CHAPTER 4
Our Vocational Journeys | 87

CHAPTER 5
Discerning Our Callings | 108

CHAPTER 6
Living the Called Life—Dangers and Warnings | 128

PART III: VIRTUES FOR THE JOURNEY

CHAPTER 7
Virtues for Beginning the Journey
—Attentiveness, Humility, and Gratitude | 155

CHAPTER 8
Virtues for Continuing the Journey
—Fidelity, Justice, and Courage | 174

CHAPTER 9
**Virtues for Completing the Journey
—Hope and Patience** | 198

Bibliography | 221
Index | 229

Introduction

PERHAPS THE BEST WAY to introduce this book is to share with you David's story. Today David teaches science in a Catholic high school in the upper Midwest, but he began his career as an engineer for a corporation. He was very good in his work as an engineer, and his salary was substantially more than what he would earn teaching science in a Catholic school; and yet, despite his success, the financial rewards, and the promising career that lay ahead of him, David felt something was missing. He was prospering, but dissatisfied; successful, but discontented.

After much discernment, and long conversations with his wife and some close friends, David left his job as an engineer and began a quite different journey as a high school science teacher. The transition was not easy; in fact, in many ways, David's life became harder because he experienced challenges, frustrations, and setbacks in the classroom that he had never faced as an engineer. During a particularly trying period, his wife asked, "Why don't you go back to your old job?" Without a hint of hesitation, David replied, "Because I've found my vocation." That simple sentence said it all. In taking the risk to leave a job in order to answer a calling, David discovered that to find a calling is to find a good way to live. We agree. To find a calling is to find a good way to live. That insight inspires and shapes this book.

Like David, all of us wrestle with questions that can lead to long late-in-the-night conversations: What is a good life? What would it mean to live one's life well? What gives life meaning and purpose and hope? What fulfills and completes us? Or, more bluntly: How do we avoid wasting our lives? How do we avoid making them little more than a chronicle of endless regrets? Thinking of ourselves as called helps us answer these questions in liberating and hopeful ways. Contrary to the prevailing narratives of consumerism and materialism that press us to believe that meaning and purpose and happiness come from living for ourselves, when we respond to, enter into, and embrace a calling, we discover that we come to life and are fulfilled when, instead of putting ourselves first, we transcend ourselves in love and service to people and projects worthy of the gift of ourselves. We shrivel when we live for nothing more than ourselves; we flourish when we come out of ourselves in order to live for something larger and more compelling. By connecting us to something greater and vastly more satisfying and hopeful than what the gospel of consumerism, materialism, and self-centered individualism promises, our callings (even the most ordinary and mundane ones) save us from ourselves. That is why to have found a calling is to have found a good way to live.

As we hope is clear throughout this book, when we live vocationally, we inhabit the world differently. We think more about giving than taking, more about responding to people's needs than safeguarding our own. Our driving desire is not to insure our own comfort and safety, but rather to make things better for others. Living vocationally impacts every dimension of our lives. It changes how we see ourselves and how we understand our place in the world. It affects how we approach other people because when we live vocationally we recognize that some of the most important callings of our lives can come so unexpectedly and in the most ordinary moments of life. Living vocationally also changes the choices we make and the reasons we make them, because now our decisions and actions must serve the callings to which we have committed our lives. Perhaps most importantly, if we live vocationally the world will be better because of us. That's because callings—even something as simple as comforting a child or preparing a good meal—always increase goodness. Callings, no matter what form they take or how long they last, are fundamentally creative endeavors by which we make our own irreplaceable contribution to something important, whether that's our family, a religious community, a friendship, the church, the surrounding society, or global community.

Throughout the book we speak less of *having* a vocation or *possessing* a calling and much more of *living vocationally* to emphasize that vocation pertains not just to certain areas of our lives, but is rather about all of life. Living vocationally creates a way of being in the world that shapes our lives as a whole. This is why we will continually stress that calling extends far beyond our jobs or our careers, and pertains to much more than whether we marry, join a religious community, or remain single. Our lives are composed of many callings, some of which are more important and enduring than others, but all of which contribute to the narrative of our lives. Living vocationally attunes us to the array of callings that can come to us—responding to a stranger in need, being there for a friend, listening to a child tell a story—and in broadening our understanding of vocation teaches us that the discovery of our callings must be guided by the discernment of the person we are meant to become. Who we are and what we are making of ourselves is a more crucial issue for vocational discernment than trying to determine the right career choice. This is not to say that the careers we pursue don't matter, but it is to claim that trying to decide on a career is not nearly as significant as deciding the kind of person we should be and how we want to shape our lives as a whole. Put differently, living vocationally reminds us that the most important question is not about *making a living*, but about *making a life*.[1]

Moreover, to speak of living vocationally testifies that our callings are dynamic, evolving realities that change over time as we change with them. This does not mean that we forsake our callings—although under certain circumstances it might—but that we grow in them and understand them more completely as we live them. There are also different chapters to our callings. At times, living our callings is relatively easy, uplifting, and fulfilling; but at other times living our callings can be disheartening, confusing, exhausting, and even painful. This is one reason why throughout the book we use the metaphor of "journey" to describe what it means to live vocationally. To speak of our callings as journeys acknowledges that they are dynamic, unfolding realities, that there are stages to living our callings (even unexpected detours), but also that they are thoroughly historical realities because we live our callings in particular times and places. We may shape history in living our callings, but we are also assuredly shaped by history—as well as the social, cultural, economic, political, and religious situations in which we live. Too, to describe our callings as journeys suggests that they have a beginning, a middle, and an end. Most of all, it is fitting to speak of callings as journeys because to take up a journey is not to wander aimlessly, but to be moving both *toward* something and *for* something. The metaphor of journey reminds us that there is a trajectory to human life that gives meaning and purpose and hope to everything we do.

This is why it is also fitting to envision our callings as stories.[2] Good stories have a beginning, a middle, and an end, are held together by a plot, and are full of interesting characters. The same can be said of our callings. To answer a calling is to begin a story. Some of those stories may be no longer than a few pages, some may extend for several chapters, and some may read like a long and gripping novel. We tell the story of our lives through our callings; we add to, revise, and enrich the story as we live it. There is a "plot" to our vocational narratives because our callings reveal the most important goals of our lives and how we hope to attain them, which is something, as

---

1. Fong, "Theological Exploration of Vocation," 6.

2. Henry, "Vocation and Story," 165.

every good story illustrates, that is seldom easily achieved. And, just like a good story, there are a multitude of characters in our vocational narratives because we cannot live our callings without the help, guidance, and support of others. Too, just as we understand a story better the more deeply we enter into it, so too do we gain insight into who we are and where we are headed as we enter into and live our callings. There are many different kinds of callings, but our most basic vocation is the story we are called to bring to life, to grow in and be faithful to, every day of our lives.

And yet, the very idea of calling reminds us that our own story is not sufficient. As we are called, we are invited by another to live into a story that is not fundamentally our own. Calling creates a new story, but as it does so it fits it within a much larger and more truthful story through which that new story can be rightly understood and lived. For Christians, that framing narrative is the story of the God who enters the world to redeem it, who is revealed first to Abraham and the people of Israel and then through the life, teachings, and ministry of Christ to his disciples. This book offers a Christian theology of vocation because we are Christian theologians who believe that the story of God and God's dealings with the world that unfolds in the Bible and is continued in the church—a story that is aptly called "salvation history"—offers the fullest, most truthful, and hopeful account of who we are and the meaning and purpose of our lives. It is in light of that story that we best understand why we are called, what we are to do with our callings, and why, even when they seem too much for us, our callings are gifts of God's goodness and love.

This does not mean that one has to be Christian to have a vocation or to experience the richness that comes from living vocationally. Nor does it mean that only Christians can appreciate and learn from a Christian theology of vocation. God calls everyone, Christians and people of other faith traditions or of no faith traditions at all. God calls believers, skeptics, and passionate nonbelievers, to contribute to God's work in the world through lives of love, goodness, justice, and compassion. The roots of a theology of vocation may lie in Christianity, but Christians have no monopoly on vocation because they know God's grace is at work in the world in surprising ways; thus, they can learn from anyone what it means to live a called life. Christians grow in their understanding of vocation when they are willing to enter into dialogue with people whose beliefs and convictions may be other than their own. This stance of open engagement with others ought to characterize followers of Christ because Jesus exemplified it throughout his ministry. The Gospels vividly illustrate that Jesus persistently transgressed established boundaries in opening his life to others, an openness that provoked disdainful critique from the religious leaders of his time. Viewed in light of the Gospels, the call for Christians to imitate Jesus by crossing religious, cultural, and philosophical boundaries does not dilute a Christian's identity or sense of calling but is, rather, what faithful discipleship requires. As Edward Hahnenberg notes, "To be open to the other is to follow Jesus, for, at the heart of his story is an opening to the other in love." In fact, Hahnenberg continues, "we have to recognize a powerful paradox: by sinking more deeply into the Christian narrative, Christians grow more open to the narratives of others."[3]

A Timely Moment for Vocation

Surprisingly, today vocation is being rediscovered. What for a while may have been viewed as an artifact from a bygone past—more a museum piece than anything having contemporary relevance—has been taken down from the shelf, dusted off, and seen in fresh new light. "Vocation" has been moved out of the museum and onto the campuses of a growing number of North American colleges and universities, where it is engaging and energizing faculty, staff, administrators, and especially students in new and powerful ways. What accounts for such a dramatic relocation? For the resuscitation of a concept many had presumed was thoroughly, and maybe even appropriately, dead?

In our universities and colleges, two initiatives have had a far greater impact than anyone anticipated. The first began in 1999 when Lilly Endowment Inc. approached a number of colleges and universities about the possibility of establishing programs for the exploration of vocation for faculty, staff, and students on their campuses. Eventually, eighty-eight schools received sizable grants to develop these programs, which collectively became known as Programs for the Theological Exploration of Vocation (PTEV). In many respects, these programs were a leaven that transformed the culture of these institutions by showing the benefits that ensue when higher education broadens to embrace questions of calling and vocation, of meaning and purpose, and of what constitutes a truly good life. When PTEV ended, the leaders of numerous institutions—both of those that had received the initial grants and of those that did not—looked for ways to continue and even expand programs dedicated to the exploration of vocation. This resulted in NetVUE (Network for Vocation in Undergraduate Education), a network of now more than 250 colleges and universities that have programs dedicated to fostering vocational exploration among undergraduates. NetVUE

3. Hahnenberg, *Awakening Vocation*, 184.

began in the fall of 2009 and is administered by the Council of Independent Colleges (CIC).

Thus, far from being viewed as staid and useless, vocation has "caught fire" as interest in it continues to grow in US higher education and beyond. Something important is happening, something promising, energizing, and hopeful. But it requires more than well-developed plans and talented leadership in order for such programs to succeed. If this is a "moment" for vocation, it must be because vocational exploration is tapping into something deeper, something that cannot be ignored without grievous cost to ourselves. We think it is the deep human need to live for something far more meaningful and promising than one's pleasure, wealth, power, or possessions. We think it is because, instead of letting us be comfortably and chronically absorbed with ourselves, living vocationally rouses us to transcend ourselves in love and service to others. We think it is because vocation draws us into a way of being that incorporates us into stories, communities, and projects that are greater than ourselves. We think it is because living vocationally offers us a way out of lives marked by emotional and spiritual malaise, ways of living that suffocate hope rather than engender it. We think it is because when you live vocationally you lead a life that is not death-in-life but that really is life. Why does engagement with vocation matter? Because it helps us live better and fuller lives, genuinely magnanimous lives marked by expansive love, generosity, concern, and service to others.

We completed *Living Vocationally* and submitted it to the publisher just as the COVID-19 virus was beginning its rampant and relentless spread across the United States and around the world, and shortly before protests against police violence, systemic racism, and growing social and economic inequality called attention to the sins of injustice and the urgent need to address them. Far from making vocational reflection a superfluous luxury, we believe these crises—and any that lie ahead—make it all the more urgent because to live vocationally is to be continually attentive to how each of us, rather than turning in on ourselves, is called to be responsive to the unfolding events of our world, particularly how they impact the well-being of others. Indeed, even when no crisis threatens (if that day will ever come), thinking and living vocationally is always pertinent because doing so gives shape to a genuinely good life, one in which we characteristically seek ways to make life better for others by doing what we can to build a more just world.

The Origin and Shape of the Book

We chose to write this book together not only because we are friends who for almost forty years have learned from, helped, encouraged, and supported one another, but also because we believed that doing so would illustrate how any person's callings are intertwined with and dependent upon the callings of others; in other words, God blesses us as we live our callings through the friends we meet along the way. The book began as Paul's sabbatical project, but it wasn't too far into his sabbatical that Paul reached out to Charlie to see if he would be interested in writing a book on vocation together. Although each of us is the principal author for certain chapters, we read, commented on, and offered suggestions for how each other's chapters could be improved—the kind of thing good friends do for one another when they are talking not only about books to be written, but about how to live better lives.

The book is divided into three parts. Part I is "Preparing for the Journey" because the first three chapters examine what would be important to know before embarking on one's vocational journey. Chapter 1 ("An Invitation to the Called Life") explores some of the blessings and benefits that come from living vocationally, but also some of the challenges that are part of every vocational journey. The chapter focuses on the fundamental vocation every person has to discover the unique human being he or she is called by God to become. Overall, the chapter is an argument for why living vocationally is an inherently good and hopeful way to live. Chapter 2 ("Vocation—Exploring the Traditions") introduces the reader to a Christian theology of vocation by investigating how Christians, from the earliest days of the church, have understood themselves as people who have been called by God to participate in the work of God in the world. This overview reveals pivotal moments in Christian thinking on vocation, noting how the tradition has been contested and reformulated through the centuries. The latter part of the chapter considers other ways of thinking about callings, some of which are not explicitly religious, and concludes with a brief account of what other religions of the world can teach us about vocation. The third chapter ("Stories of Call") looks at some classic call stories, particularly, but not exclusively, from the Bible, to consider what they may teach us about how we experience and respond to calls in our own lives. Even though classic call stories are often dramatic, we can discern patterns and characteristics in them that are instructive for us today as we take up our own vocational journeys.

The second part of the book is "The Journey of the Called Life." It begins with chapter 4 ("Our Vocational Journeys"). There we explore why journey is a fitting metaphor for living vocationally. The first part of the chapter examines the different stages of our vocational journeys by noting important life transitions, such as the transition from adolescence to young adulthood, which is a key moment for vocational exploration, or the passage from middle adulthood to late and older adulthood, a transition that brings the painful reminder that we cannot pursue every calling we would like and that even the most cherished calls of our lives will end. The second half of the chapter lays out why thinking of our callings as journeys is not only more realistic than envisioning them as carefully planned trips where everything is clear from the start, but is also reassuring since it prepares us for the challenges and surprises, the blessings and the tribulations, that are part of any real journey. Chapter 5 ("Discerning Our Callings") begins with a framework for vocational discernment that proposes three principles to guide how we think about discernment, and then offers a six-step process for discerning our callings. While the chapter acknowledges the stress and anxiety that can accompany any attempt to discover our callings, it seeks to ease that stress and anxiety with the conviction that the God who calls us is a God who loves us and wants our good. Part II concludes with chapter 6 ("Living the Called Life—Dangers and Warnings"). Just as highways are marked with signs calling our attention to things ahead that could endanger us if we are not careful, we must also be alert to mistaken understandings of vocation that, at best, will mislead us and, at worst, could harm us by robbing us of a promising way to live. Those dangers include too closely identifying call with choices, as if "choice" is the best way to think about callings; assuming that living vocationally will happen without struggle and without substantive change in ourselves; and conceiving vocation so broadly that it loses any substantive meaning. The chapter concludes with the story of Paul Kalanithi, a doctor whose vocational journey provides a memorable account of why, even when it asks everything of us, to have found a calling is to have found a good way to live.

The third part of the book, "Virtues for the Journey," is written with the conviction that we need to become certain kinds of persons—persons whose character has been formed by the virtues—in order to take up, continue on, and complete our vocational journeys. Chapter 7 ("Virtues for Beginning the Journey") focuses on attentiveness, humility, and gratitude. We call them "situating virtues" because they help us settle into our callings and, by rooting us in specific times and places, help us attend to our callings every day. Chapter 8 ("Virtues for Continuing the Journey") reminds us that callings don't take care of themselves; indeed, if we take our callings for granted, they will die. This is why in order to remain engaged with our callings and to deal with all that can weaken them, we need virtues such as fidelity, justice, and courage, each of which the chapter examines. We argue that fidelity is absolutely crucial to sustain us on our vocational journeys and that justice and courage serve and strengthen fidelity. Chapter 9 ("Virtues for Completing the Journey") considers hope and patience. Hope reminds us that our callings orient our lives to a future fulfillment, that they have an ultimate goal or *telos* that Christians call the reign of God. Hope keeps us focused on that goal and fortifies us against the temptation of despair by which we forsake the most promising possibility of our lives. Patience is an ally to hope because patience teaches us not to grow despondent or disenchanted when hope's promise seems far beyond our grasp.

A Word of Thanks

No one writes a book without accumulating debts of gratitude. We want to especially thank Shirley Roels, the first Director of NetVUE, and David Cunningham, who succeeded her in 2017. Shirley and David encouraged us to write this book—we can even say they urged us on by regularly inquiring about its progress! Their support and enthusiasm convinced us it was worth doing and kept us going when we were sidetracked by other projects and responsibilities. So much of the renewed interest in vocation is due to their wholehearted and steadfast commitment to NetVUE. Without them, "vocation" might still be on a shelf in a museum. Readers will quickly note how much we depended on and benefited from the three volumes on vocation that David Cunningham edited for the NetVUE Scholar's Project. We also want to thank Sandy Murphy and Rebecca Lahti of St. Norbert College. At Paul's request, they generously shared with us what they have learned from helping students discern their callings. Thanks to them, we gained a better sense of the questions, reflections, and concerns students raise when thinking about how they might be called, a better sense of why they were attracted to thinking about vocation, but also why it sometimes made them nervous and a little afraid. And we want to thank Rodney Clapp of Wipf & Stock. We shared our ideas for the book with Rodney several years ago and his consistent encouragement—and patience—helped us make the transition from talking about the book to writing it. His support for us over the years, and his kindness, have been a great gift.

Finally, we wish to extend our deepest gratitude to Stanley Hauerwas, to whom we dedicate this book. We became friends many years ago in Stanley's graduate classes at the University of Notre Dame. More than anyone else, he challenged us to take theology seriously. And if we were to be writers and theologians and teachers, then we had better take that seriously too. He said this, of course, in many colorful ways; but it impacted us mostly because of how he embodied it. He demonstrated to us what living the called life really involves, both in its daily toils and struggles and its deep and abiding joy. In faithfully living his own callings, he helped us discover and embrace our own. Our gratitude to him is as deep and enduring as it is joyous.

Every book has an audience in mind. *Living Vocationally* was written in the hope that it might be useful to undergraduates—especially juniors and seniors—who are thinking about who they want to be and how they want to shape the rest of their lives. But we wrote the book to also appeal and be useful to adults who have already taken up—and may be far along— their vocational journeys. Nothing we say should be relevant only to young adults not only because the vocational discernment that is begun in late adolescence is ongoing, but also because we only understand what it means to live vocationally when we are well into the journey that every calling brings. We hope the book adds to conversations on vocation that have been underway the last several years. More than anything, we hope readers will agree that to have found a calling is to have found a good way to live.

PART I

Preparing for the Journey

CHAPTER 1

An Invitation to the Called Life

To be human is to live a called life. To live a called life is to live an inherently good life. To have embraced, entered into, and been faithful to our callings is to have lived one's life well. For Christians, *calling* or *vocation* is a fundamental way of thinking about ourselves and our place in the world because Christians believe that we are called not just once, but continually. Every day God is summoning us, appealing to us, inviting us to respond, because it is through our callings that we serve the plans and purposes of God. Indeed, in faithfully living our callings our own individual stories are taken up into the larger narrative of God's creative and salvific love.

These convictions inspired, energized, guided, and informed everything that follows in this book. Seeing ourselves as people who are called changes how we understand ourselves and our place in the world in genuinely hopeful ways. It sets us on a trajectory where we will transcend ourselves in goodness and love, because when we live vocationally our primary concern is not how we can promote and advance ourselves, but how we can make life better for others by being continually attuned to God's call. Too, as the language of "living vocationally" suggests, we believe that vocation is about all of life, not just our professions and careers. We don't leave questions about callings and vocations behind when we have settled into jobs, married, and begun to raise families, because vocation introduces us to a way of being in the world that permeates every aspect of our lives every day of our lives.

Thinking of ourselves as called changes the way we inhabit the world. It changes the choices we make and the reasons that we make them. It enriches our everyday existence by expanding both our sense of *possibility* and *responsibility*. It reshapes how we see and approach other people because to live vocationally is to know that callings can come to us from the people we least expect. Even more, Christians believe that living vocationally frees us to imagine both who we are and what we do—as well as why we are here and where we are going—in truly creative and liberating ways. It beckons us to go deeper, to leave the trivial and superficial behind as each day we strive, in all the often very ordinary settings of our lives, to have a positive impact on the world by using our gifts to do good. And at a time when so many people seem to sleepwalk through life, never stopping to ask questions of deeper meaning and purpose, never wondering if what they have been taught about happiness, peace, and genuine fulfillment is true, a Christian theology of calling attests that to live vocationally is to have discovered the kind of life that really is life, a life whose happiness is not counterfeit, whose fulfillment is not shallow and empty, and whose peace is not shattered by the slightest disappointment. When we live vocationally, Christianity teaches, we will be stretched and challenged, and sometimes may be spent and exhausted, but we will never seem more dead than alive.

To see ourselves as called is to have discovered a good way to live. This is why anyone who lives a called life, despite the sacrifices, setbacks, or surprises it may bring, will be no stranger to joy. The purpose of this book is to explore why that is true through a Christian theology of vocation. In this opening chapter we will examine some of the blessings and benefits that come from living vocationally. We will consider why living vocationally leads to a genuinely good and fulfilling human life, and why, by contrast, disregarding our callings, running from them, repressing them, or simply denying that we are called, constitutes a life that is less than fully human.[1] We will also address two of the more difficult challenges that are part of every vocational journey. But we will begin by exploring the foremost vocational question of all: the unique human being each of us is called by God to become. It is good to start there not only because the call to become who we are meant to be unifies all the other callings of our lives, but also because, as the following story illustrates, discovering who we are meant to be and becoming that person is a powerfully liberating benefit of living vocationally.

Being Who We Are Meant to Be

In *Let Your Life Speak*, Parker Palmer shares the story of his own vocational journey. For a long time, it was a journey marked by confusion, unexpected detours, plenty of wrong turns, and definitely more darkness than light. But the main problem was that he was trying to be someone he was never meant to be.

1. Badcock, *Way of Life*, 13.

After graduating from college, Palmer, convinced that he was called to ministry, enrolled at Union Theological Seminary in New York City. But the lousy grades, stress, and unhappiness that marked his first year were unmistakable clues that serving the church as a minister might fit others very well, but certainly didn't fit him. From there, Palmer headed west to begin doctoral studies in sociology at the University of California in Berkeley; after Berkeley, he settled in Washington, DC to work as a community organizer. Nonetheless, five years working in "the rough and tumble" of community organizing left him burned out and exhausted.[2]

Palmer's geographical journey from the East Coast to the West Coast, and then back east again, was a metaphor for the turmoil afflicting his soul. He was a gifted, privileged individual with a glittering future ahead of him and no shortage of promising opportunities. But he was miserable, and it wasn't until he was thirty-five that he realized why. Looking back, Palmer learned "that it is indeed possible to live a life other than one's own."[3] As he eventually surmised, despite our best intentions and the most laudable goals, we can live deeply divided lives, lives that leave us anxious and conflicted as well as restless and empty inside. This division most often arises when we live unreflectively, never taking time to scrutinize who we really are and, in light of that, what callings might be best for us. There was nothing wrong with any of the careers Palmer envisioned for himself except for the insurmountable—and painfully discovered—truth that they were never meant for him. The tension, anxiety, depression, and distress that shadowed him during the day and woke him up in the middle of the night were invincible indications, as Parker belatedly realized, "that the life I am living is not the same as the life that wants to live in me."[4]

Palmer was living "from the outside in, not the inside out," paying more attention to the hopes and expectations of others, to society's script about what constitutes a good and successful life, and to his own misguided assumptions about himself, than to the truth of his own soul.[5] Looking back, he summarizes what it took him so long to understand: The "deepest vocational question is not 'What ought I to do with my life?' It is the more elemental and demanding, 'Who am I? What is my nature?'"[6]

As Palmer confirms, and as we will reiterate throughout the book, vocation goes much deeper than what occupation one has or even what we

2. Palmer, *Let Your Life Speak*, 19–22.
3. Palmer, *Let Your Life Speak*, 2.
4. Palmer, *Let Your Life Speak*, 2.
5. Palmer, *Let Your Life Speak*, 3.
6. Palmer, *Let Your Life Speak*, 15.

do or accomplish from day to day; at its heart, it is about our person. The Gospels tell us that each of us is a uniquely created child of God, born and bred with a set of gifts and experiences that equip us for fullness of life. Such fullness is possible when we live from the truth of our own unique being. When we do, we discover that both who we are and what we do matters. We learn that even the most ordinary actions and routines of our lives can make a difference in ways we never expected. Such lives, even if they might appear to be small and insignificant can, as we will show later in the chapter, rightly be described as *magnanimous* because they continually aspire to what is truthful and best, and because through them we become more genuinely and fully human by growing in justice, love, compassion, courage, and all the other virtues that make for a good life. But, again, this is only possible when we first discover and embrace the deep-down truth of who we were created to be. Living vocationally must always start there.

The theologian Gordon Smith agrees. In *Courage & Calling*, Smith says, regarding our callings: "The first command is simply 'Know yourself.'"[7] This is the starting point for living with integrity and authenticity because we cannot grow as persons, we cannot truly be of service to others, and we certainly cannot flourish, if in pursuing what we imagine is our calling "we violate who we are."[8] We are never called to be somebody we are not. "If we seek to be anything other than who we are," Smith warns, "we live a lie."[9] Even though other people (including, sometimes, those closest to us), institutions, and certain social and cultural messages may encourage us to live falsely, to live a lie is morally, spiritually, psychologically, and emotionally damaging; it is to waste the only life we will ever have. This is why our core calling is to *be ourselves*. Many callings of our lives come and go, while others may span decades. All of them, though, take their place within one calling that never ends—the one that truly extends from the beginning to end of our lives: "to discover who we are so that we can live our lives in such a way that we become the people we are truly meant to be."[10]

But we need to be careful in how we understand what it means "to be ourselves" and we are rightly wary when we are relentlessly encouraged to do so. Language about "becoming who we are meant to be" or "discovering your true self" is quite prevalent (some would say depressingly prevalent) in our contemporary culture. It's the cultural gospel that is endlessly preached to us in commercials, in popular psychology, and in sterile spiritualities.

7. Smith, *Courage & Calling*, 37.

8. Smith, *Courage & Calling*, 37.

9. Smith, *Courage & Calling*, 38.

10. Neafsey, *Sacred Voice*, 52.

You can find it in any number of popular songs and self-help books, and even in some churches. Unfortunately, this cultural gospel does not seem like good news because people in Western developed countries are living increasingly divided and depressed lives, even while pursuing their own self-discovery! One reason the imperative "to discover our true self" hasn't brought the bliss it promises is that we are told there is a pure, utterly original self sleeping deep inside us that only needs to be awoken and brought to life; but there is nothing about that self that needs to grow, to change, or to be formed. Or we are told that whatever our self is, it is purely our own invention. We are free to create whatever self we want and whatever that self is will be our true self. Of course, the unspoken message is that we can create any kind of self we want because ultimately it doesn't matter. The danger in both understandings of the self is that it makes an idol of the self and imprisons us in a world that is no bigger than ourselves. No wonder that what results is not peace and fulfillment, much less joy, but loneliness and despair.

Exactly how we arrived at such misguided understandings of the self involves a long story, but part of it relates to what it means to be truly happy, to live full and genuinely good human lives. In our culture, we tend to imagine happiness as a feeling, a kind of satisfied state of being we might arrive at, like entering a palace of blissful pleasures and satisfaction. As opposed to this, a long tradition of philosophy since Aristotle, as well as a theological tradition especially connected with St. Thomas Aquinas, understood happiness not so much as a feeling, but as a whole way of being extended over a whole life. Happiness, for Aristotle and Aquinas, was not primarily an emotional state, but an activity, specifically the activity of being increasingly formed in the habits and qualities of character that both named the virtues. One became a self—a genuine individual—as he or she acquired, grew in, and practiced the virtues. In this respect, the self was neither a wholly interior reality, deeply hidden within us, that we eventually discovered, nor something we created *by* ourselves and *for* ourselves; rather, the self was what a particular way of life, extended over time, made possible. For both Aristotle and Aquinas, becoming one's true self requires taking up a journey. And the journey not only requires others, but is also one of growth and ongoing transformation.

Claiming the Image of God that Is Specially Our Own

Still, what was absolutely crucial for Aquinas and other Christian theologians was their conviction that our authentic and truly unique self, far from being something we created on our own terms, was rooted in, and inseparable from, the image of God that is stamped on each human being and that is specially our own. Christianity holds that every human being without exception is a living, breathing image of God, a unique manifestation of God; or, as the Quakers say, a "spark" of the divine. Christianity teaches that every one of us brings something irreplaceable and unrepeatable of God to life in the world. When we live from, and more fully into, this image, we embody a particular aspect of the goodness, beauty, and glory of God in ways no one else can. This is why for Christians our foundational calling—the one on which every other calling must be built—is to recognize, cherish, and nurture the *imago Dei* that is distinctively ours. That *imago Dei* is our truest identity, our genuine self, and most trustworthy clue to the person we are meant to become. That *imago Dei* reveals not who somebody else is meant to be, but the person we are meant to be and *must be* if we are to grow, find peace, and be a force for good in the world.[11] The Anglican theologian and former Archbishop of Canterbury Rowan Williams captured this well when he wrote that "in the most basic sense of all, God's call is the call to *be*: the *vocation* of creatures is to exist." By "exist" he means to live fully as God has uniquely created us to be. As he went on to say, "the vocation of creatures is to exist *as themselves*" because God never desires for us to be anything other than the beloved image of God that God created us to be.[12]

These words are immensely reassuring because they tell us that the path to life is not something that we have to create ourselves, or even discover on our own, but rather is something that unfolds before us when we answer the calling to become the person God's love envisions us to be. We take up the path to life when we affirm the person we were created to be, when we live *each day* more fully into the image of God that has blessed and graced us from the beginning. When we do so we not only begin to love ourselves in the most fitting and life-giving way, but also are freed from constantly comparing ourselves to others (or wishing we were them), a tendency that may be second nature for most of us, but which is usually a dreadful waste of time. If I affirm, embrace, and am grateful for the person God has created me to be, I don't expend energy trying to be someone else. If I am at peace with this core truth of my being and do my best to live from it, I can appreciate who others are and celebrate and be blessed by their gifts, just as I want them to be blessed by who God has created me to be and by the gifts God has entrusted to me. As Gordon Smith explains, "To think vocationally means to make an appraisal of the self. We look at ourselves; we identify, accept and embrace who we are called to be. This focus

11. Wadell, *Happiness*, 122–23.

12. Williams, "Vocation (1)," 149.

on ourselves frees us from comparing ourselves to others. And this liberates. For when we refuse to compare ourselves to one another, when we reject envy and jealousy of others, of their gifts and abilities and opportunities, we are freed to be who *we* are."[13]

Undoubtedly, one of the reasons that living vocationally is so appealing is that it gives us the freedom to be who we are by bringing to life the person God's love has created us to be. But it can take an awfully long time for us to find the courage we need to seize that freedom. Sadly, we can spend large chunks of our lives running from our true identity, suppressing it, or continually denying it. We can spend an awful lot of time trying to be somebody other than the truly original image of God that we are. Sometimes this is because we are afraid to be who we are. We are worried we will be judged, rejected, and even unloved; consequently, instead of embracing our true self and working to bring it more fully to life, we exchange it for a self we think will be pleasing to others. Other times we try to be somebody we aren't because we live in a society that encourages inauthenticity, that wants us to live falsely. It may seem odd to say that our society encourages conformity and inauthenticity. After all, doesn't it continually bombard us with messages exhorting us to be ourselves and to let our own colorful individuality shine? Aren't we constantly told that we must dare to be unique, whether it's in the clothes we wear, the gadgets we buy, the food we eat, or the stores where we shop? But the real intent of these messages is to make us uneasy with who we are, to make us anxious and uncertain, so that we begin to build an image of ourselves that runs counter to the grain of our soul.

In *Becoming Who You Are*, the Jesuit priest James Martin notes that we live in a culture that "tempts us to think that if only we were someone else— better looking, better educated, better moneyed—we would be happier. All we need to do is to be other than who we are."[14] That's the message of many commercials and businesses make millions selling us products that promise to give us a newer and better self. Martin himself fell into this trap; he spent years cultivating a false self, working hard to be someone other than who he really was. He earned a degree from a prestigious school of business and entered the corporate world of New York City. He had a good job, was on the threshold of a promising career, and was surrounded with friends. And yet, only a few years into his job, he found himself doodling "over and over, in small letters: 'I hate my life.'"[15]

---

13. Smith, *Courage & Calling*, 96.

14. Martin, *Becoming Who You Are*, 31.

15. Martin, *Becoming Who You Are*, 21.

A career in business certainly can be a calling for many, but it wasn't Martin's; in pursuing it he was forcing himself to be someone he wasn't. This left him mentally and emotionally drained and morally and spiritually famished. He may have been successful, but it was killing him. Looking back, Martin writes: "The self that I had long presented to others—the person interested in climbing the corporate ladder, in always being clever and hip, in knowing how to order the best wines, in attending the hottest parties, and getting into the hippest clubs, in never doubting my place in the world, in always being, in a word, *cool*—that person was unreal. That person was nothing more than a mask I wore. And I knew it."[16] What he later discovered—and what put him back on the path to life—is that "God calls each of us in every situation to be ourselves: nothing more and, more importantly, nothing less."[17] If we are not to lose our way in discerning and living our callings, we must take that truth to heart. It is where living vocationally must always begin.

Discovering Ourselves by Committing Ourselves

We receive insistent messages in our contemporary culture to "be yourself." And yet, if we unreflectively follow these messages, we will, ironically, be led further away from ourselves. This is because the call to become ourselves should not be confused with obsessively focusing on the self. We do not become more fully ourselves by becoming more self-absorbed. In fact, just the opposite is true: We learn what it means to become ourselves only by moving outside of ourselves in committing to projects, persons, and communities by which we transcend the self. Indeed, we discover ourselves only as we follow the call to serve others. This is one of life's profoundest mysteries—one that lies at the very heart of why calling is such a crucial theological idea. Perhaps it is not surprising that we so often get it wrong because we can easily assume that in order to know how we are called or what calling might be best for us, we must first have a totally clear understanding of our unique and authentic self by itself. We must, we assume, gaze inward before moving outward.

While we need theology to fully appreciate the significance of this mystery, we can begin to recognize something of how it works from our life experience. For one thing, if we wait until we are absolutely sure about who we are before we offer ourselves to some person or project, we will never commit ourselves to anything; indeed, we may spend our lives on

16. Martin, *Becoming Who You Are*, 19.
17. Martin, *Becoming Who You Are*, 41.

the sidelines, missing the most promising callings of our lives. While we shouldn't jump mindlessly into a calling, more often than not we discover who we are called to be not *prior* to making commitments, but *through* them. In some of the most important areas of life, knowledge and understanding do not precede commitments, but follow them.

This reminds us of a point made earlier: human beings are made to journey and grow. To be sure, each of us is called to a particular and unique journey and story, but it is never a story of the self by itself, but rather always one that connects us with and to one another. Our self is not something static and unchangeable that we quickly comprehend, but a mystery that we only gradually come to understand, a mystery that unfolds throughout our lives as we encounter other people, enter into relationships, are formed by different experiences, and respond to countless challenges.[18] This is why we'll never really know what it might mean for us to be true to ourselves without first saying "yes" to something.

In her study of Josiah Royce's philosophy of loyalty, Hannah Schell notes that for Royce "commitment to a cause is precisely how a self becomes a full person—a person with purposes and plans, concerns and cares. . . . Without plans or purposes, individuals are not yet *persons*."[19] Those causes, plans, purposes, cares, and concerns to which we are committed could be a friend or community, a church or civic organization, a team to which we belong, or a social justice issue about which we feel strongly; indeed, it could be any calling that engages and energizes us enough to elicit loyalty from us. Virtues are characteristic ways of being and acting that make both who we are and what we do good and, for Royce, loyalty is the foundational virtue of our lives—essential if we are to live with integrity—because we come to know who we are and what we are about only as we learn to be loyal to the persons, communities, causes, and concerns that define our lives. As Schell summarizes, it is "a mistake to imagine that we can ascertain who we are—to 'find ourselves'—prior to making a commitment to undertake meaningful deeds."[20]

Not just any cause, project, or purpose will do. Royce taught that the "cause to which one is loyal goes beyond the individual person and cannot be merely an expression of self-love or the seeking one's own private advantage."[21] In other words, I'll never find myself if I live only for myself. We glimpse our authentic self, and slowly grow into it, only by giving ourselves

18. Guinness, *Call*, 24.

19. Schell, "Commitment and Community," 245.

20. Schell, "Commitment and Community," 247.

21. Schell, "Commitment and Community," 245.

to persons, communities, causes, and concerns that call us out of ourselves and bind us to something larger than ourselves.[22] In this way, self-discovery comes through self-forgetfulness, the self-forgetfulness that binds us to others for the sake of projects worthy of our lives.

One objection to this way of thinking is that committing to persons, communities, and causes could hamper the process of self-discovery precisely because commitments close off options and limit possibilities. If we bind ourselves to persons, causes, and concerns prematurely, no matter how worthwhile they might be, won't this deny us the time, experimentation, options, and flexibility we need to come to know who we are? Won't it lead to a misleading or distorted understanding of ourselves?

These are serious questions. One response is to emphasize that the commitments by which we gain a better sense of who we are called to be do not have to be permanent; in fact, for young adults they usually shouldn't be. Young people should be wary of making lifelong commitments too soon. They need to be able to try different things, to explore a variety of possibilities, and to be able to forsake some temporary commitments in order to consider other ones. For example, the commitments that students make to causes and projects during their college years should typically be provisional, not something that will define the rest of their lives.

At the same time, making commitments in early adulthood—having to choose some possibilities over other ones—teaches us that in order to make anything real, including ourselves, we need to decide among alternatives, all of which might be good but all of which cannot be equally pursued. Students who might find several possible majors interesting and rewarding know they'll never finish college unless they focus on some while letting others go. The same is true of careers, hobbies, and talents to develop, or people with whom to spend the rest of our lives. As Margaret Farley observes, "Without commitment in relation to some possibilities in my life, I am left only with potentialities. Commitment limits self-process, but it is also what makes it possible."[23]

Farley reminds us that we are brought to a clearer, surer sense of who we are as we make commitments throughout the different stages of our lives. We don't gain our identity by holding back, by playing it safe, or by always keeping our options open. Our identity is formed through our families, through the key relationships of our lives, through our most formative experiences, but also through the risks we take in our commitments. So while we may be reluctant to promise ourselves to something because we

22. Schell, "Commitment and Community," 245.

23. Farley, *Personal Commitments*, 44.

worry that saying yes to it will mean we'll need to say no to many other things, the truth is that we don't really come to life—we don't really "catch fire"—until we can give ourselves wholeheartedly to the persons, communities, causes, and projects that matter most to us and are truly worthy of the gift of our lives. People who live vocationally know this is true. It is why they seem more fully alive—more fully engaged with life.

Discovering Something Truly Worthy of Our Life

> To journey for the sake of saving our own lives is little by little to cease to live in any sense that really matters, even to ourselves, because it is only by journeying for the world's sake—even when the world bores and sickens and scares you half to death—that little by little we start to come alive.[24]

We have suggested that living vocationally connects us to our true selves—to the *imago Dei* that is uniquely our own. But, in the process, it also frees us to do something genuinely worthwhile with our lives. Instead of floating through life on an ocean of distractions, bouncing from one thing to the next, or aspiring to nothing loftier than our own pleasure, comfort, and gratification, our callings give us "a vision of something to live for," a vision to guide and inspire our lives in a way that is genuinely and richly fulfilling.[25] Callings bestow meaning and purpose on our lives as a whole, including the mundane routines that characterize most of our days.

And yet, our desire for meaning does not guarantee that something is genuinely valuable. Something is not meaningful simply because I want or desire it. Similarly, the language of "calling" cannot be a license to christen any way that I might live as acceptable simply because I have decided that it is "meaningful to me." Rather, as the above passage from Frederick Buechner attests, the only way to be truly and fully alive is by devoting our lives to something other than ourselves. This doesn't mean that we shouldn't care for ourselves—for our physical, mental, emotional, and spiritual well-being—but it does mean that we grow, flourish, and are fulfilled only when we devote ourselves to the good of others. Human beings are "wired to serve," made to expend themselves on behalf of others.[26]

This is another way of understanding the *imago Dei* because to live according to the God in whose image we are created is to live with generosity,

24. Buechner, *Sacred Journey*, 107.
25. Clapper, *Living Your Heart's Desire*, 13.
26. Schuster, *Answering Your Call*, 2.

love, and service. Our callings tap into this fundamental truth of our nature because they draw us out of ourselves in response to the needs of others. Whether it is helping a friend through a difficult time, being patient with family members we have been given to love or befriending an elderly person who is lonely and afraid, as we respond to the various callings of our lives we learn to serve and in learning to serve make something worthwhile of our lives. Moreover, as we respond to all the callings that comprise our lives, we discover that happiness and fulfillment come not when we seek them directly, but in the self-forgetfulness that characterizes those who love and serve others, often at great cost to themselves.[27]

Finding Ourselves by Forgetting Ourselves

Almost everyone has heard the famous prayer attributed to St. Francis of Assisi. Even though it was really anonymously written, it describes well the life and calling of St. Francis: "Lord, make me an instrument of thy peace. Where there is hatred let me bring love . . ." The prayer asks for the power to respond to what is dark in the world—hatred, despair, malice, animosity, and discord—with the light that comes with love, gentleness, generosity, forgiveness, and peace. It concludes with these words: "for it is in giving that one receives, it is in self-forgetting that one finds, it is in pardoning that one is pardoned, it is in dying that one is raised to eternal life."

The final lines of the prayer echo what Jesus said to his disciples as he began to explain to them that he was going to have to go to Jerusalem to suffer and die: "If any want to become my followers, let them deny themselves and take up their cross and follow me. For those who want to save their life will lose it, and those who lose their life for my sake, and for the sake of the gospel, will save it. For what will it profit them to gain the whole world and forfeit their life?" (Mark 8:34–36)[28]

Both the St. Francis prayer and these words from Jesus further illumine the key theme of this chapter. To live a called life is to find oneself. We all want to find ourselves; as we have said, the message is plastered all over our contemporary culture. But what does it mean to find ourselves? And how do we do it? The promise (and challenge) of a called life is that we find ourselves only as we forget ourselves. Of course, it is not easy for human beings to forget themselves; next to the angels, we are the most self-aware of God's creatures, something our capitalist culture incessantly takes advantage of

27. Schuurman, *Vocation*, 124.

28. Unless otherwise noted, all scriptural quotations are from the New Revised Standard Version of the Bible.

as it tells us what we should desire, how we should look, what we should value, and especially what we should do with our money. How can we forget ourselves when we are constantly told to think about ourselves, even when so much thinking about ourselves leaves us anxious and depressed?

The prayer, and Jesus' words, call us to a way of being and acting that cultivate the self-forgetfulness that makes us whole: giving, pardoning, taking up our cross, becoming an instrument of peace. Here again the paradox of calling presents itself: It is only as we follow the call out of ourselves that we find ourselves. Put more strongly, we cannot do this (loving, giving, serving, forgiving) *so that* we can find ourselves; rather, we must be so captured by what we are called to do that it, not ourselves, becomes the focus of our lives. It is only when our lives become the genuine gifts that they are meant to be that we discover who we really are—that we see the image of God in us most clearly—and are truly free.

This is appealing, but it clearly isn't easy. For while we are meant to transcend ourselves in love, we are also, each of us, possessors of what the novelist and philosopher Iris Murdoch has called "the fat relentless ego,"[29] an ego that greedily seeks to follow its own way, to pump itself up, or to come out on top. Thus, perhaps it is no surprise that shortly after Jesus tells his disciples to take up their cross and follow him, they start bickering about who among them is the greatest (Mark 9:34); in fact, two of them, James and John, call Jesus aside to say, "Teacher, we want you to do for us whatever we ask of you," which turns out to be sitting "one at your right hand and one at your left," the two most prominent positions in the coming reign of God (10:35–36).

Callings Always Worthy of Our Lives

Still, the promise and hope of living vocationally stems from the unassailable fact that we are, thankfully, meant for more than our fat egos can possibly imagine; indeed, this is one reason the very idea of receiving and responding to a call appeals to us whether we are Christian or not. We are naturally inclined to see ourselves as people who are called because we rightly surmise that the only way that we can be delivered from ourselves (and from the suffocating and joyless task of feeding our fat egos) is by answering a calling. In fact, every one of us feels the tug of a variety of callings and knows we must muster the courage to respond because the only way we can ever *find* ourselves is by moving *out of* and *beyond* ourselves.

29. Murdoch, "On 'God,'" 52.

This is why, for example, virtually every human being has an innate hunger and thirst for justice. That hunger and thirst are signals from a calling, even if many of us may seldom heed it. To follow the call of justice is always worthy of our lives because when we do, we actively contribute to the life abundant that God wants for all men and women, indeed, for the whole of creation. When we work against dehumanizing structures, institutions, policies, and practices; when we speak out against bigotry and discrimination; when we align ourselves with the plight of migrants and refugees; when we denounce bullying, torture, cruelty, and ridicule; when we reach out to victims of human trafficking, sexual, or domestic abuse; when we build homes, communities, and societies in which the needs of the poor are genuinely acknowledged and addressed; and when we extend justice to other creatures and species, we are expending ourselves in ways that are worthy of our lives. We are living vocationally because we are making life better for others and, in doing so, coming more fully to life ourselves.

The call to work for justice never ceases; indeed, the brokenness of our world runs so deep and is so pervasive and enduring that doing what we can to mend it is always a worthy calling.[30] None of us has been untouched by the brokenness. People struggling to survive in countries torn apart by endless war or ethnic conflict surely know that the world is broken and needs healing. So do people in neighborhoods where barely a day passes without someone being wounded or killed by guns. So do children whose parents have divorced or who were raised in homes where love was missing. So do families in which people have stopped talking to one another for reasons that are typically embarrassingly trivial. So do people who suffer from grudges, petty resentments and jealousies, and malicious gossip.

Brokenness abounds because breakdowns in love and justice, respect and understanding, are everywhere, so much so that we are tempted to concede that it's the way the world works. But to accept discord and division as the way things must be is like choosing to take a sip of poison every day. Human beings are created for community. As living, breathing images of a God who is best understood as a communion of unbreakable love, we are created for intimate relationships of love and without these we die. We come to life not through hostility and animosity, and not through selfishness, ingratitude, and self-righteousness, but in families, friendships, communities, and societies where people look out for one another and realize that everyone flourishes when the common good becomes far more important than anyone's personal privilege. This is why in addition to the justice that sets things

30. Miller, *Living Faith*, 86–88.

right, the world cries out for a love that can comfort and heal, a love that can bring dead things back to life and that can make broken things whole.

The biblical word for this is *Shalom*. Shalom is typically translated "peace," but it is the peace that results not just when wars have ended and hostilities have ceased, but when every person lives in right relationship with every other person—as well as with other creatures and the natural world—so that all of us together are flourishing. The call to work for Shalom is also always worthy of our lives. Shalom is shattered by sin, destroyed by greed, selfishness, and indifference, and eroded by words that wound and actions that diminish. Every human being is called to contribute to the restoration of Shalom by working for justice and peace in every sphere of their lives, doing what they can to mend the brokenness whenever and wherever they can. We answer this call every time we allow love to triumph over animosity and selfishness, compassion to triumph over apathy and hardness of heart, and forgiveness to triumph over bitterness and permanent alienation.

These words—*justice, love, peace, community, compassion,* and *forgiveness*—name the deepest longings of our hearts. They also come to us as a calling, for we know that these longings cannot be fulfilled without work. With help from God and others, we are capable of giving ourselves to this work. When we do, we are drawn into the larger narrative of God's creative and salvific love. There we find freedom and life because, as we press on to respond to first this and then that need or hurt or injustice, which, if our eyes are open, we will see at every turn in our lives, we forget ourselves by transcending ourselves in love and service to others. When we live vocationally, our lives become gifts. When our lives become gifts, we are most fully alive.

Are Lesser Callings Still Worthy Ones?

One reaction to singling out working for justice and peace, and being agents of healing and reconciliation, as callings worthy of our lives is that for many of us, they sound nearly unattainable; beautiful and inspiring, and absolutely necessary, but beyond our reach. How can we confront injustice, mend brokenness, and be agents of Shalom when we have classes to attend, papers to write, children to raise, jobs to go to, friends to visit, families to support, or even just bathrooms to clean? Besides, couldn't thinking of our callings always in such large, sweeping terms like "defending justice" or "working for peace" cause us to overlook the very callings we most need to hear? Possibly, but, in fact, we have opportunities to act justly (or unjustly) or to work for peace (or sow discord) each day with family members, friends, others with whom we work, or in the messages we send on social media—we just don't tend to notice these or to think of them as callings. This tells us that we do not have to step out of our present life to find ample ways to answer the call to be just, loving, compassionate, and peaceful.

Once we begin to live vocationally, we discover that worthy callings are always within reach. A person who keeps her promises, honors her commitments, and is trustworthy and responsible is already living worthy callings. Someone who is diligent and dependable, who perseveres through hardship, and who each day seizes opportunities to do good already knows the rich meaning and purpose that come from living vocationally. A professor who is always prepared for class, who looks for ways to improve his teaching, who cares for his students, and who is thoughtful and supportive of his colleagues is also doing something genuinely worthwhile with his life.

What might seem to us lesser callings are still perfectly good and important ones, and a Christian theology of vocation can help us understand why. It is easy to wonder if anything we do really makes a difference, but a Christian theology of vocation reassures us that our actions do matter because God works through us and with us to achieve God's plans and purposes. Christians believe that God *calls* us because God *depends* on us. God wants to care for the world, but does so through the kindness, generosity, thoughtfulness, and consideration we show one another each day. God wants to bring love, justice, and goodness to life in the world, but does so through the good that we do in our families and friendships, in our schools and places of business, in our communities and societies. "God has chosen to work in this world through the agency of human hands," Lee Hardy explains. "In responding to our callings, we are actually participating in God's care for humanity and the earth. We are God's co-workers."[31]

For Christians, it is through our callings, including the smallest and seemingly most insignificant, that we contribute to Jesus' central mission of bringing the reign of God into being, which is the fullness of life that God envisions for everyone and everything that God created.[32] As Germain Grisez and Russell Shaw stress, "each of us has a unique contribution to make in *continuing* Jesus' work in our own lives and in today's world."[33] This is why even if we are never able to see it, and even if it fails to make the difference we might hope, any act of kindness, any expression of love, any deed of justice, and any gesture of compassion is never wasted. Even the smallest acts

31. Hardy, "Investing Ourselves," 30, 32.

32. Badcock, *Way of Life*, 52.

33. Grisez and Shaw, *Personal Vocation*, 116.

of goodness that may seem eminently forgettable to us "contribute in some way to God's mission, to the care and redemption of all God has made."[34]

Of course, most of our days are comprised of routines, many of them tiresome. Students study, go to class, perhaps go off to work, spend time with their friends, and catch a few hours sleep. After they graduate, the focus shifts from going to school to going to work, settling down, and perhaps raising families; the routines change, but they don't disappear. That so many of our days are the same—just one thing after another—can make us doubt the value of who we are and what we do, to the point that we slowly disengage from our callings.

A Christian theology of vocation rescues us from this danger because it assures us that our lives, far from being nothing more than a succession of disconnected events, are participating now in a compelling narrative of lasting significance—the narrative of God's redemptive love. Knowing this brings a "unity, solidity, and coherence" to our lives that otherwise would be missing.[35] To see ourselves as called saves us from lives of insignificance; indeed, seeing ourselves as called gives deep meaning to the ordinary details of life because it incorporates us into a greater story, one that existed before us and will continue after us. Without this greater story to give a framework to our lives, they become incoherent in themselves. Without this greater story, we are tempted to think that we can establish our own significance and bestow meaning on our lives without reference to anything outside of or larger than ourselves, but we will always be foiled. Apart from a larger narrative that can carry our lives, we cannot understand who we are or what we are about in any satisfying or sustainable way. A considerable blessing of living our callings is that they provide a plot or story line for our lives, one that can incorporate all the various dimensions of our lives, including the most mundane.[36] We may not know exactly what the next chapter of the story will be—or perhaps even the next page—but our lives are marked by the peace, freedom, and hope that come from knowing that the story to which we are contributing is unquestionably good.

Living Magnanimously

Our callings give us opportunities to recognize, respond to, and grow in goodness in all the richly diverse ways that can be done. This is true whether we are talking about the callings we commit to for most of our lives or the

---

34. Schuurman, *Vocation*, 40. See also Brouwer, *What to Do?*, 105.

35. Guinness, *Call*, 176.

36. Guinness, *Call*, 177.

ones that unexpectedly come our way for a time. Through all of them we have opportunities to grow, to deepen, and to be morally and spiritually transformed by transcending ourselves in love, kindness, and service to others. To seek to be that kind of person and to have that presence in the world is to live a *magnanimous* life, which is another significant benefit that comes from living vocationally. We can even say that living our callings both *requires* magnanimity and also *results* in magnanimity, and that magnanimity is necessary for a full and flourishing life.[37]

Magnanimity is a strange-sounding and largely forgotten virtue; most of us have never heard of it. Yet it is unwise to neglect magnanimity because it protects us from slipping into ways of living that diminish us. Without magnanimity, we will never grow to become who we might be; we will never achieve the greatness to which God calls us and makes possible for us, and thus will leave this world with mountains of regret. If this sounds overstated, consider this: magnanimity equips us to respond to every opportunity— and these come every day—to love and to do good. Without it, we will pass them all by because seeking to love and to do good asks something of us.

Thomas Aquinas defined magnanimity as "a certain aspiration of the spirit to great things," adding that a magnanimous person is someone who has "the spirit for some great act," which aptly captures what it takes to live our callings.[38] Magnanimity literally means to be of "great soul" or "great spirit," and describes a person who, instead of settling for what is easiest or most convenient, strives for what is best in every dimension of life. Magnanimous people are not afraid to lift their sights high in order to pursue what is most promising for human beings. They have high expectations for themselves, set challenging goals, and consistently strive to become more than they already are by responding to the call of good in all the ways it presents itself.

Magnanimous people know that we most often achieve greatness not by singularly momentous acts, but by the quiet and often unnoticed goodness that comes with being responsible to our callings. They may fall short; they may even occasionally fail. But magnanimous people never allow those momentary defeats to lower their hopes, to turn them away from what is best, or to relinquish the worthy and promising life they have come to know through their callings. They are committed to excellence not because they see themselves as better than others but because they want to do their best with the gifts that have been entrusted to them and the opportunities that

---

37. Some material in this section is taken from Wadell, *Happiness*, 99–101.

38. Aquinas, *Summa*, II–II, 129, 1. Quotations in this chapter are from the Ross and Walsh translation.

come their way. If asked to explain why they won't settle for less demanding ways to live, they'll say that God and others deserve their best.[39]

In an address he gave to students of Jesuit schools in 2013, Pope Francis surprised his audience by saying that the most important element to their education was "to learn to be magnanimous." He told the students that magnanimity "means having a great heart, having greatness of mind; it means having great ideals, the wish to do great things in response to what God asks of us." His words illustrate the inseparable connection between magnanimity and vocation because in order to live out our callings we need to be people of great heart and mind, and of great ideals; and we need to be people who are continually open to what God asks of us. But Francis went on to say that we do great things not by neglecting the mundane parts of our lives, but rather by responding generously and graciously to them. We live magnanimously, he suggested, when we "do well the routine . . . daily actions, tasks, meeting with people—doing the little everyday things with a great heart open to God and to others."[40]

Thus, living vocationally not only requires magnanimity, but also leads to magnanimity because we achieve excellence in our lives, aspire to what is best, and remain fixed on what is worth living for by responding generously to our callings. It takes magnanimity to be loyal to our friends and in our marriages, to do the best that we can in our studies and in our jobs, and to be generously attuned to the needs and well-being of others. But it is also true that doing all these things craft a magnanimous life, a life that gifts us with meaning and purpose and happiness and peace precisely because it asks much of us. Simply put, the only life worth living is a magnanimous life and the only way to live magnanimously is by giving ourselves wholeheartedly to our callings, the lesser ones as well as the greater ones.

Sometimes talk about "aspiring to greatness," "seeking excellence," or "pursuing what is best" can make magnanimity seem like a rare and rarified virtue, a luxury for the special few who are not bogged down by the ordinary responsibilities of life. But magnanimity has nothing to do with wealth, talents, fame, and long lists of achievements—nor is it only for people with time on their hands, like celebrities or rich philanthropists. On the contrary, anyone can be magnanimous; it simply requires that we generously respond to the demands of the different callings of our lives. Weary parents who would rather relax watching television but instead help a son with homework exhibit magnanimity. Students who stay committed to working for justice and peace when it seems they will never be achieved

---

39. Smith, *Courage & Calling*, 86.
40. Francis, "Free to Choose Good," 122.

are magnanimous. Friends who are patient with one another's shortcomings also exemplify magnanimity. In every case, these people aspire to what is best and unquestionably demonstrate that they have the "spirit for some great act."

Perhaps the reason most of us are unacquainted with this virtue is because we live in a culture that seldom encourages it. If we equate a good life with wealth, material comforts, pleasure, entertainment, the constant gratification of our desires, and the freedom to do whatever we want, magnanimity won't matter because we will have settled into a life that's all about us and, therefore, asks nothing of us. If what we aspire to aims no higher than a life of comfortable survival, magnanimity will be irrelevant. And if we believe a life of calculated self-interest is better than a life of service, magnanimity will seem hopelessly naïve and foolish.

In fact, if that is what we believe, instead of cultivating magnanimity, we will have become skilled in *pusillanimity*, the vice that most directly opposes magnanimity. It is even less known than magnanimity (and harder to spell) but perhaps all the more prevalent. Aquinas described pusillanimity as a "pettiness of mind" by which a person stops aspiring to what is best because it asks too much.[41] Instead of raising her sights to what is truly good and worthwhile, she opts for what is easiest or immediately more appealing. As the word suggests, a pusillanimous person has puny hopes, puny dreams, puny goals, and puny expectations of life. She is like the man in the Gospel who buried his talent instead of developing it; like him, she gives up without even trying. Instead of growing and being challenged, the pusillanimous person glides through life as a spectator taking in the sights, enjoying herself as she becomes comfortable with mediocrity.

This is why pusillanimity is incompatible with living vocationally. Our callings open up the horizons of our world and continually call us out of ourselves on behalf of others. The pusillanimous person shrinks the horizons of his world to what is manageable and comfortable and predictable; for him, life is all about playing it safe. Our callings can sometimes leave us out of control, and thus open to risks and surprises, but the pusillanimous person has to be in control. This is why he is content with a life that asks little of him, a life in which he has decided not to grow, not to change, and definitely not to be challenged, all of which happens when we live vocationally. A life consistently spent settling for less—a life that never offers a single moment of self-transcendence—may be comfortable and secure and full of pleasures, but it is also empty, meaningless, and bereft of happiness

---

41. Aquinas, *Summa*, II–II, 133, 2.

and hope. Our callings require the courage to be magnanimous and train us further in it; this is an indisputable benefit of living vocationally.

Challenges in Living Our Callings

This chapter has focused on the blessings and benefits that come from answering, embracing, and faithfully investing in our callings. But callings also bring challenges, sometimes considerable ones. To conclude the chapter, we will consider two of the most common challenges that are part of most vocational journeys.

The first is the painful awareness that we cannot pursue every calling for which we might be suited—callings that are needed, appeal to us, and for which we have the appropriate gifts. One reason is simply because we are finite creatures who are restricted by space and time, and have limited resources and energy. No matter how well intentioned, we cannot possibly respond to every call that comes our way; to attempt to do so would leave us worn out and depleted. A second reason is that the callings to which we have already committed ourselves ordinarily have priority over callings that come later, even if we find those later callings more compelling and appealing. I may be strongly attracted to a particular calling, but if answering it means that I abandon or neglect callings to which I have already said yes, then ordinarily I should not respond. As disappointing as that may be, I must recognize that there are others who are available to answer the call in ways that I cannot. Third, our ability to respond to callings is limited by age. For younger persons, it may be too soon to respond to a calling; for older persons, it may be too late. Having to pass on a calling is never easy because we know that the callings that we cannot answer remain undeniably good; indeed, the fact that we must refuse certain callings evokes regret.[42] Acknowledging this regret is an important way of honoring the indisputable goodness of callings that we cannot accept.[43]

A second challenge to living vocationally is how hard it can be to do justice to all the different callings of our lives. Living vocationally would be blissfully easy if we only had to deal with one call, but that's never the case. Consider all the callings of our lives. We are called to be true to ourselves and to live with integrity. Religious people are called to center their lives on God and each day to nurture their relationship with God. Spouses and partners are called every day to support and love one another, and to be present to each other. Parents are called to care for their children, to

42. Mahn, "Conflicts in Our Callings," 54.
43. Mahn, "Conflicts in Our Callings," 48.

guide them through the early years of their lives, and to help them grow into thoughtful and responsible adults. Friendship is a calling that demands the ongoing investment of ourselves in another person's well-being, especially if the friend is struggling. Students are called to be responsible to their studies, to grow intellectually, morally, and spiritually, and to use the years of college to reflect on who they are meant to become. Whether or not we think of our jobs as callings, they demand considerable time and energy of us, which makes it difficult to deal with the other callings of our lives. And all of us are called to do what we can in response to the needs of the local community, the larger society, and the world. How can we possibly give all of these callings the attention they deserve?

In the best of all worlds, our callings would always exist in harmony, each of them complementing and balancing one another to create a beautiful life. There are times when this seems to happen, but there are also periods when our callings compete and even conflict with one another, and these tensions may not be easily resolved. At such moments, we feel pulled in several different directions all at once. Students experience this when a troubled friend needs somebody to listen, there's a paper due the next day, and there're problems brewing at home. Single parents know the pull of conflicting obligations when it is time to go to work, but there's a sick child at home who needs them. Adult children struggle with the tension that can arise among callings when they try to balance care for their aging and infirm parents with the needs of their homes and the demands of their jobs.

The virtue of magnanimity will help us through such periods. We should be aware that there will be times in our vocational journeys when one or more of our callings suffers because we have to give disproportionate attention to another call. This is to be expected and lived through as faithfully as we are able. But we should also recognize that if the demands of some callings mean that others are consistently overlooked or neglected, we may have to decide, after careful discernment, that some of our callings must be relinquished. We can do this within the larger picture provided by the framework with which we began this chapter: our fundamental calling is to be fully ourselves, that is, the person God wills us to be, serving him gladly with the time and place and people we have been given.

Conclusion

This chapter has considered some of the benefits and blessings that come from living vocationally. There are many and we will continue to explore them throughout the book. But in a Christian theology of vocation, none matters more than the freedom and joy that flow from becoming the person God's love created us to be. This is why the fundamental calling of every human being is to discover, claim, love, and live from the unique image of God that is especially their own. And yet, the only way to know what the image of God is for us and the only way to bring it to life is by transcending ourselves in love and service to others. When we answer the invitation to a called life we discover the paradox at the heart of a Christian theology of vocation: We will never find ourselves, much less become ourselves, if we only live for ourselves. This is why we are most fully alive when we make our lives gifts for others.

Living vocationally isn't easy. If you want your life to be trouble free, decide now never to answer a calling. People who live vocationally will readily attest that callings bring challenges, setbacks, doubts, hardships, and sometimes heartbreaks. But they will also readily attest that there is no better way to live because when we respond to the callings of our lives, in ways we may never fully appreciate, we become active participants in the narrative of God's creative and redemptive love, which means our lives, no matter how unspectacular they may seem to us, are gifts that bless the world. That is what becomes possible when we have the courage to live vocationally. And it is why when we see ourselves as called that we have discovered a good way to live.

CHAPTER 2

Vocation—
Exploring the Traditions

ONE DOES NOT HAVE to be Christian to live vocationally, but one does have to be familiar with how Christians have understood "calling" or "vocation" because both terms are rooted in the Christian tradition. Vocation comes from the Latin word *vocare*, which means "to call," and from the beginning Christians have believed they were called by God. Thus, in this chapter we will continue our exploration of vocation and what it might mean to live vocationally, first, by investigating how thinking about vocation evolved in Christianity. We will then examine other approaches to vocation, noting how a Christian theology of vocation provides a framework for a variety of ways to think about calling, some which may not be explicitly religious at all. The final section of the chapter will briefly consider how some other religions of the world can enrich our understanding of vocation. By the end of the chapter it should be clear that there are many ways to think about God calling us to use our gifts to make the world a better place.

Vocation and the First Christians

From the very beginning Christians have understood themselves to be called. Calling was not something added on to their lives, but rather what gave them a distinctive identity and purpose. They were a people called *by* God, *to* God, and *for* God. This is suggested by the word the New Testament uses for church, *ekklesia*. *Ekklesia* combines two Greek words, "*ek*," which means "from" or "out of," and *klesia*, which means "calling." Thus, the early Christians recognized themselves as a people who had been called out of their individual lives by God into a community. Like their Jewish ancestors who were called by God to be a blessing to the nations by embodying God's love, mercy, and justice in the world—especially God's concern for the poor and outcast—Christians knew they were brought together by God for a special purpose or mission. They were the "people of God" called to do the work of God. Their calling was not primarily about them, but about what God wanted to achieve through them. Too, the focus of their calling was not about how it might benefit them, but about how through them God's message of salvation might be announced throughout the world. As 1 Peter 2:9 testifies, "But you are a chosen race, a royal priesthood, a holy nation, God's own people, in order that you may proclaim the mighty acts of him who called you out of darkness into his marvelous light."

Their collective vocation was to further the creative and redemptive work of God in the world by following, imitating, and learning from the life, teachings, and ministry of Jesus. No follower of Jesus was exempt from this vocation. To enter the church, Christ's body in the world, was to be called out of the narrow boundaries of one's individual life in order to participate in a purpose much larger than one's self, the purpose of proclaiming and advancing the reign of God. This is why the first Christians understood calling in a much broader and more comprehensive sense than we often do today. For them, calling did not refer to a job or an occupation, but to a whole way of life, a distinctive way of being in the world.

In the early church's theology, Christians entered the story of Jesus and became part of the community that promised to make that story their own when they were baptized. They believed that to be baptized was to respond to God's offer of salvation in Christ. It was to answer God's *call* to grace and freedom and fullness of life by abandoning the darkness and destructiveness of sin in order to take Christ's life as the model for their own. For them, baptism was truly a sacrament of conversion because it dramatically symbolized leaving behind an empty and unpromising way of life in order to enter into a radically new and abundantly more hopeful way of life. The sacrament itself indicated that the changes brought about by baptism were profound. The exorcism and renunciation of evil, immersion into water, a dying and rising, being clothed in a new garment and anointed with oil: all these were powerful reminders that a rupture had occurred between their past life and the new one they were entering. To become a Christian was to die in order to be reborn, a truth eloquently expressed by Paul, who wrote: "So if anyone is in Christ, there is a new creation: everything old has passed away; see, everything has become new!" (2 Cor 5:17). Some early Christian writers understood the consequences of being baptized to be so extreme that they compared baptism to a change of citizenship or a transfer of one's loyalty and allegiance. To be baptized was to take on a new identity, to become part of a new community, and to commit to learning new beliefs, customs, traditions, and practices. It was very much like leaving the country of one's birth in order to become a "citizen" in the reign of God.

This overview of how the early church interpreted baptism lifts up four essential aspects of how it understood "calling." First, the early Christians believed that their vocation was rooted in and defined by their baptism. Baptism gave them the foundational calling of their lives and they lived that calling by continually partaking of the new way of life that baptism made possible for them and to which it continually summoned them. In short, no Christian had to search for or worry about discovering their calling because as soon as they were baptized they were called.

Second, since through baptism Christians "put on Christ" and strove to become "another Christ" by continually conforming their lives to Christ, every Christian participated in the collective call of discipleship. To be baptized was to become a disciple, a "student" of Christ, and this meant, in effect, enrolling in school together with other students, a school Christians call the church. In the church every member *together* helped one another grow in the attitudes, concerns, dispositions, and virtues of Christ. The vocation of being a disciple marked a Christian for life. It was the calling in light of which they understood who they were and what they were to do with their lives. It was the one calling they could never exhaust, the one calling, short of death, that would never leave them.

Third, since baptism entailed an ongoing reorientation and transformation of one's whole life, leaving no dimension of life untouched, every other calling was secondary to the fundamental call of discipleship. Should a Christian pursue a particular career? If it helps her grow in discipleship, well, perhaps yes; however, if it hinders, weakens, or contradicts her baptismal calling, then the answer clearly is no. Should she get married, remain single, or join a community? Such questions can be answered only when seen in light of the foundational calling of baptism and a life of discipleship. If getting married, remaining single, or joining a community draws one closer to Christ and helps one grow in love of God and others, they are fitting callings. The relationship between the call to discipleship and other callings tells us that for the early church any secondary calling was meant to serve the primary calling that came with baptism.

Fourth, by linking calling to baptism, the first Christian communities emphasized that calling applies to everyone in the church, not just a distinguished few. To be a Christian is to be called, no exceptions, no excuses. This broad and expansive understanding of vocation made the idea of calling something very natural in the early church. For the baptized in the first few centuries after Christ, the language of calling helped them understand who they were and how they were to live. It gave them a clear identity and sense of purpose and meaning. In Christ, they were called to holiness of life. In Christ, they were called to an exorbitant love of their neighbors, including their most resolute enemies. In Christ, they were called to the world-saving work of building the reign of God, a work begun by Jesus and then entrusted to them as his followers.

A Narrowing of Vocation

In October 312, Emperor Constantine was victorious at the battle of the Milvian Bridge and attributed his victory to the God of the Christians. Shortly after, he ended the persecution of Christians in the Roman Empire by legalizing Christianity. By 380 Christianity had become the official religion of the empire. And so began a decisive change that influenced Christian thinking on vocation for centuries.

Here's what happened. Prior to its legalization by Constantine, Christians were a growing, but relatively small and often persecuted minority on the margins of the empire. Because many of their beliefs and practices threatened the customs of the empire (e.g., not worshiping the Roman gods, refusing to offer sacrifices to the emperor, and typically refusing to fight in the emperor's wars), some Christians were martyred; consequently, to be baptized was not only socially and politically costly, but potentially quite dangerous. But once Christianity was legalized, and especially when it was pronounced the official religion of the empire, to be a Christian was not only acceptable, but also socially advantageous. No longer on the margins, Christians became the rulers and decision-makers who occupied positions of power and prestige. On the one hand, this was a benefit for the church because the persecution was over and because, thanks to its new status, membership in the church increased significantly. But, on the other hand, as the church moved from the fringes of society to the center, it found it easy to modify the gospel and the teachings of Jesus to accommodate the needs of the empire. The radical demands of discipleship no longer so clearly applied to all of the baptized; indeed, to practice them across the empire could even seem irresponsible as Christians wielded power amid the complex, and often bloody, dynamics of the real world.

In response to this change, some men and women fled to the desert to pursue a more radical life of discipleship, one characterized by intense prayer; fasting and other ascetical practices; poverty, celibacy, and obedience to a spiritual master. Their goal was to imitate Christ as much as possible in every area of their lives. If Christians were no longer being killed on account of their faith, this new disciplined way of life could constitute a "spiritual" martyrdom through which men and women offered their whole lives to God. This was the beginning of monasticism. Some monks lived alone (the Greek word *monos* means "single" or "alone") while others gathered in communities.[1]

Monasticism brought a certain renewed health to the church. The women and men who adopted this new way of life recognized the dangers of diluting the teachings of Jesus in order to fit more comfortably into the surrounding society. In this respect, monasticism, which began as a protest movement, "validated ways of life that embraced radical countercultural expressions of faith."[2] These monks and nuns did not believe that Jesus meant his teachings to be nice ideals that were much too lofty to follow in one's life. As Keith Graber Miller writes, they "sought a closer relationship with God, a relationship similar to that which nearly all Christians had shared in the earliest centuries of the church: They were those who wanted commitments of faith to still matter, to demand something of them."[3]

Nevertheless, and unfortunately for Christian theology of vocation, the view developed that there were two distinct classes of Christians. There were the spiritual virtuosos who had withdrawn from the world in order to commit themselves entirely to Christ, the specially called ones; and then there were the vast majority of Christians who, unable to make that full-fledged commitment, more or less muddled along. This "Doctrine of the Two Ways" resulted in a more stratified and hierarchical understanding of the church. Men and women who entered the religious life or priesthood were the ideal Christians who gave up much in order to embrace what came to be endorsed as a higher and more perfect way of life.[4] These specially called ones committed themselves to the "evangelical counsels" or "counsels of perfection," namely, the religious vows of poverty, chastity, and obedience. More ordinary Christians, who came to be known as the laity (from the Greek *laos* for people), had to live with the humbling truth that they did not have it in them to aspire to what is best.

So it was that a "hierarchy of holiness" developed in which holiness became the almost exclusive reserve of monks, nuns, and priests. Holiness was possible for this spiritual elite, but largely out of reach for ordinary Christians who, at most, did their best to avoid the ever-present snares of

1. Cahalan, "Called to Follow," 31.
2. Cahalan, "Called to Follow," 35.
3. Miller, *Living Faith*, 34.
4. Cahalan, "Called to Follow," 31.

sin. If the first Christians affirmed that baptism called every believer to a life of holiness, this now became the special vocation of clergy and religious. The link between holiness and the religious and priestly life was also forged by the conviction that a life committed to celibacy and virginity was unquestionably better than marriage and life in the world—even though this understanding grew principally out "of Greek philosophy and its persistent dualism"[5] between body and spirit. As Darby Ray bluntly states: "Bodies were generally viewed as a hindrance to salvation—a source of temptation and a constant reminder of one's corruptibility and finitude, of how far from God one really was."[6]

The calling of the Christian to a life of discipleship was therefore disassociated from the more common, ordinary and material human activities relating to family life, or farming, or commerce, or politics. Such activities characterized the lives of most Christians, but were not seen as potential paths to holiness. "The world of work, temporal affairs, marriage and family was at best neutral, and more often a hindrance, to sanctity," Edward Hahnenberg writes. "Most medievals simply assumed if holiness is to be attained by lay folks, it is achieved despite their life in the world, not because of it."[7] Real Christians left the darkness of a fallen and corrupt world to pursue holiness in the only place it could confidently be found—in monasteries and convents located safely apart from the world.[8]

The result, already apparent, was that the understanding of vocation narrowed significantly. If Christians of the early church were taught that as soon as they were baptized they received the call to discipleship, now the language of calling or vocation became almost exclusively associated with religious life and the priesthood.[9] This shift can be partly explained by a change in the practice of baptism. In the early church, infants were typically not baptized because only an adult could freely decide to make the life-changing commitment to follow Christ. However, with the development of the doctrine of original sin and Augustine's teaching that anyone who died unbaptized was damned, the practice of baptizing infants became the rule rather than the exception. This changed the theology of baptism from a response to the call to follow Christ to a cleansing from original sin.

5. Hahnenberg, *Awakening Vocation,*

6. Ray, *Working,* 69.

7. Hahnenberg, *Awakening Vocation,* 10.

8. Fortin, *Centered Life,* 46.

9. Miller, *Living Faith,* 35.

Instead of being primarily about discipleship, baptism came to be viewed predominantly as what one needed to avoid being shut out of heaven.[10]

This alternate way of understanding baptism, and so also calling, lingers. Generations of Catholics were taught to pray to know if they had a vocation, which meant to discern if they might be called to the religious life or priesthood. If you were called to the priesthood or religious life, you had a vocation; if you weren't, you didn't. Even today when Catholics talk about a "shortage" of vocations or are urged to "pray for vocations," they are referring to the lack of priests and religious. This would make no sense to Christians of the early church. How could the church lack vocations when everyone receives one in baptism?

A Broadening Again

Neither did it make sense to Martin Luther (1483–1546), the Augustinian monk whose fiery challenges to the Roman Catholic Church sparked the Protestant Reformation. Luther vehemently rejected the view that only monks, nuns, and priests had a vocation.[11] And he just as vehemently critiqued the "spiritual elitism" that held that the priesthood and religious life were "higher" or more "perfect" states of life and thus the only sure paths to holiness. For Luther, the "Doctrine of the Two Ways" was heretical because it denied a principal element of biblical theology: through baptism all Christians become part of the priesthood of Christ. It is baptism, not ordination, that consecrates one as a priest, and since all Christians are incorporated into the priesthood of Christ, there are not two states or classes of Christians, but only one, namely "the status of being 'in Christ' by virtue of baptism."[12] There is a fundamental unity and equality among all Christians because of a common faith and a common baptism.[13] People may have different roles in the church, but, as St. Paul teaches in 1 Corinthians 12, these different roles do not make any person more important than any other person; rather, they are simply different ways of serving the church as one body.

For Luther, the fundamental vocation of all Christians is to love God and our neighbors. Every Christian shares the same calling to become part of the people of God and the priesthood of Christ, and to grow in holiness through loving God and one's neighbor. Luther referred to this as the "general calling" of every Christian. Precisely how each individual could best live

10. Cahalan, "Called to Follow," 32.

11. Badcock, *Way of Life*, 34.

12. Badcock, *Way of Life*, 34.

13. Hahnenberg, *Awakening Vocation*, 12–13.

out this calling depended on the unique circumstances of their lives; this more particular path Luther named one's "external calling." Reformers following Luther often spoke of the "general calling" as the "spiritual calling" of every Christian, and of the "external calling" as one's "particular calling."[14]

In broadening the idea of calling to include all Christians, Luther also connected vocation to ordinary life. One did not have to flee the world to the desert, enter a monastery or convent, in order to follow Christ because if the central vocation of every Christian is to love God in loving their neighbors, this can be done anywhere. Christians grow in holiness not by loving some imaginary or idealized neighbor, but by loving the neighbors right in front of them, the men and women they encounter every day at home, in the workplace, and in their communities. Husbands fulfill their callings by loving their wives, parents by loving their children, politicians by working for justice and the common good, and friends by seeking one another's good. "For Luther, life in the world is not a distraction from the life of holiness," Hahnenberg writes. "It is precisely the place where we live out our God-given call."[15] In fact, Luther, who left the monastery to become a husband with a family, criticized priests and religious for running from the demands of love. Leaving the world to enter a monastery was not a higher form of love, but "a flight *away from* the love of neighbor that God commands," a love that is meant to be practiced in the web of relationships that make up our everyday lives.[16] Luther felt this so strongly that he urged "the celibate monks and priests of his day to break their vows, get married, and have children." For him, far from being a more perfect form of love, priesthood and the religious life made loving too easy.[17]

Luther's vision reoriented how calling could be understood in his time. First, by affirming that every state of life could be a calling, Luther suggested that we do not need to search far and wide to know our callings because more than likely what God calls us to do is right in front of us in all the different roles and relationships that make up our lives.[18] Our collective calling is to love our neighbors and we have all been given neighbors to love by God. They may not always be easy to love; in fact, at times we may not even like them, but loving them is what we are called to do. For Luther callings were not principally understood as a means to self-fulfillment, but as the way we are called to be attentive and responsive to the needs of our neighbors.

14. Schuurman, *Vocation*, 17.

15. Hahnenberg, *Awakening Vocation*, 12.

16. Hahnenberg, *Awakening Vocation*, 13.

17. Schuurman, "To Follow Christ," 57.

18. Hahnenberg, *Awakening Vocation*, 15.

Precisely because it is often not easy to love all the "neighbors" who move in and out of our lives, living our callings requires self-denial and self-sacrifice, effort and perseverance, patience and generosity. Still, we may find that it is exactly by pursuing such a life that we are fulfilled, even joyous.[19]

Second, in claiming that we fulfill our central calling to love God and our neighbors through the roles, occupations, and relationships of our lives, Luther attributed religious meaning to the ordinary activities of everyday life. Luther meant to abolish the distinction between the sacred and secular worlds—there is only one world and all Christians are called to serve in it; if we are to love, do good, and grow in holiness, it is only in that world. This means that anything we do, no matter how small, no matter how mundane, is spiritually significant if done as an act of love. A simple act of kindness, a word of encouragement, an expression of care, or being patient with people who are difficult to love, all are holy, all are acts of worship and praise to God, if prompted by love. "What matters ultimately before God is not *what* one does," Luther stressed, but "*how* one does it."[20] As Schuurman emphasizes, Luther's understanding of call "sanctifies *all* of life, inviting Christians to offer every aspect of life as their divine worship."[21]

Third, for Luther, as Christians followed their particular callings they participated in and extended God's redemptive work in the world, a world that was created to bring glory to God but was now wracked by sin. Luther believed that every person had a "station" or "standing" (*Stand* in German) in life that they were providentially assigned by God. In whatever role one found oneself, that was God's will for her. Those roles put people at different levels of society, but no matter where one stood in the social hierarchy, it was where God had assigned them to love and do good.

Luther's description of the different "stations" or "standings" can be interpreted in terms of a medieval and feudal view of society as an organism in which every member has a part.[22] Understood in this organic way, no one person's work is any more valuable than any other person's work. Government official, entrepreneur, merchant, farmer, or street sweeper, all work is essentially equal because it is all needed; through work in its various forms, no matter how humble or seemingly insignificant, each person can love God, serve others, and contribute to the common good.[23] Too, if God ordered the world and our place in it as a way for God to continue to

19. Schuurman, "To Follow Christ," 79–80.

20. Hahnenberg, *Awakening Vocation*, 14.

21. Schuurman, *Vocation*, 6.

22. Badcock, *Way of Life*, 40.

23. Ray, *Working*, 72–74.

love and care for all of God's creation, then God's providential care for the world works not apart from or independently of our callings, but through them. God's love, justice, mercy, compassion, and kindness are mediated through the particular callings each person inhabits in society.[24] Through our callings we become "coworkers" with God, channels through which God continues to bless, heal, and build up. As Badcock writes, "By means of these standings or offices of life and society, God's loving purposes in creation are fulfilled."[25]

Yet even though such new emphases in Protestantism rightly worked to broaden the idea of vocation after the narrowing that occurred in Christendom in the previous centuries, they also brought new risks that continue to threaten a robust theology of vocation. Because he believed that one's station in life was "ordained by God" and part of God's plan or design for the world, Luther upheld an essentially conservative view of society that uncritically endorsed the institutions, structures, and overall ordering of that society. Citing Paul's words in 1 Corinthians 7:20 ("Let each of you remain in the condition in which you were called"), Luther maintained that the state or role "into which we are born is the one in which we should die," and that no matter how bleak our circumstances might be, it is "God's intention for us and should be honored as such."[26] Even though it is true that the people of Luther's time had neither the options nor social mobility that many people have today, his claim that the way things are is the way God wills them to be risks giving theological legitimacy to social structures, beliefs, and practices that are unjust and, therefore, need to be criticized, reformed, and, in some cases, abolished.[27]

John Calvin

Luther's contemporary John Calvin (1509–1564) largely agreed with Luther's theology of vocation, but differed from Luther in identifying one's particular calling more exclusively with one's work and the importance of being busy and productive. The difference is subtle, but important. For example, Luther disdained the monastic life because, as noted above, he saw it as fleeing one's responsibilities to love one's neighbors. But Calvin despised monasticism because he judged it to be a life of idleness. The monastic life did not lead monks closer to God; rather, it made them lazy because by

24. Kleinhans, "Places of Responsibility," 105.

25. Badcock, *Way of Life*, 36.

26. Ray, *Working*, 75.

27. Schuurman, "To Follow Christ," 74–75.

devoting so much of their lives to prayer, the monks failed to develop the gifts God had given them, gifts meant to be put *to work*. For Calvin, "we are born to work," to be busy and productive.[28]

Calvin felt that human beings were restless, unsettled, fickle creatures. God rescues us from that troublesome condition, Calvin taught, through our callings. The work we are called to do not only helps us "know who we are and what we should do with our lives," but also provides a focus, order, and stability to our lives without which we would dangerously go astray.[29] Calvin believed we would much more likely stay out of trouble if we diligently applied ourselves to the work to which God has called us. But he also believed that in devoting ourselves to our callings we could be sure that we were "living as we were created to live" and "doing what God intends us to do."[30]

Calvin's thinking on these matters allowed him to avoid the strong emphasis in Luther on "station." Our callings, Calvin taught, are not determined by our station in life but rather by our gifts. He believed that God has given everyone gifts to serve the common good.[31] For society to prosper, each person must discover and use their gifts for the good of the whole. Like Luther, Calvin did not view callings primarily as a means to self-fulfillment, but as the way God calls us to use our talents for the benefit of society. Any occupation that did not contribute to the common good could not possibly be one's calling. As Calvin saw it, we are obliged to look for work that brings the greatest advantage not to ourselves, but to the larger society—and this will not always be in the highest paying job.

But, unlike Luther, Calvin did not maintain that it was God's will that we stay in the station in which we were born. If our station in life does not allow us to use our God-given gifts, then we must search for a place where we can; indeed, it is our duty to do so. It is good neither for society nor for us if we remain in situations where opportunities to use our gifts are rare. Even more, if prevailing social structures and practices prevent us from using our gifts "in ways that truly serve our neighbor and honor God, then the social structure must be changed. The Calvinist impulse," Lee Hardy observes, "was to bring existing social institutions into line with our vocations, not our vocations into line with existing social institutions."[32] In this respect, Calvin's view of society was more dynamic and flexible than

28. Hahnenberg, *Awakening Vocation*, 19.

29. Ray, *Working*, 77–78.

30. Ray, *Working*, 79.

31. Ray, *Working*, 78. See also Hahnenberg, *Awakening Vocation*, 19.

32. Hardy, "Investing Ourselves," 33.

Luther's. In insisting that people find work that aligns with their gifts, Calvin allowed—even encouraged—a social mobility that Luther did not.

Beneficial, but Flawed

In many ways, Luther and Calvin rescued and reinvigorated Christian thinking on vocation. However, we must be careful not to uncritically endorse the Protestant reformation of vocation. If Protestantism saved vocation from its captivity in an impoverished Catholic spirituality, in many respects it seems only to have led to a different kind of captivity. As this brief survey has shown, the Reformers effectively and forcefully reminded Christians that they all had a vocation. In retrieving this broader understanding of vocation, they rightly rejected the narrower and more exclusive understanding of vocation that resulted from the Doctrine of the Two Ways. Yet, following Dietrich Bonhoeffer, A. J. Conyers notes how quickly and easily the new concept of vocation, broadened in these ways by Protestantism, could also be secularized into what Max Weber three centuries later identified as the "Protestant work ethic."[33]

Two obvious dangers flowed from what became an almost completely secular understanding of vocation. The first was that vocation became almost exclusively connected to work. If Luther and Calvin rightly criticized the narrowing of vocation that happened in Catholicism, their efforts, albeit unintentionally and for different reasons, also resulted in a much narrower understanding of calling, one that has prevailed over several centuries as, perhaps especially in Protestant circles, calling became synonymous with one's career or profession. Moreover, once vocation was so tightly linked to being an employed, productive member of society, to be unemployed was judged to be lazy, which was soon understood as the greatest vice. After all, if God is understood as a worker who created the world and all things in it and who ceaselessly continues to sustain it, men and women, as God's images, most resemble God through their work. Consequently, to be unemployed is a serious moral failure. By not working, one is both refusing to use one's gifts to glorify God and to serve the common good, and refusing to do what most makes one like God.[34]

The second danger in moving to a purely secular understanding of vocation is that the emphasis both on one's station and one's secular occupation as the place where we find our calling frequently led to an uncritical affirmation of worldly structures, institutions, and powers, many of which

33. Conyers, *Listening Heart*, 27.
34. Ray, *Working*, 81.

earlier Christians would have regarded with considerable suspicion, especially as disciples of a man who had been unjustly killed by them. This was
increasingly so as vocation was viewed more as a way to serve an expanding capitalist economy than as a way to serve God. As Dietrich Bonhoeffer
insisted, vocation "in the New Testament sense, is never a sanctioning of
worldly institutions as such; its 'yes' to them always includes at the same
time an extremely emphatic 'no,' an extremely sharp protest against the
world."[35] Monastic Christianity had provided the "no," a sharp protest
against the world, even if it might also have failed to offer a way for non-
monastics to see their lives as a response to God's call to work with God
in the sanctification and redemption of the world. Bonhoeffer called these
"'two disastrous misunderstandings'" of vocation "'the secular Protestant
one and the monastic one.'"[36]

Karl Barth

Bonhoeffer's contemporary Karl Barth (1886–1968), probably the most
significant Protestant theologian of the twentieth century, was well aware
of how the Protestant emphasis could go awry. Barth applauded Luther and
Calvin's affirmation that God calls *all* Christians (not just priests, monks,
and nuns), but feared that the growing tendency to identify one's calling
almost exclusively with one's work resulted in many Christians forgetting
that their primary vocation was not to a job, but to the Christian life. Luther and Calvin's sense of the relationship between a Christian's primary
calling (in baptism) and her secondary or particular callings was gradually
reversed. Over time, the call to be a Christian—the call to discipleship—was
overshadowed by other "callings," especially those having to do with the
world of work; indeed, it was almost entirely forgotten.[37] And if it was not
forgotten, Barth alleged, God's call became so closely identified with a person's work that the two became virtually indistinguishable; consequently,
not only was the sovereignty of God's call weakened but, in an increasingly
secular world, it eventually disappeared. Barth addressed the problem by
continually reiterating that "the divine call to be a Christian transcends all
human callings."[38] According to Barth, in the New Testament to be called
is always first and foremost to be summoned to the new way of life that
is made possible in Christ. That calling is not one among others; rather, it

35. Bonhoeffer, *Ethics*, 255.
36. Conyers, *Listening Heart*, 27.
37. Hahnenberg, *Awakening Vocation*, 99.
38. Hahnenberg, *Awakening Vocation*, 100.

is the calling that every other calling should serve. As Schuurman writes, "God's call to be a Christian must qualify every aspect of life: marriage and family, employment relationships, political life, as well as the life of the church."[39] No dimension of life should remain untouched or unchanged by that foundational calling.

Barth believed that people lived out their baptismal calling to new life in Christ through the particular settings and circumstances in which they found themselves. Barth called these "places of responsibility" and used that phrase to stress that God calls each of us as particular people in particular historical circumstances, in particular relationships and communities, people with particular gifts and opportunities, backgrounds and experiences, but also particular limitations and restrictions.[40] God's call addresses not only *who* we are, but also *when* and *where* we are. It is not an abstract, generalized call that comes to us as if we were anybody living anywhere at any time, but a call that meets us in all the unique features of our lives.

The great value of Barth's approach is that it takes seriously the fact that every human being is a unique individual living in a particular context at a particular time. God does not call us to be or to do everything; rather, God calls us to be ourselves (not someone else) and to do what we can to contribute to the creative and redemptive work of God, not in some far-off future world, but exactly where we find ourselves today. Knowing that our calling will emerge from the particularities of our lives makes it easier to discern what that calling might be, though not necessarily easier to accept. As Hahnenberg affirms, "For Barth, each of us has—each of us is—a 'unique opportunity.' I am placed here and now as the person that I am. What does the world around me need? What am I able to provide?"[41]

The place in which we find ourselves inevitably falls short of what God wants the world to be. Not only because of human finitude, but also because of human sinfulness (both personal and social), the world continually needs to be transformed, continually needs to be brought to greater approximations of justice and peace. Thus, to be called *from* where we are necessarily means to "grapple" with the world that we know, protesting its inequities, lamenting its injustices, and doing what we can to overcome them.[42]

---

39. Schuurman, *Vocation*, 35.
40. Hahnenberg, *Awakening Vocation*, 119.
41. Hahnenberg, *Awakening Vocation*, 122–23.
42. Schuurman, "To Follow Christ," 67.

A Catholic Response

It may have taken 400 years, but eventually the Catholic Church embraced the broadened understanding of vocation to which the Reformers pointed. At the Second Vatican Council (1962–1965), in *Lumen Gentium*, its document on the church, the Catholic Church affirmed that through baptism every Christian becomes a member of the priesthood of Christ. There are not two classes of Christians, but only one; indeed, there is a fundamental equality and unity among all Christians because at baptism every person is consecrated a priest of Christ and *called* to imitate and bear witness to Christ.[43] Whether single, married, ordained priest, or religious, every Christian is first of all a member of the priesthood of Christ and given the vocation of being Christ for others. Moreover, holiness is no longer the exclusive vocation of priests and religious; rather, the council insists that "all the faithful, whatever their condition or state are called by the Lord—each in his or her own way—to that perfect holiness by which the Father himself is perfect."[44] Lest any doubt remains, an entire chapter in *Lumen Gentium* is devoted to the subject of holiness, a chapter aptly titled: "The Universal Call to Holiness." It emphasizes that the fundamental calling of all Christians—the vocation every Christian shares—is to holiness of life by following in the way of Christ. Too, if to be holy is to be godly, and if God is love, Christians grow in holiness as they grow in love.[45] *Lumen Gentium* agrees with Luther: we are holy when we love God and our neighbors. We are holy when we manifest love in all the ways love can be practiced in every situation of life.

While there is a common vocation to holiness, there are different ways to pursue holiness. *Lumen Gentium* notes that priests pursue holiness primarily through their ministry to the church, and monks and nuns through the special character of their lives. But the majority of Christians follows Christ, lives the gospel, and grows in holiness through the various roles and settings of their everyday lives.[46] This means one thing for spouses and partners and parents, another thing for single persons, and another thing too for adolescents or young adults. More recently, in his 2018 apostolic exhortation *Gaudete et Exsultate* ("Rejoice and Be Glad"), Pope Francis confirmed that every Christian is called to holiness, but likewise stressed that there are many paths to holiness. Instead of "hopelessly trying to imitate something not meant for them," Francis wrote, each person must "discern

43. Flannery, ed., *Lumen Gentium*, 10.
44. Flannery, ed., *Lumen Gentium*, 11.
45. Flannery, ed., *Lumen Gentium*, 42.
46. Flannery, ed., *Lumen Gentium*, 31.

his or her own path,"[47] the path that best enables them to build with Christ "that kingdom of love, justice and universal peace."[48]

At the Second Vatican Council the Catholic Church also recognized that one did not have to flee the world to find God, to respond to a calling, or to grow in holiness. The council endorsed a much more positive view of the world, acknowledging that God's grace, love, and goodness are present everywhere. One could follow Christ and bear witness to the gospel not only in a monastery or in the priesthood, but equally as well in marriage and family, the workplace, and the larger community. The distinctive calling of the laity—what the council called the "special vocation of the laity" and the "apostolate of the laity"—was to "contribute to the sanctification of the world" and "manifest Christ to others" by bringing the gospel to bear on every area of life.[49] Thus, every Christian truly is an apostle because every Christian, *Lumen Gentium* insists, is given the mission of carrying forward the work of Christ. Laymen and laywomen fulfill their distinctive apostolate by doing what they can to further the reign of God in the world.[50] They faithfully live that sacred calling when they work for the ongoing humanization of the world and the flourishing of all persons and creatures in all the different roles, responsibilities, and relationships that make up their lives. It is through them, the council asserts, "that the world may be filled with the spirit of Christ and may the more effectively attain its destiny in justice, in love and in peace."[51]

Other Approaches to Vocation

Karl Barth was one of a few honored non-Catholic guests present at the Second Vatican Council where the universal call of all Christians to holiness was articulated in *Lumen Gentium*. This emphasis on the centrality of holiness is a sign, perhaps, of an emerging consensus in contemporary Christian thinking about call. In some ways, the focus on holiness rightly returns a theology of vocation to the call to discipleship that Jesus issued as he first walked the shores of the Sea of Galilee. "Follow me," he says to Andrew and Peter, James and John. And, without a moment's hesitation, they got up and followed (Mark 1: 16–20). None of them knew where they were going. If they had known precisely, they might have remained with

47. Francis, *Gaudete et Exsultate*, #11.

48. Francis, *Gaudete et Exsultate*, #25.

49. Flannery, ed., *Lumen Gentium*, 31, 33.

50. Flannery, ed., *Lumen Gentium*, 36.

51. Flannery, ed., *Lumen Gentium*, 36.

their nets; after all, the path that the subsequent story traces contains many twists and turns as well as dark spaces—including suffering and persecution and death. Knowing that they could not foresee all that might lie ahead of them, yet intrigued, even compelled, by the person they saw and heard, they got up and followed.

The simplicity of Jesus' summons is matched by the complexity of our humanity. The call came to Andrew and Peter, James and John, in the same way. But none of these four young men, nor others who joined later, travelled the path in precisely the same way. Their call was the same; it was, as it is for all Christians, a universal call to embark on a life of discipleship that can make us holy, that leads to God. But although they were brothers, Andrew was not Peter and James was not John. Likewise, each one of us is profoundly different, born at different times in different places with different gifts and responsibilities, different struggles and different burdens to carry. The general call to grow in holiness as we make our way to God is the same for everyone. But how each of us is specifically called to do so may differ in surprising and quite interesting ways. Thus, even though "holiness" may sound boring, in fact there is nothing more attractive, truly personal, and beautiful. Discovering the continuity and similarity of all of our calls, while at the same time discovering how different and fundamentally unique God's call is to each of us, is a daily task. The questions this task poses are not easy, but we think they are exciting and invigorating, as we hope the rest of this book will show.

In light of these reflections on the inescapably *personal* character of vocation, the fundamental vocational question that every person faces is not "What should I do?" but, more importantly, "Who should I be?"[52] In this perspective, *being* precedes *doing*. What will we make of ourselves? What kind of person will we be and what kind of life will we craft for ourselves? What will be the guiding convictions, the pivotal beliefs, and the principal values in light of which we shape our character? Will others be better because of who we are? We all face these questions; we must if we are to live thoughtfully and well. While these questions might be pertinent for our careers and professions, they obviously transcend them. As Jerome Organ says, "We are called not just to a job (nor even to a career), but also to a *life*; this demands a broader account of what we might *do* with that life."[53]

Parker Palmer, whom we introduced in chapter 1 and who has written extensively about callings, consistently affirms, as emphasized in that chapter, that our most important vocation is to become the person we are meant

52. Organ, "Of Doing and Being," 225.
53. Organ, "Of Doing and Being," 226.

to be. For Palmer, our deepest calling is to discover, claim, and grow into our authentic self.[54] In more explicitly religious language, Mark McIntosh claims that God calls "everything that exists into the fullness of being."[55] Consequently, the core calling of every human being is to respond to that summons by becoming the unique person that God is calling into life. McIntosh pictures every human life "as a pilgrimage in response to divine calling, and our particular vocation as a journey into those patterns of life that allow us to be truthfully and wholly the persons God is calling into being."[56] Instead of simply existing, which would be a waste of our lives, we should continually grow into the truth of ourselves, a truth that reflects God's special love for who we uniquely are.

In chapter 1 we spoke of the unique identify that is born from God's special love for us as the "image of God" that is particularly our own, and said that we are called to live from this deepest truth of our being. It is only then that we can, as McIntosh said, "be truthfully and wholly the persons God is calling into being." However, as A. J. Conyers helpfully reminds us, the image of God, especially as understood by theologians such as Origen, Augustine, Aquinas, and Luther, "is not a settled fact but a promise."[57] Rather than being something static and unchanging, the image of God that is entrusted to us should grow and develop so that we achieve greater likeness to God by living in greater conformity to the ways of God—that is the "promise" to which Conyers refers. The danger of taking the image of God as a settled fact is that it can easily lead us to presume that human knowledge and desire, in its present and given forms, are sufficient to guide all of creation. Obviously, the whole of human history has shown that this is not the case. What we want now, what we have become capable of bringing about with all our quite remarkable human powers, is not necessarily what ought to be.

This is why another important way to think about vocation is to see ourselves called to ongoing growth and conversion. If this does not happen, not only will the various callings of our lives atrophy, but, even worse, they can become a means of justifying whatever happens to be or whatever we happen to want. Recognizing this, the Jesuit theologian John Haughey, guided by the work of Bernard Lonergan, argues that a most basic human calling is to an ongoing process of intellectual, moral, affective, and religious conversion. Haughey understands this call to conversion to come from

54. Palmer, *Let Your Life Speak*, 16.

55. McIntosh, "Trying to Follow," 120.

56. McIntosh, "Trying to Follow," 120.

57. Conyers, *Listening Heart*, 27.

"reality itself." To be human is to be in a world that continually calls us to
transcend ourselves by breaking out of a self-enclosed existence in which,
instead of respecting what is real and true, we impose "on reality what we
would like it to be."[58] We answer the call to *intellectual* conversion when
we commit to knowing what is true and real rather than being governed
by prejudices, biases, and self-absorbed fantasies.[59] We respond to the call
to *moral* conversion when, instead of living only to satisfy our wants and
pleasures, we seek what is truly valuable and strive to live according to what
is genuinely good.[60] *Affective* conversion begins when we move out of ourselves in response to the ever-present call to love, a call that comes to us
daily in every person and creature we encounter. And we achieve *religious*
conversion when we truly *abide in love* for God and others so that all of our
choices are inspired by love.[61] As Haughey summarizes, "The unceasing and
most universal level of call is to be authentic by living in reality, by judging
what is and being responsive to it, by judging what is not real and nam-
ing it as such."[62]

Twentieth century American theologian H. Richard Niebuhr proposed
that being human is essentially a matter of being responsible.[63] Following
Niebuhr, Margaret Mohrmann suggests that our core vocation is to become
responsible human beings, people who recognize the complex relationships
that constitute our lives and the obligations and responsibilities they create.
The call to live responsibly ought to characterize our whole way of being
because we live in a world that continually asks something of us. This understanding of vocation manifestly extends the meaning of calling beyond
our career or profession or a state of life such as marriage. We are called to
be responsible in every dimension of our lives: yes, in our professions, but
also in our home life, in our friendships and other relationships, in our local
communities, and in how we respond to the challenges of the larger world.
As Mohrmann explains, "Responsibility is the center of what we do and of
who we are; our moral goodness depends on how well we do it."[64] We are
called to live responsibly not only because in doing so we become more
fully human, but also because genuine community and genuine peace are
possible only as every human being answers that call.

58. Haughey, "Three Conversions," 2.

59. Haughey, "Three Conversions," 3.

60. Haughey, "Three Conversions," 4–5.

61. Haughey, "Three Conversions," 7.

62. Haughey, "Three Conversions," 3.

63. Niebuhr, *Responsible Self.*

64. Mohrmann, "Vocation Is Responsibility," 27.

Steven Garber further develops this "call" to responsibility by arguing that each of us is "responsible for the way the world is and ought to be." Thus, our "common vocation" is "to care not only for our own flourishing, but for the flourishing of the world."[65] For Garber, the principal vocational question is quite straightforward: "'Knowing what you know about yourself and the world, what are you going to do?'"[66] Garber's insight does not negate the point, made earlier, that vocation is first about who we are and, secondly, about what we do. His point reminds us that even though we can distinguish *who we are* (being) from *what we do* (action), we cannot ultimately separate them because authentic "being" requires knowledge of who we are in the world, not only as we (and it) are now, but also how it (and we) might become. Illumined by faith, this knowledge leads necessarily to action.

Similarly, Caryn Riswold stresses that living vocationally today requires a trenchant and abiding awareness of the dehumanizing forces at work throughout the world—everything that impedes human flourishing—and a commitment to do what we can to overcome them. As she notes, many people are "encouraged to think of themselves as less than fully human";[67] moreover, each day they are prevented from knowing what a fully human life might look like. Thus, the call to work for a more just and humane world must be at the forefront of any relevant theology of vocation, especially for those fortunate enough to have largely escaped these dehumanizing forces. In *Awakening Vocation*, Edward Hahnenberg insists that in a world of so much injustice and cruelty and oppression, of so much misery and grief, where so many human beings struggle every day to survive, we are all called out of ourselves to respond to the cries of the suffering.[68] We must allow our journeys to be interrupted—and even redirected—by the affliction of others, recognizing that the very presence of a suffering human being calls us to do what we can to help. Without excuses and without delay, we must do what we can "to take the crucified people down from the cross."[69]

Vocation in Other Religious Traditions

In the first part of this chapter we gave an overview of how calling or vocation has been understood in the Christian tradition. It is important to know

65. Garber, *Visions of Vocation*, 18.

66. Garber, *Visions of Vocation*, 51.

67. Riswold, "Vocational Discernment," 73.

68. Hahnenberg, *Awakening Vocation*, 222.

69. Hahnenberg, *Awakening Vocation*, 225.

this story if we are to investigate further how call might be understood to-day, including how we might discover what God is calling us to in our lives.

As we have seen, the idea that we are "called" is a central focus of the Christian tradition. That tradition is filled with interesting stories of different people being called by God, some of which we will consider in the chapters that follow. Reflecting on these stories, and considering some key theological concepts that relate to call, can help us get a firmer grasp on the "grammar" of call. To use a word well in a particular language, speakers need to have a sense of the nuances of its meaning within that language. As they learn this they come to know the grammar of that term and thus are better able to distinguish between good and bad, legitimate or illegitimate uses of the term. *Call* is a term that can be easily misused, but within a tradition, it becomes easier to notice when it is. For instance, if someone says that God is calling him to buy and sell slaves, or commit adultery, or take vengeance upon his enemies, and if, when pressed, he acknowledges that the God he thinks is calling him to do these things is the God of Jesus, he must confront the teachings and life of Jesus, which clearly indicate that the God known in Christ would never "call" anyone in this way.

Outside such a tradition, the grammar of call will be more difficult to discover. For the purposes of this book, we will consider the term principally from within the Christian tradition. It is important to stress, however, that the term is not exclusive to Christianity. And, in fact, Christians should be familiar with, and open to, its use in other traditions. Christians do not have a corner on God's call. Indeed, what they know of God indicates plainly that God calls not only them, but all human beings into friendship with God and one another. Moreover, God is at work in the world, and this work is for everyone to participate in, not only Christians. It should not surprise us, then, that the belief that God calls us is found in other religious traditions—even if the idea appears in ways that are sometimes dissimilar to the Christian understanding of calling.

Judaism, for example, has "no concept of vocation or calling" if we understand that to mean that today God directly speaks to and calls particular individuals. According to Amy Eilberg, "The predominant position of classical Jewish sources is that after the deaths of the literary prophets of the Bible, God never again spoke directly with individuals. Thus, the notion of God communicating God's specific desire for a particular person's life choices is foreign, if not vaguely offensive."[70]

However, this does not mean that the Jewish people as a whole do not have a calling. Jewish people are called to holiness of life by observing

---

70. Eilberg, "*Hineini*," 5.

God's commandments and by the "wide range of ritual, ethical, communal, and interpersonal practices" that accompany them.[71] By faithfully following these commandments, they honor and serve God, live in relationship with God, and make their way to God.[72] They are called, through a series of liturgical and ritual blessings, to regularly give thanks to God for God's goodness to them. The purpose of these blessings is to summon them "to pause at as many moments as possible throughout every day, remembering the presence and blessings of God, orienting one's life around these gifts and the obligations they create."[73] Jewish people are likewise called to repentance for sins, to making amends for the harm caused by wrongdoing, and to doing what is necessary "to become a person who could never again commit such an act."[74] Overall, the primary vocation of the Jewish people is "to place God at the center of their lives, as a constant source of guidance, orientation, and concern,"[75] and to commit themselves to the "repair of the world" (*tikkun olam*) by working for justice, peace, and human rights for all persons.[76]

The idea of calling is particularly strong in Islam. In the most basic sense, "God calls human beings to submit—to become Muslims."[77] Muslims honor this calling in lives of obedience to God, in placing themselves at complete service to God, and in prayer and good works.[78] Prayer is especially important because through prayer Muslims acknowledge their dependence on God and confess their indebtedness to God. Prayer also chips away at pride, a vice that hinders the freedom that is found in acknowledging that human beings belong to God and are answerable to God.[79] Interestingly, Islam teaches that people know that God's call is extended to every person because that call "is 'written on' the hearts of human beings" and is manifest in "signs" in the natural world, in family and social life, in history and personal experience.[80] But because we often miss the signs—or refuse to see them—"God sends prophets to remind people of the reality in which they live."[81] Perhaps most importantly, an integral part of every Muslim's call-

71. Eilberg, "*Hineini*," 6.
72. Eilberg, "*Hineini*," 7.
73. Eilberg, "*Hineini*," 8.
74. Eilberg, "*Hineini*," 9.
75. Eilberg, "*Hineini*," 11.
76. Eilberg, "*Hineini*," 20.
77. Kelsay, "Divine Summons," 101.
78. Kelsay, "Divine Summons," 82.
79. Kelsay, "Divine Summons," 102.
80. Kelsay, "Divine Summons," 101.
81. Kelsay, "Divine Summons," 101–2.

ing is to share what they have with the poor, to combat injustice, to spread
compassion, and to work for peace.

There are amazingly diverse expressions of Hinduism, but enough
common characteristics to glean some understanding of what it can teach us
about vocation. A basic tenet of Hinduism is that all things are related. There
is no such thing as a completely separate individual because everything in
the universe is interconnected and every being is dependent on every other
being. Each person "exists in a complex web of relationships that includes
other human beings, other species, and the natural world."[82] Because of the
"interdependent character of life," the primary calling of every human being
is to live and act in ways that "contribute to the sustenance of the whole"
and to the nourishing and flourishing of all persons, indeed, the whole of
creation.[83] To do so is to live according to *dharma*, which essentially means
"to support or sustain." As Anantanand Rambachan writes, "*Dharma* refers,
therefore, to all beliefs, values, and practices that are viewed as promot-
ing the well-being of the universe."[84] The opposite of *dharma* is *adharma*,
which consists of beliefs, attitudes, practices, and actions that, instead of
contributing to harmony and well-being, result in "disunity, fragmentation,
and chaos."[85] Self-centeredness, greed, excessive ambition, insensitivity, and
indifference would all be examples of *adharma*. In Hinduism, nothing de-
stroys *dharma* more than living as if I am the only thing that matters.

In order to fulfill this fundamental calling of contributing to the well-
being of all living beings, each person must find work that is in harmony
with his or her nature.[86] Hinduism teaches that our callings must align
with our dispositions, our interests and gifts, our temperament and personality.[87] Our callings should be "fitting" inasmuch as they genuinely express
who we are and enable us to grow and to be fulfilled as we live them. By
contrast, to pursue any work or occupation that is clearly at odds with our
nature will not only lead to "frustration and unhappiness" for ourselves,[88]
but will also hinder our ability to contribute to the common good. Hinduism does teach that our nature and, therefore, our callings, can change, but
there should always be harmony between who we are and what we do.[89]

---

82. Rambachan, "Worship," 116.

83. Rambachan, "Worship," 116.

84. Rambachan, "Worship," 109.

85. Rambachan, "Worship," 117.

86. Rambachan, "Worship," 110.

87. Rambachan, "Worship," 129.

88. Rambachan, "Worship," 111.

89. Rambachan, "Worship," 111.

Still, while we must be attentive to ourselves in discerning our callings, we must also remember that our callings should benefit others and enable us to contribute to the "universal community" of which we are a part.[90] When they do so, all of our actions—indeed, our whole life—become an act of worship and praise to God who exists in all living things.[91]

A fourth religious and philosophical tradition that can enhance our understanding of vocation is Confucianism. Unlike Christianity, in which the ultimate goal is salvation through everlasting communion with God and the saints, in Confucianism the goal is "perfected moral character, meaningful human relationships, and an ordered, harmonious society."[92] This is achieved through the cultivation and development of one's character, which is the primary calling of Confucians.[93] The development of the self includes every dimension of our lives: our minds and hearts, our attitudes, habits, and dispositions, our feelings, our beliefs and convictions, and even our bodies. Self-cultivation occurs especially through education; notably, in Confucianism the purpose of education is not to prepare one for a job, much less to create "narrow specialists," but to cultivate genuinely good human beings who know how to live well with others.[94] The formation of one's character also happens at home, in friendships, at work, "through an engagement with the arts, sports, literature, even good conversations over a nice meal and wine."[95] As Mark Berkson elaborates, "Any activity that challenges a person, brings them into a community of fellow practitioners, and enables the cultivation of virtues and the pursuit of excellence can be seen as a calling if pursued for the right reasons, regardless of whether it provides an income."[96] Perhaps the best way to capture how Confucianism understands vocation is to say that "the ultimate calling for each of us is to become a benevolent human being," people who have good will toward one another, who consistently want what is best for one another, and in doing so learn how to live in right relationship with others. We both learn and exemplify what benevolence practically means when we fulfill our obligations in all the different relationships of our lives.

We cannot possibly do this on our own. Like Hinduism, Confucianism holds that human beings are radically and inescapably social beings. There

90. Rambachan, "Worship," 117.
91. Rambachan, "Worship," 119.
92. Berkson, "Cultivation," 164.
93. Berkson, "Cultivation," 175.
94. Berkson, "Cultivation," 175.
95. Berkson, "Cultivation," 176.
96. Berkson, "Cultivation," 176.

is no such thing as a truly separate and autonomous self because our self is constituted, shaped, and continually transformed by all the various relationships of our lives. Who we are—and who we will become—is a reflection of these many relationships. "We are who we are," Berkson explains, "because of those we have loved, lived with, and learned from."[97] Consequently, we need the help, guidance, insight, and instruction of others (including our ancestors) to truly learn what it means to be human. Self-cultivation occurs in healthy families, healthy friendships, and healthy communities. But it also has to be mutual. The "vocational vision" of Confucianism is a society in which each person helps other persons become better human beings.[98] I do not simply take whatever you give me in order to improve myself, but also give whatever I can so that you too can become a better human being. In this respect, as Berkson summarizes, "In the Confucian vision, *we are all calling each other.*"[99]

Conclusion

In this chapter we have explored different ways that calling or vocation has been understood. We gave foremost attention to how thinking about vocation has developed in Christianity. Our survey revealed that even though the Christian tradition never abandoned the idea of calling, some accounts of vocation were definitely misguided, particularly when moving from a religious to a purely secular understanding of calling. Once calling was separated from baptism, the conviction that it is important for all Christians to consider was not only diminished, but also seriously threatened. We should not imagine that we are immune from such abuses or threats. Nevertheless, there is much happening today that suggests this is an opportune time to once again consider how thinking of themselves as called by God might rightly guide the lives of all Christians. The topic is being discussed in new and interesting ways by contemporary Christian theologians. But Christians do not have a monopoly on vocation; indeed, their own understanding of God attests that God calls every person, Christian or not, religious or not, to contribute to God's work of transforming the world in justice, love, and peace so that all God's creatures can flourish.

As we have seen, there are many ways to think about our callings, both what they might mean and how they might be experienced in our lives. What this survey of the "landscape" of vocation has shown us is that calling

97. Berkson, "Cultivation," 167.

98. Berkson, "Cultivation," 174.

99. Berkson, "Cultivation," 174.

means so much more than figuring out possibilities for a career or searching for that fitting person with whom to spend the rest of our lives. Every day we are called, every day we are summoned to respond to a world that continually beckons to us, continually asks us to contribute to something larger than ourselves, something momentous, meaningful, and immensely hopeful. We become better human beings when we respond to those callings.

CHAPTER 3

Stories of Call

IT IS GOOD NEWS to receive a call. Why? Because living a called life is to live into our real selves, and also to live a life aimed toward something that is truly worthy. However, to qualify this—or, really, *because* of this—following a call will not make our lives easy. Following worthy things takes effort and sacrifice. Despite the fact that we sometimes confuse them, we all know deep down that an easy life is not the same thing as a good life.

This is one reason why we *need* to be called: without the call, and left to our own devices, we will more likely take the easy path. It is sometimes necessary, it seems, that we be picked up and placed on the more difficult path, which is also the one that will carry us toward something better. Some of the oldest stories of call, especially those in the Bible, begin with this idea: we need someone—actually, God—to push us out on an uncertain and potentially dangerous path in life. Naturally, we will resist this. But if we go, it will be good for us, and good for many others as well, since God's call always takes us out of ourselves, out of our small, self-involved world, to life in and for community. But this can be like pulling teeth. And, it often involves a story—one where someone is interrupted in their daily life by God or God's messenger and, after some discussion that often involves resistance on the part of the one called, is given a mission, and placed on a new path of life

In this chapter we want to explore some important stories of people being called, beginning especially with those in the Bible. The Bible is an ancient text, of course, and for that reason it may sometimes seem distant from us. But in fact, often the pattern of call we discover in the Bible's stories is repeated. There seems to be a kind of logic to it. In this chapter we want to notice something of how this logic works, and also consider how stories of call that come to Christians (and others) often follow patterns we first find in the biblical stories of call.

The Biblical Tradition of Call

The God of the Bible tells the prophet Jeremiah that he has "appointed" him to be a prophet before he was born. The prophetic life was what he was meant for. Nevertheless, when Jeremiah hears this, he objects, offering excuses like "I'm only a boy," or "I do not know how to speak" (Jer 1:6).

Jeremiah gets a very tough assignment. He has to predict the destruction of Jerusalem by the Babylonian empire, saying this again and again, directly and forcefully to the people of Judah. And they respond with disdain. How unpatriotic and even blasphemous to say that our God will not protect us from our enemies, that they will destroy everything that we hold dear, and we will have to suffer! Jeremiah's calling was no fun for him. "I have become a laughingstock all day long; everyone mocks me. For whenever I speak, I must cry out, I must shout, 'Violence and destruction!'" (Jer 20:7–8). He becomes depressed and even curses the day he was born (Jer 20:14). Yet he persists, banking on the promise God gave him when he called: "Do not be afraid of them, for I am with you to deliver you, says the LORD" (Jer 1:8). Later, when Jeremiah's prophecies come true, and after all the violence and destruction, he is able to offer words of comfort to the Judean exiles in Babylon who, having survived through their suffering, can reawaken to hope.

The Bible is full of stories of calls like Jeremiah's. More than any other book, it is because of the Bible that we talk about "call" at all. That makes it the right place to start in any attempt to understand what call might mean, especially for Christians. The fact is, religious traditions are the natural home of talk about call. After all, if there is a call, there must be a caller. In the Bible, the caller is the one God who created everything and everyone, and who remains throughout history intimately involved with how it all turns out. The Bible is God's story, a story in which people like Jeremiah are offered a role. Call in the Bible, we might say, is an invitation to enter with your life the place that God gives it in God's story.

An implication of this biblical understanding is that in following the call we learn more about what God is doing—who, really, God is. When people in the Bible are called they are invited not simply to come to know a plan about their lives but to know and interact with a person. As he follows his call, Jeremiah becomes friends with God, which he shows most clearly when he tells God off. True friends, after all, hold each other accountable. "I lay charges against you," he says to God. "Why does the way of the guilty prosper?" (Jer 12:1). The reason Jeremiah can say something like this to God is because he thinks he knows God's character. As Jeremiah has learned, God has created all that is, and has generous intentions for what he created and for his people, whom he wants to live justly and righteously. If all of this is true of God, then why do the wicked prosper?

While Jeremiah becomes intimate with God through his call, we need also to remember that, even before the occasion of his calling, he was a member of a people who passed on knowledge about what could reasonably be expected of God. Prophesying around the time of the fall of Jerusalem in 586 BC, Jeremiah was an inheritor of a long religious tradition about the God of Israel, who had directed Abraham and Sarah in their wanderings, led his people out of slavery in Egypt in partnership with Moses, and saved Israel from their enemies by leaders like Deborah and David. This tradition already included stories of call. As Jeremiah's call came to him, he could understand and test it in relation to this tradition. Because he knew the stories of people like Abraham or Moses or Deborah, all Israelites who earlier received calls, Jeremiah was in a position to understand his call when it came—and this also put him in the position to engage with God, even talk back to him, as many "called ones" before him had done.

Calls make the most sense in the context of such a tradition. This does not mean you must belong to a religious tradition to be called, but rather that such traditions carry a history of a God who calls that gives you a leg up as you try to understand any call you might think you have. In such a history, if a call comes to you, it is not because you are so special and exceptional, but because this God is at work in the world; and he does this work through people like you. Any "people of God," however they might name themselves, are learning to find themselves within this work, guided by others in their tradition who have been called before.

This does not mean there is a standard script for God's call. In the biblical tradition, there seems to be little restriction on who God might call, or how and when he might call. The biblical God not only calls Christians and Jews, but also calls or speaks through others who seem to claim neither tradition, like a mysterious King Melchizedek (Gen 14) who shows up to bless Abraham, or Jethro, a "priest of Midian," who is kind to Moses and gives him crucial advice about how to lead the Israelite people (Exod 3 and 18). Christians actually believe that God calls us all, whether or not we believe in advance that he is there, and irrespective of what sort of idea we happen to have of him. To be called by this God means to join in what he is doing in the world. Anyone can do this—and God seems to want everyone who is willing to join in.

As Jeremiah's case also shows, while Christians believe we can gather from the biblical tradition a broad sense of God's intentions, just exactly what God is doing in the world at any particular time is sometimes very surprising. This means that if we are to join in God's work, heed the call, we will need to be ready to puzzle it through. This is helped by an intimacy with God like the sort Jeremiah developed, which included questions and negotiations and sometimes even vehement objections to what God seemed to be doing.

The demand for this is often the strongest when the story needs to take a new turn. New turns, new conditions, require change and innovation; calls within them are not predictable. No one would have predicted that God's plan for Israel included the destruction of the temple and of the holy city of Jerusalem—no one, that is, except Jeremiah who got the news from his call. Similarly, after sticking with his call, Jeremiah was able to give voice to surprising new things to his people about what God was doing: "The days are surely coming, says the LORD, when I will make a new covenant with the house of Israel and the house of Judah" (Jer 31:31).

So calls can be surprising and puzzling, and they can mark changes in the histories of individual persons and the communities they belong to. Yet even the surprise makes sense only if we have something to measure it against. The philosopher Alasdair MacIntyre has argued that human beings think and reason well only within a tradition.[1] A tradition carries a set of shared goods, and judgments about them, that it passes on to us. Religious traditions do this as they carry a vision of how we can live well in community, pursue justice, and endure suffering. MacIntyre also has shown how important stories are in passing on a tradition and in teaching us to make judgments within our own storied lives. We depend on narratives to set the meaning and context of our judgments about what we should do or what kind of people we should strive to be. Religions traditions not only tell stories of the lives and experiences of people that are worth imitating, they are also carried along by these stories—and this, they suppose, gives us access to the storied life of God. Indeed, we know human beings (and God) only within a story; our capacity to tell our own or another person's story is what also allows us to ascribe unity to that person's life, and also explain at various points why they did what they did, and evaluate whether it was good that they did it.

Stories of call fit into this narrative pattern; they tell us not only about the call itself, but about the person who is called and, in the Bible, the one who calls: God. Considering at least some of these stories in some detail is important if we wish to understand what living vocationally might mean in light of the biblical tradition. In the following sections we will look more closely at the stories of the calling of three important biblical characters:

---

1. See MacIntyre, *Three Rival Versions*. MacIntyre's is perhaps the most important voice in moral philosophy over the past fifty years.

Moses, Isaiah, and Paul. As we begin to do this, it is worth stopping to summarize four general points that seem to recur in the Bible's stories of call.

First, the tradition rests upon the idea that God wants us to be fully ourselves as we were created to be, but we often stray from this, and need to be brought back. And so, the biblical God calls us back to ourselves; we need, in fact, to be restored and healed. Call involves a personal kind of healing, which comes from beyond us, even as it is also what we most desire. As William Cavanaugh puts it, the "healing of our weakness depends on recognizing the source of our being outside of ourselves, but this source is simultaneously within us; we find ourselves precisely by finding God. Thus, vocation is both a call from outside the self that draws one outside the confines of the small self and it is also, at the same time, a discovery of our deepest desires and our true self."[2] Call in the Christian tradition is also a rescue: we are called out of something, or told by God to leave something behind and move on to something better—which is the very thing we were made for in the first place.

Second, the call is about more than our own well-being. God in the Christian tradition is doing something in the world: he is redeeming it. This requires work, the most difficult and serious and complex work there is— although also the most meaningful and joyful. It is at its core a work of love. The God of the Bible invites us into this work; in fact, he depends on us to do it. God works through us, itself a sign of his love. In a particular time, God knows much better than we do what this work is. He knows where he needs us. And so, Christians believe, he calls us into specific places and within specific communities to do something, to participate somehow in the redemption of the world.

These two points, about our rescue and restoration in call, and the work it involves, inform the biblical story from the start. In Genesis 1–11 we hear not only about how God created us to be his friends, we also learn of how this goes terribly wrong, leading to trouble of all sorts, such as fratricide, when Cain kills his brother Abel, or unbridled ambition, when people make the most of the current technology to leave their place on earth behind, attempting to build a tower called Babel that reaches all the way to heaven. In the story, God acts in response to this trouble—to the fact that human beings have strayed from what God willed them to be in creating them—by calling Abram (later Abraham), whom he tells to "Go from your country and your kindred and your father's house to the land that I will show you" (Gen 12:1). Because of this call we have the Jewish people, through whom "all the families of the earth shall be blessed" (Gen 12:3). With the first call

---

2. Cavanaugh, "Actually," 43.

of Abraham the rescue begins; and it is carried on through him and Sarah as they respond to the call, becoming part of God's redemptive work

The call of Abraham also demonstrates a third point that fills out the Bible's picture of call: the occasion of a call—when God speaks it and we hear it—very often marks a significant turning point in the story, certainly of the one called, and often enough in the larger story of God's redemptive work in the world. Often there is a radical disruption, a sea change in life. With call one kind or form of life is ended and a new one begun. Abraham and Sarah had a settled place in family life in Haran, but were suddenly yanked from this by God's call, becoming the wandering nomads who produced God's chosen people. Or, the disciples were tending their nets by the Sea of Galilee, along comes Jesus who says "Come, follow me," and they drop their nets and take up a course that leads them to become apostles of a new movement that eventually spreads around the world.

The radical disruption we often find in biblical calls heightens the drama—which makes for a good story. We remember many biblical stories of call, like Abraham's or Moses's or Jeremiah's or Paul's, because of the drama in them: God suddenly breaks in, confronting someone, and afterwards everything is different. The difference, in fact, amounts to a new kind of life that the call has begun in us. This third feature, so often found in biblical stories of call, needs qualification. We can recognize that the Bible tells a dramatic story which highlights turning points, but the story is also of a people who have lived with God, in a more or less ordinary way, for thousands of years. Jeremiah was one of a kind, as was the dramatic destruction of the holy city; we need not imagine that to be called we must mimic his radicality, or his suffering. Similarly, the first disciples will remain the first; we don't need to think that our call is invalid if it does not create a new world movement.

On the other hand, all calls are dramatic in another sense: they play a dramatic role within our story as it connects to God's. We shouldn't expect our calls to be as exciting or mysterious as Moses's when he is confronted in the wilderness by a burning bush or Saul's (Paul's) when he is struck from his horse by a blinding light. Nevertheless, there is a different kind of drama that does come to us all, namely that the occasion of our calling becomes a swing point in how we eventually come to tell our stories. Call stories in this way always inform life stories; they play a key role in the "drama" that is our own story as well as the larger story of a whole people.

This leads to a fourth crucial feature of the biblical idea of call: we learn to tell the stories of our calls only after we have lived them for some time. This is true not only for us personally, but also of religious communities and traditions. The Israelites can tell the story of the call of Abraham best when they are able to see what unfolded from it: the chosen people. On the biblical model, key moments are determined not simply by what happens to us, but by the larger story of God's activity in the world, an activity into which we are invited by God's call. Then, and only then, can we notice and articulate how God called us, how what we heard and how we responded matters both in our own history and that of God's dealings with the world.

In sum, four things about the logic of call are worth remembering as we consider the Bible's stories of call: (1) We are called from one kind of life to a better, fuller one, and this often involves a sort of rescue or salvation. (2) This new, different life draws us to participate in God's redemptive work in the world; by calling us, God's work becomes also ours. The occasion of our being called from some earlier way of living into the heart of God's redemptive work (3) marks for us a before and after moment in our lives, a point at which a new sort of life began. Yet (4) we can best identify this before and after only as we are able later to tell the fuller story not only of our lives but of God's life in the world that we have been invited to join.

So, for Christians, ideas about call begin within the stories of the Bible. But, as the features of these stories also show, call is not enclosed within this tradition. The calls we learn of in the Bible meet people where they are, and invite them to something new and exciting, even if this means joining in some difficult work. And, once God's call is followed, it becomes key in locating who we are and where we are headed. Importantly, the God of the Bible calls us all and offers us redemptive work to do. This also means that we can expect to find stories of call outside the biblical story—ones we can learn a great deal from such as, for instance, the call of Muhammad or Gandhi. The God of the Bible is at work in the world, redeeming it; he knows what this work involves in a specific time and place far better than we do. Christians believe what they have been given in the Bible is a story, or series of stories, that guide us as we look to understand our own callings, and to remind us that we have them.

Moses Is Called into Service

The Jewish people acclaim Moses as their greatest leader ever. Yet he had a rocky start. As we are told in the early chapters of Exodus, hidden by his mother in a basket in the river, Moses initially survived Pharaoh's genocidal intentions. Fortuitously, the baby and basket were found by Pharaoh's daughter, who brought Moses home and raised him in the household of the king of Egypt. As Moses grew, undoubtedly his privilege puzzled him. Likely he asked himself, "Am I oppressed or the oppressor?" Under the attentive watch of his sister Miriam, who knew where he was and even arranged that his own mother care for him, Moses could not entirely forget his Israelite roots. But the Israelites were persecuted, and Moses had a cushy life as an Egyptian. Could he really claim solidarity with his people?

Moses's identity issues became urgent when he noticed an Egyptian beating an Israelite. Impulsively, he killed the Egyptian and quickly hid his body in the sand, hoping no one had seen. But they had, as he discovered the next day. Puffed up with righteous indignation, he urged one of his fellow Israelites to stop fighting with his kinsman. The man replied: "Who made you a ruler and judge over us? Do you mean to kill me as you killed the Egyptian?" (Exod 2:14). Soon the news that Moses was a killer reached Pharaoh, who commanded that he be apprehended and killed. Moses had little choice but to run away, deep into the surrounding desert.

We can only imagine what Moses was feeling at this point. His connection to Pharaoh and all Egypt was severed: he had killed one of his own privileged class, and now there was a price on his head. There was no going back to that life. But he fared no better with the Israelites to whom he was only a golden boy. They wanted nothing to do with his entreaties for moral reform. The best he could hope for was to leave all the confusion behind and start over in the wilderness of Midian. And this seems to unfold rather happily. He is shown kindness by a desert dweller named Jethro (also called Reuel), who welcomes Moses into his family, even giving him his daughter Zipporah in marriage, and the couple quickly bears a son. So Moses settles into a pastoral life, grazing Jethro's flocks on the mountains.

This is when Moses is called. God suddenly appears in a burning bush. "I am the God of your father, the God of Abraham, the God of Isaac, and the God of Jacob . . . I have observed the misery of my people . . . I have also seen how the Egyptians oppress them. So come, I will send you to Pharaoh to bring my people, the Israelites, out of Egypt" (Exod 3:6–10).

So begins a long dialogue between Moses and God all about Moses's calling. The back and forth between the caller (God) and the called (Moses) makes this the longest call story in the Bible. At its heart is Moses's reluctance to follow the call, which he expresses in various ways. Moses first asks about his own identity—"Who am I that I should go to Pharaoh, and bring the Israelites out of Egypt?" (Exod 3:11). Yet, quickly, this shifts to a question about God's identity. Perhaps this is because God answers Moses's identity question not by focusing on Moses's resume, all his talents and his experiences, or even on the reasons why God has singled him out with his choice for leadership, but rather by simply saying "I will be with you" (Exod 3:12). By contrast, Moses seems quite concerned about God's resume, and so asks for his name—receiving the famous reply: "I am who I am" (Exod 3:14).

Here we learn one of the most important lessons about call in the Bible. Receiving a call is not like applying for a job. One might say that Moses is well suited for the difficult work of confronting the Pharaoh and freeing the Israelites—he is a Levite (Israel's priestly tribe), knows the workings of Pharaoh's court, had recently gained experience in the desert, etc., etc. Yet in all the call stories of the Bible never are we given a list of the extraordinary credentials of the one who is called. In fact, it is usually the opposite: Jeremiah is too young, Moses, as we learn a few verses later (Exod 4:10), is slow of speech, Gideon is the least of the least of the tribes of Israel, David is the youngest of many brothers who his father Jesse does not even consider for leadership, Peter is a common fisherman.

The point is not that God calls incompetent or ill-equipped people. It is rather that in the call the focus is not on the person who is called and all he or she has to offer, but rather on the God who calls, his purposes, and his assurances that he will accompany those he calls. This is one of the many reasons a call is not a career. "My career" features me; "my call" does not, at least not in the same way. It rather features the God who calls us.

"Bringing the Israelites out of Egypt" is not on Moses's agenda. His story previous to his call indicates that he cares for the Israelites, that he is aware of the injustices they are suffering, and that he thinks something should be done about this. Yet doing something about it is not on his life's program, especially as it stands at this point. Amidst all the turmoil of the past few years, Moses seems to have pushed any noble thoughts about helping his people out of his mind and is now happily raising a family, caring for sheep, and making this new place, Midian, his own. He is not in the market for a new job; if God had put out an ad, he would not have applied. In the call God proposes to Moses a program that is far larger than any of this; not surprisingly, his imagination cannot reach for it. Indeed, he tries to fight it off, one objection after the other. What if the people don't know the God I supposedly come in the name of? (Exod 3:13). What if they're unconvinced by my story of God appearing to me? (Exod 4:1). What if I fumble in my speech? (Exod 4:10).

In the subsequent dialogue God meets every one of Moses's objections with a promise of strength through companionship. The "I will be with you" with which the conversation begins is repeated, with specifics added: God explains who he is, not only with the mysterious "I AM" but also with an ancestral history of his dealing with the Hebrew people in the past; Moses is given some things to do with his wooden staff to help convince the people; God promises to teach Moses speech and send along the more articulate Aaron to speak for Moses. God never suggests that his plan for liberation will be easy or that Moses will not confront significant obstacles if he agrees to the call. Such obstacles can be faced as they arise, so long as Moses counts on the promise made repeatedly in the call: that God will be with him throughout.

Near the end of the long story of Moses's call the mood shifts. Moses has raised various objections about what might happen if he agrees to do what God wants. God has responded to each with some specific remedies aimed at the worries Moses has expressed. Yet at the end of it all Moses sighs: "Oh my LORD, please send someone else." This brings a different kind of response from God: "Then the anger of the LORD was kindled against Moses . . ." (Exod 4:13–14). The anger responds to the fact that Moses, with this last objection, breaks the mood that has held throughout the course of the call as God and Moses have made their respective points to one another. Here Moses looks for a way to end the call, to hang up the phone. He is saying, in effect, "I do not want to live a called life. I know my people are in trouble in Egypt, and I am glad, God, if you have a plan to help them, but I would really rather not be involved."

Moses needs to be saved from himself. The land of Midian has been good both to and for Moses. He fled there to escape hatred and animosity coming from both the Egyptians and the Israelites. Here in the wilderness of Midian he has been welcomed by foreigners; he is rejuvenated, and his strength has returned. But there is temptation in this. Perhaps because of his earlier failure at leadership, Moses seems to have become content with life from the sidelines. He does not want what God is planning since it interferes with what he is now happily doing. Save the people, God, but leave me be. "LORD, please send someone else."

Moses needs to be rescued from defining his life on his own terms. In this way his call story clearly illustrates the first feature of biblical calls as noted above: if he follows it, the call will take him from one form of life to a new one, one that is better and fuller, even if also more challenging. Moses might stay in Midian with Jethro's family where, after a crisis, his life has become well-ordered and pleasant. Now, in the midst of this pleasant life, he has been confronted in the burning bush by a mysterious God, who just now is inviting him to join in a different sort of project: the liberation of the Israelites from slavery in Egypt. God and Moses will work together, and with others. It is difficult work, and Moses will be stretched by it. Yet, despite its difficulties it is an abundant and deeply meaningful life, of an entirely different order than the one he is now living. Midian is good for a time, but it is not the promised land.

The salvation or rescue offered to Moses in the call combines exactly with the salvation that comes to the people. God intends to draw them out from Egypt and transform them, opening a new kind of shared life precisely at this place in the wilderness where Moses is now standing, at Mount Horeb (or Sinai), where he hopes to strike a covenant with them and begin to teach them what it really means to be "people of God." The rescue in both cases comes in terms of a new sort of work Moses and the people can enter if they follow the call.

Here the second feature of biblical calls mentioned above is plainly displayed. The new life to which we are called is always a life of participation in God's redemptive work in the world; in heeding the call God's work becomes also ours. By leaving the relative comfort of Midian and following the call back to Egypt, where his people suffer and the cruel Pharaoh reigns, Moses will learn to live a story that is not just his but his people's, and ultimately also the story of God.

Almost everyone knows the story that unfolds after Exodus 4 when Moses, after many stalling attempts, accepts the divine call and returns to Egypt to confront Pharaoh and free the Israelites. Subsequently he leads them across the Red Sea and back to Mt. Sinai where, functioning as mediator between the Israelites and the mysterious God who called him, Moses receives God's law and proclaims it to the people. It is a great and inspiring story. But what happens to Moses at the end of it all? We know this story less well, but it is a revealing one. As we learn as the Torah concludes, after a long song and few last words of advice, Moses dies, shortly after climbing Mount Nebo to look over to see the promised land. At this point the Bible adds two final points about Moses: First, "He was buried in a valley in the land of Moab, opposite Beth-peor, but no one knows his burial place to this day." And second, "Never since has there arisen a prophet in Israel like Moses, whom the LORD knew face to face" (Deut 34:6, 10).

If the story were only about Moses, the first comment about not knowing where his bones are would seem sad. Shouldn't we know the place of his burial so we can honor Moses for all his hard work? But as the second comment suggests, if you want to honor Moses, look to the people who live with his memory and whose lives were made possible by his willingness to follow the call. And look also to the God who remains present, whose face was reflected for a time in the face of Moses. This is the sort of life story call makes possible. If my story is not about me, but about the people, and about God's work to shepherd them through, I can expect, and accept, that following the call will bring a certain diminishment of my individual life—although this is also the source of its ultimate enhancement: that it was lived for others.

By the logic of call in the Bible, those who follow the call do not become heroes but rather servants. The surprise in the biblical call is that, if I follow it, I will discover that the call is not mainly about me or my life, but rather about what my life points towards. There is a kind of diminishment in this; in a way, I become smaller as I follow God's call. But this is because of the much larger thing that comes into focus as I live the call. In the New Testament, John the Baptist plays the role of harbinger, the one who prepares the way for Jesus, Israel's messiah. This is why he says, knowingly, "He must increase, but I must decrease" (John 3:30). There is a kind of death in this. It is significant, perhaps, that we are told of John's call in the New Testament story, as if it needs to happen before the bigger thing it points to can be fully revealed.

This is true of Moses. He leads the Israelites to the brink of the promised land but does not enter. Instead, he dies and is buried in obscurity. Again, this seems sad for Moses, kind of a raw deal. But when we remember that Moses's call was never about Moses for himself, but rather about Moses for the people, it seems rather fitting. Indeed, we can see the logic in it, echoed in our time. Dr. Martin Luther King, Jr., in whose bones the story of Moses resonated, similarly responded to a call from God, first to be a minister of the gospel and then the leader of the civil rights movement in America. Like Moses, his extraordinary career is well known. Yet there seems a cruel twist at the end with his assassination at age thirty-nine in Memphis on August 4, 1968.

But Dr. King's last public words point us beyond his life to what it served. The night before his death, as he closed his final speech delivered at the Masonic Temple in Memphis, King indicated he knew his time was short. "Longevity has its place," he said, but not for him. Rather, "I just want to do God's will. And He's allowed me to go up to the mountain. And I've looked over. And I've seen the promised land. I may not get there with you. But I want you to know tonight, that we, as a people, will get to the promised land!"[3]

Like Moses, King knew the significance of his life before it ended: it was not to be found in how it ended, nor in all the fame it has since brought to his name, but rather in the larger story for which it was lived. And this was possible only because of his willing response to the call of God to offer his life in service to his people—and therefore to a larger story, the one God is telling about how all of us are drawn together upward to full unity and peace in the Promised Land.

Isaiah's Fear Is Turned to Confidence

Moses, as Deuteronomy tells us, was the greatest prophet in Jewish history. His life and service set the context for the work of all other biblical

3. King, *Dream*, 203.

prophets. Similarly, we can hear the echo of his call in many subsequent biblical calls. For instance, and as we have noticed, the prophet Jeremiah pushes back against God's call because he is too young and a lousy public speaker—just like Moses.

A few generations prior to Jeremiah, Isaiah receives his call after he is transported in a vision to see God in the temple. God is too big for it. "Holy, holy, holy," say the winged creatures in the vision, "the whole earth is full of his glory." And "the pivots on the household shook at the voices of those who called, and the house filled with smoke." Isaiah is mortified and humbled: "Woe is me!" he says, "I am lost, for I am a man of unclean lips, and I live among a people of unclean lips; yet my eyes have seen the King, the LORD of hosts" (Isa 6:3–5).

The vision takes Isaiah more quickly through the paces than Moses in his call story, not just because the vision gives no room for mistaking who God is, but also because it makes Isaiah profoundly aware of his own and his people's sin. The reference to unclean lips is to false speech, lies. What is false must be burned away. And so the winged creature flies to Isaiah and touches his mouth with a burning coal. As the creature declares, "'Now that this has touched your lips, your guilt has departed and your sin is blotted out.'" The vision is so powerful that Isaiah is seemingly overwhelmed. Unlike Moses, who takes a while, he seems instantly transformed. When God asks for assistance, Isaiah offers eager consent rather than reluctance and resistance. "Then I heard the voice of the LORD saying, 'Whom shall I send, and who will go for us?' And I said 'Here am I; send me!'" (Isa 6:7–8).

Despite such differences, the call of Isaiah is like the call of Moses in that it induces fear, which arises because each encounters someone, something, that is vastly superior to him. Isaiah is immediately aware of his unworthiness and feels the need to avert his eyes—and this is like Moses who at the site of the burning bush removes his shoes and hides his face: "he was afraid to look at God" (Exod 3:6).

Fear marks our memory; it unsettles us as it suddenly brings us face to face with ourselves: our mortality, our frailty, and our relative smallness. In fact, in biblical call stories a state of fear and dismay is frequently the starting point. Its presence, however, is temporary, for something is almost always done to assuage it. For instance, when the angel of the Lord announces the good news of the messiah's birth to the shepherds, we hear: "and the glory of the Lord shone around them, and they were terrified." But the angel said to them, "Do not be afraid: for see—I am bringing you good news of great joy" (Luke 2:10). Or when Mary hears from the angel Gabriel that she is to bear the messiah, the text tells us she was "much perplexed"—to which

Gabriel responds: "Do not be afraid, Mary, for you have found favor with God" (Luke 1:29–30).

It is not only in the Bible that we find fear in stories of call. As Muhammad receives his call, he is confronted by the angel Gabriel who at first instructs him to read, pressing him with a cloth on the forehead with such force that Muhammad fears he will die. Moving from the cave in which this occurs, Gabriel comes again, and Muhammad stands transfixed. According to Ibn Ishaq's record of Muhammad's recollection of the event, "I stood gazing at him, moving neither backward nor forward; then I began to turn my face away from him, but towards whatever region of the sky I looked, I saw him as before."[4]

We should know, of course, that it is a rare person who has such dramatic encounters with the divine. But the drama we find in call stories such as Moses's or King's or Isaiah's or Muhammad's makes them riveting and memorable. We might forget all the things that God and Moses say to one another in Moses's call story, but we do not forget the burning bush. Similarly, in Isaiah's account, the image of strange, majestic creatures flying about and all the rumbling and the smoke—these things stick with us. This is partly due to their strangeness; like Moses, we are curious and want to have a look. But at a deeper level, it is the element of fear that first registers with us. What does fear have to do with call?

Very importantly, we need not expect that as we are called we will be overwhelmed by fear. It is a common mistake to await such a decisive and overwhelming encounter, assuming that without it God has not really yet called us. We are told stories of call in the Bible and other sacred texts not to make us hold out until their details are replicated in our own callings, but rather so that we can learn something from them about the logic or grammar of call. What we see in stories like Isaiah's is that in his call he is brought into contact with something that is awesome. This leads to fear of a certain sort which is acknowledged and addressed in different ways in many biblical call stories.

In our time we tend to think that fear is always bad; yet in the Christian tradition we find it counted among the seven gifts of the Holy Spirit. How can fear be a gift? As St. Thomas Aquinas describes it, fear arises from some perceived evil, such as the threat of death. We rightly fear close encounters with fierce creatures whose power greatly exceeds ours, such as a lion. We know they might kill us. Is this the fear Isaiah feels, that the thundering God might kill him?

---

4. Ishaq, *Sirat Rasoul Allah*, 21.

Isaiah makes no mention of a fear of death. Rather, what seems at the root of his fear is that he feels terribly unworthy. God is encountered not so much as a killer but as a judge. Aquinas believes God is rightly feared because from him comes the "evil" of punishment. But, as he further clarifies this point, God's punishment is not an evil "absolutely" but rather "relatively"; in fact, it is really a good since it aims not at death but rehabilitation, healing, cleansing.[5] When we human beings fear punishment from God, we demonstrate an awareness of our need for such changes in ourselves. In strange and frightful encounters like the one Isaiah has, we recognize not only that we are fragile and vulnerable creatures, subject to harm and death, but also that we are sinners in need of redemption—and this is a need we cannot fill for ourselves. Isaiah expresses this clearly, both for himself and for his people. "Woe is me, for I am a man of unclean lips, and I live among a people of unclean lips."

In this story, and in the others mentioned, the fear that arises in the divine encounter is addressed shortly after it arises by God or those who speak for God. "Be not afraid," Gabriel says to Mary. In Muhammad's case, he receives comfort from his wife Khadija, who is convinced he will be a great prophet of Allah. For Isaiah, the coal is brought to his lips and he is purified. In none of these stories do we get the idea that the human who encounters God is wrong to feel fear. Rather, they treat it as if it is the most natural thing—what human beings might be expected to feel as their first response to God. With this in mind, we can perhaps begin to understand how fear might be a "gift," especially as a first response. As goes the proverb: "The fear of the Lord is the beginning of wisdom, and knowledge of the Holy One is insight" (Prov 9:10).

When someone is afraid they are not, at the moment of their fear, secure in their own abilities; they are not, as we like to say, very "self-confident." If we are thinking of "call" as if it is mainly a pep talk to get out there and do something great, then this lack of self-confidence due to fear will seem counter-productive. As coaches often note, the key thing is to get their athletes to believe in themselves and their abilities. The locker room before the game is not the place to incite fear of the opponent; instead what we need is to build up self-confidence: "You can do this! You can go out there and dominate!" In our time this approach has spilled off the sports field into almost every aspect of our lives: we believe that without exuding self-confidence we will be no good at our business dealings, our jobs, or in our relationships. Yet, ironically, with all its talk of self-confidence,

---

5. Aquinas, *Summa*, II–II, 19,1. Quotations in this chapter are from the translation by the Fathers of the English Dominican Province.

our age remains permeated by fear. This is sometimes expressed as a fear of death, but also of so many other things: of disease, of loneliness, of failure, of embarrassment. Perhaps its most common form is a nagging, ever-present anxiety: we are not sure what we are afraid of, but nonetheless we feel it. Far from a gift, this fear seems like nothing but a curse that clings to our lives, dragging them under.

What is interesting about Isaiah's call is how quickly his fear, and the lack of self-confidence it reveals, turns to a readiness, a confidence even, to serve. His response to his call is perhaps the most eager and enthusiastic in all of the Bible. Whom shall I send? asks God. "Here am I, send me!" responds Isaiah—this after moaning, just three verses before, "Woe is me!" What made the difference? There is only one possible source: the coal bought from the altar to cleanse his lips, and the words accompanying it from the winged creature, "your guilt has departed and your sin is blotted out."

Here we can see an absolutely crucial feature of call, which distinguishes it dramatically from a pep talk, and so also marks the difference between how we typically think of our need for self-confidence and the biblical idea of empowerment to serve, as it is manifest in these ancient stories of call. The vision of Almighty God instills fear in Isaiah, and he recognizes how insignificant and imperfect he is in comparison. In this state, if Isaiah were responsible for generating his own confidence, if he felt the need to buck up, assert himself and take on the job, he would fail—and the knowledge of this would crumble him to pieces. But Isaiah does not need to do this; in fact, his call is showing him this. The gift of the fear, which comes in the truthful awareness of his own inadequacy and sin, causes him to give it up. When he gives it up, he can receive the cleansing that comes in the gleaming hot coal brought from the altar. Once cleansed he can step forward, for, after all, this same great God has asked for assistance.

Fear is the first term in the grammar of call. It comes as our small, selfish worlds are busted open by a visit from, or a vision of, or a recognition that there is, something indescribably bigger and more powerful than we are. In stories like Isaiah's, it is followed, first, by the clear realization that, by ourselves, we can never measure up and, second, that, actually, we don't need to since the God whom we initially rightly feared is also the very one who calls for our participation and pledges to enable us and accompany us. This second realization depends on the conviction that this God of great power is, in fact, best named as Love. This is how "perfect love casts out fear" (1 John 4:18). In the face of love, how can we resist responding to the call that comes with it? "Here am I, send me!" And so, we are empowered to accept the call as ours.

The third characteristic of biblical calls listed earlier in this chapter was that call brings profound change in our lives, and often also in the lives of our people. With it, one kind of life is ended and a new one begun. There is drama in this; often in the biblical calls it is accented by fearful encounters that rocket the ones who are called beyond any self-satisfied complacency and put them in touch with who they really are as sinful, mortal creatures. As such they feel a profound sense of their dependencies, and quickly realize that if they accept the call they cannot depend on their own strength. It is important to add, however, that the drama need not spring always from an explosive divine encounter. What is necessary, rather, is that the one who is called reaches this essential realization: that the capacity to follow the call is not manufactured within us but comes from beyond us as we are cleansed and equipped to act by Almighty God. Our identity as one who is called is rooted here, in a much different soil than the "self-confidence" we are frequently told we must have if we are to succeed in a competitive world.

As it turns out, it is a very good thing that Isaiah does not depend on his own strength, for his call is exceedingly difficult. In his time, the great Assyrian Empire draws near, crushes Israel, and forces Judah into servitude. Isaiah's task involves crying out in warning, year after year, to a people whose ears are clogged with their own self-confidence. How long must I cry? he asks. "Until cities lie waste without inhabitant, and houses without people, and the land is utterly desolate," comes the reply (Isa 6:11). In volunteering for this call, Isaiah volunteers for a life of suffering. But, as he can recall later, he initially stepped forward with confidence not in his own strength and worthiness, but rather in the power and purpose of the transcendent caller, who lifted Isaiah's fear by blotting out his sins. In his difficult life he has many more occasions in which he might reasonably feel fear. Yet, as we read later in the prophetic writings gathered under his name, such occasions are addressed with the profound reminder that Isaiah did not call himself; rather, the work of his call is given him by Almighty God, who is also his companion throughout all its human struggles. As this God says, "I, I am he who comforts you; why then are you afraid of a mere mortal?" (Isa 51:12).

Saul Is Placed on a New Road

For dramatic and fearful encounter, it is difficult to beat the call of Saul, who becomes St. Paul, the great missionary, letter-writer and theologian of the latter half of the New Testament. When we first meet him, he is the zealous Jewish enemy of the Christian church, which he considers dangerous and heretical: "Saul was ravaging the church by entering house after house; drag-ging off both men and women, he committed them to prison" (Acts 8:3).

This zealous work is interrupted as Saul is on his way with his compan-ions on the road from Jerusalem to Damascus where he plans to capture and imprison more Christians.

> [S]uddenly a light from heaven flashed around him. He fell to the ground and heard a voice saying to him, "Saul, Saul, why do you persecute me?" He asked, "Who are you, Lord?" The reply came, "I am Jesus, whom you are persecuting. But get up and enter the city, and you will be told what you are to do." The men who were traveling with him stood speechless because they heard the voice but saw no one. Saul got up from the ground, and though his eyes were open, he could see nothing; so they led him by the hand and brought him into Damascus. For three days he was without sight, and neither ate nor drank. (Acts 9:3–9)

As we read this passage we feel as if someone has suddenly switched on a very bright strobe light, and we are stumbling about, trying to get our bearings. Saul is literally knocked over by Jesus' call. The disorientation comes from the blinding light and the strange voice, and the fact that the others present hear someone, but can't see him. But it also comes from the fact that Saul is completely surprised by the person who addresses him. He was quite sure about Jesus: he's the enemy. But now, suddenly, he's brilliantly present and wants to take over Saul's life.

Jesus' introduction of himself as the one whom Saul is persecuting cuts deep into Saul's self-understanding. Saul would describe what he is doing as a work of righteousness. Unlike Moses, who seems to be hiding out, avoid-ing the fate of his people in the desert, Saul is fully in the fray. But he is going the wrong way, and in the process he is causing others to suffer unjustly. Jesus voices this; he speaks for the ones who are right now Saul's target, the persecuted ones. Sometimes biblical calls involve coaxing; Moses's seems to. But this one is a confrontation. It brings the sudden and jarring message that what you thought you were doing, what you were aiming your life at, in full conviction that it was right and just so to do, is leading nowhere. In fact, you are on the road to hell. This realization cannot but blind. You are suddenly aware that you absolutely cannot continue as you were. But as for what to do otherwise, you have no idea!

All this shakes Saul to his foundations. He was pursuing what he thought was right, within a religious and social context in which his identifi-cation of Christianity as a great threat to Judaism (Saul was a Pharisee, Jews well known for their biblical scholarship and serious approach to morality) was no doubt confirmed and bolstered. Turning from this was no small thing; a minor adjustment in Saul's life plan would not do. But how, then, was he to find out how to move on from such a confrontation with Christ and his own folly?

We have been warning against the presumption that our call stories must resemble the ones we find in the Bible on all their dramatic points. And here again we can caution against expecting our calls, like Saul, to knock us off our horse. On the other hand, the fear Isaiah had of God was real and, as we saw, even good. Too, as we have seen with Isaiah, even if we don't have a vision of flying creatures bearing fire, we can learn from his story the importance of fear in call, and why it might be a gift. Similarly, we can acknowledge that, like Saul, we might have been led astray by the moral training we have gotten from our youth onwards, in a culture and in communities that are carried along by certain assumptions about what is right. Like Saul, we are trained by our culture and even by our religious communities to have certain aspirations for ourselves and our lives. We embrace these and pursue them, as a matter of course. In our time and culture this has specially to do with the pursuit of the American dream—which is really a dream about having money, possessions, security, and comforts. Perhaps some of us who are convinced we are morally and religiously on the right path need to be confronted by the folly in it, and put by our call on a dramatically different path.

Millard Fuller, the founder of Habitat for Humanity, is a case in point. In college he and a friend developed a plan to become very rich—and he did it, primarily by selling cookbooks! But in the midst of this financial success, and as he felt stress in his marriage, he became suddenly aware that he was on the wrong path. "A planned life can only be endured" was the phrase that hit him, uttered by a wise Chinese elder on a television show that Fuller happened to be watching in a hotel one night. He suddenly recognized that, despite his success, he had become captive to the plan to make more and more money, one his society offered to him and he had wholeheartedly embraced.[6] The phrase burned a hole in his soul, and he knew right then and there that he had to change.

But changed to what? Fuller was "Christian," but his Americanized faith community provided insufficient alternatives to the life he knew he had to leave. In fact, when he approached some of his Christian acquaintances about the idea that perhaps he should give away all his money, Fuller was cautioned to be more prudent. It was not until he met Clarence Jordan, the founder of Koinonia Farms in Americus, Georgia, that Fuller's inkling

6. Fuller, "Life Endured."

that perhaps he was being called to use his fortune to help the poor began to take a clearer shape, eventually the shape of Habitat for Humanity. Knowing the biblical tradition and how it presents real alternatives for life, Jordan helped shape Fuller's sense of call into an imaginative new possibility.

Saul is similarly clueless about what he should do after the jolting experience on the road. As the text tells us, he is simply to go to the city of Damascus and wait to be told what to do. Here his call is completed only as it intersects with another's, namely that of Ananias, an older Jewish Christian in the city. Despite all he had heard of Saul and his intentions to imprison Christians, Ananias follows God's command and goes to Saul, welcomes him, and baptizes him into the community (Acts 9:18). This action on Ananias's part reminds us of how a tradition provides guidance for those who have become suddenly aware that the path they have been following in life is leading nowhere. The Christian tradition brings to our attention genuinely different ways to live, genuinely different from those offered to us by our culture—although we need to really look for them, keeping our imaginations open. It also provides wise and thoughtful guides, such as Ananias and Clarence Jordan, who can think both well and radically about how the wisdom of the tradition might bring forth new fruit in our called lives. The great innovation that is St. Paul, with all his powerful energy and spiritual force, grows within this environment, and the world is profoundly changed as a result.

The story of Saul's call includes many of the dramatic elements we have already seen in Moses's and Isaiah's stories. Yet perhaps its most distinctive feature becomes evident only later. It is the most retold call story in the Bible. The fact that it is retold so often brings us to a renewed consideration of the fourth feature of biblical calls identified earlier, namely that we are best able to identify and tell the full significance of our callings only after we have lived them for some time.

The story of Saul's (Paul's) call is told first by Luke in Acts 9, but later twice more, as Luke records Paul himself telling it in his own defense near the end of his life and after he is arrested in Jerusalem. Paul also briefly tells it with his own pen when he writes to new Christians living in Galatia (Gal 1). In Acts 26, Luke's Paul recounts his experience to King Agrippa; when we read this account carefully we find it is subtly different from the story of Acts 9. In this second version, Jesus says what was first reported, "Saul, Saul, why are you persecuting me?"— but then adds considerably more in reply to Saul's question about who he is.

> "Who are you Lord?" The Lord answered, "I am Jesus whom you
> are persecuting. But get up and stand on your feet; for I have

appeared to you for this purpose, to appoint you to serve and
testify to the things in which you have seen me and to those in
which I will appear to you. I will rescue you from your people
and from the Gentiles—to whom I am sending you to open
their eyes so that they may turn from darkness to light and from
the power of Satan to God, so that they may receive forgiveness
of sins and a place among those who are sanctified by faith in
me." (Acts 26:15–18)

These instructions from Jesus about what he plans to do with Saul are
far more elaborate than in Luke's first account, where all he says to Saul is
"get up and enter the city, and you will be told what you are to do" (Acts 9:6).
They are expanded, now, to include what Saul sees, or will see, about Jesus:
how this will be a rescue for Saul, and how it will include Paul's key (and
surprising) mission to the Gentiles.

The difference between the two accounts suggests something important about call. The commands Jesus gives in the earlier account come to
Saul when he is unprepared to receive the reasons for them. These reasons,
and the bigger story they relate to, emerge in the second account. We can
map this difference onto Saul's own knowledge of his call. Initially, he could
not have known what Jesus's words meant, all about his salvation and his
mission to the Gentiles. Yet in the intervening years he received the formation he needed to more fully understand his call. In this way, his call,
and really *any* call, begins a story that cannot be told until the call is lived
out in response.

For Paul, the call he receives on the road to Damascus is an invitation
into an unfolding adventure whose story can be better told as it unfolds,
and fully told only much later in his life, after he has followed it out. In
a sense, the story of Paul's call cannot be completely told until his life is
over. Or, to extend that point even further, because it involves service to
Christ's kingdom, which is yet coming, it cannot be fully told even today.
It awaits completion at "the last day." This future orientation of call remains
with Paul, and all of us, since to receive and follow a call is to get going on
a path that leads somewhere; for Paul (and others such as Millard Fuller),
this meant a significant change in direction. As his story aptly shows, Saul
was traveling with great force down a road, but it was the wrong one. His
call turns his life around and starts him on a new path that leads to a totally
different destination, a whole new future.

At the same time, however, when Paul follows his call he joins a movement that is much larger than he is. Paul's call initiates him by training him
towards his true identity; to discover this he will need to be formed within
a tradition carried by a community that goes before him. This includes

Ananias (and for Fuller, Clarence Jordan). Those who are newly called cannot know where the call will lead them, but they can (and must) be formed by the people who go before them and can direct them, as well as by the work the call opens to them and the experiences it brings. As they are instructed and formed, and as they work out their call, they will gradually come to a fuller and more mature understanding of what the call really means in their lives, and even in the life of God, who is moving in the world partly by means of those whom he calls.

Conclusion

The biblical calls of Jeremiah, Moses, Isaiah, and Paul in different ways allow us to open doors into some key features we can discover about call in the Bible. The stories told in the Bible about these calls—and about any number of others who are called—are interesting, and full of wonders that are ripe for retelling. They give us an appreciation of the diversity of biblical calls, as well as point out to us how pervasive and important the notion of call seems to be within the biblical tradition. The aim of this chapter has been to give a sense of this diversity while also noting key similarities in how the God of the Bible calls. The drama of the call stories we have considered makes them exciting—and we can rightly be excited about receiving a call. Yet we should not be so overwhelmed by the drama as to miss the logic that seems to inform the view the Bible presents about what God is up to in calling us. As we receive it in the biblical tradition, call will include some element of personal rescue or redemption, which crucially includes an invitation to join in God's redemptive work. The invitation, if received, frees us from the smallness of our own isolated lives and opens a new chapter in which we no longer need to be afraid to do the difficult work the call directs, precisely because it is the work of the God who calls, and who also promises to accompany us as we are changed and remade by our callings. As such, call marks a turning point in our life, whose significance will come clear only as that life unfolds within the call, as it moves towards a new and hopeful future, stretching us with it.

PART II

The Journey of the Called Life

CHAPTER 4

Our Vocational Journeys

"IF YOU COULD DO it, I suppose, it would be a good idea to live your life in a straight line," says Jayber Crow, the barber in Port William, a fictional small town in Kentucky where Wendell Berry's novel *Jayber Crow* takes place. "But that is not the way I have done it, so far," Crow muses. "I am a pilgrim, but my pilgrimage has been wandering and unmarked. Often what has looked like a straight line to me has been a circle or a doubling back. . . . Often I have not known where I was going until I was already there."[1]

Those words aptly describe almost everyone's vocational journey. We may think when we discover a calling that our lives will neatly unfold in a straight line with everything clearly marked out ahead of us, all our days of uncertainty fading quickly behind us. Having answered a calling, we might conclude that no more decisions would be asked of us because we've said yes to something that will steer us through the rest of our lives.

But it seldom turns out that way. Answering a calling is not like going to the grocery store where we know exactly how to get there and back and can list the things we have picked up along the way. Rather, it is much more like a pilgrimage, as Jayber Crow calls it, or a journey, that takes us to unexpected places where we meet unexpected people and face unexpected challenges along the way. Even if we continually answer yes to what we have been called to, what those callings mean and what they might ask of us change as we pass through different stages of our lives. When we think of our callings not as carefully planned trips but as unfolding adventures, we are reminded that we make our way in our callings, learning about them and growing into them as we go. And, for all of us, there will be "detours," sometimes occasioned by our own failures, but also often enough caused

1. Berry, *Jayber Crow*, 133. See also Schwehn and Bass, eds., *Leading Lives that Matter*, 467.

87

by other callings that arise in our lives, perhaps requiring that we must lay one calling temporarily aside in order to respond to a more urgent one. For instance, someone we love might become chronically ill and thus we must neglect a current calling or postpone responding to another calling in order to care for them. Too, there will be painful transitions as new callings emerge and old callings are left behind. Yes, it would be easier if we could live our lives "in a straight line," but ordinarily that is not how it is with our callings, especially because we are called to be responsive to the needs of a world that is constantly changing, and we changing with it. Like Jayber Crow, we find ourselves circling and doubling back, getting sidetracked and even lost, sometimes wandering in the darkness more than ambling in the light, pilgrims unsure of where they were heading until they were already there. Looking back, we may find that our vocational journeys are marked with more zigzags than straight lines, more twists and turns and ups and downs than flat open roads.

Journey is a fitting metaphor for living out our callings. In this chapter we will examine what it means to speak of our vocations as journeys and why doing so is not only more realistic, but also, perhaps surprisingly, much more promising and reassuring than picturing them as straight paths where everything is clearly marked and every step predetermined. We will first explore the different stages of our vocational journeys, journeys that begin at birth and end at death, death that comes for some much earlier in life than for others. In the second half of the chapter we will consider how envisioning our callings as journeys both expands and enriches our understanding of what it means to live vocationally, reminding us again that vocation is about much more than our careers.

Stages of the Journey

To speak of our callings as journeys is to recognize that vocation, far from being limited only to specific periods of our lives such as young adulthood, spans the whole of our lives from infancy to old age. Of course, we may not reach old age; many who are called do not. Still, the language of calling is pertinent at any stage of life no matter how long we may live. As the contributors to *Calling All Years Good* compellingly demonstrate, vocation is not something we must occasionally consider, but is a lifelong question that gets to the heart of being human.[2] One might say that at every stage of our lives, we are being called.

---

2. Cahalan, "Callings Over a Lifetime," 1.

Childhood

But does it really make sense to say that infants are called? That they can live vocationally? In many respects, obviously not. Children who are just beginning life—taking their first steps into what for them is a completely new and beckoning world—are not yet sufficiently formed physically, psychologically, morally, emotionally, and intellectually to recognize or respond to a calling. That is why if we speak of children as being called, we must do so analogously. Yes, they are called insofar as they are awakening to the world around them, engaging and responding to it in the limited way that they can. But they cannot, in any coherent sense of the word, live vocationally because they lack the awareness necessary to understand what it might be like to be called, obviously cannot discern a calling, and certainly cannot respond to a calling with the understanding, intentionality, and freedom that will come as they age. If to be called is to receive a gift, children are not yet able to recognize and understand, much less truly accept, the gift. In this sense, the language of calling properly belongs beyond childhood when we are sufficiently developed to possess the freedom, comprehension, and moral agency needed to recognize and respond to a calling. And that is perfectly fine. Children should be able to enjoy life—truly to delight in it—before wrestling with questions of purpose and meaning and vocation. All of that will come later. In the first years of their lives, children should "just be" as they are drawn more fully to life through the love of their parents and extended families to become the persons God's love summons them to be.

But there is a way that we can speak of children as called. The story of the call of the prophet Jeremiah reveals that from the beginning of our lives God envisions something for us that as children we could not possibly know—and that's probably a good thing. As he begins his auspicious but extremely difficult career as a prophet, Jeremiah hears the voice of God say: "Before I formed you in the womb I knew you, and before you were born I consecrated you; I appointed you a prophet to the nations" (Jer 1:5). Rather than rejoicing at the news, God's declaration unsettles Jeremiah because he responds by telling God, whom he addresses as "Sovereign LORD," that he is not at all ready to take on the task God wants to give him.

Yet this may suggest something important that can console Jeremiah (along with the rest of us) as he proceeds along the winding and difficult path of this life. In following his calling, Jeremiah learns that he is not in control, the "Sovereign LORD" is, and this Lord, who loves us and is worthy of our trust, has intentions for us that will unfold in our lives. Like Jeremiah, we are called even before we are born and we will be called until we die. But in the early years of our lives we live as human beings typically do within families, learning to play and interact with other children who are both like us and also different, slowly growing into ourselves, discovering what we love, what fascinates and excites us, and whom we admire. In this respect, Jeremiah was no different from any of us. He was not some superhuman creature, but was of the earth, formed in his mother's womb, soon to be a little baby held in his mother's arms. Jeremiah, like all of us, was once a child. And, like all of us, Jeremiah the child grew up, grew old, and eventually died. This is the human journey we all share, moving from infancy to death, formed and guided throughout by the call of our creator, who is also our destination.

There are parallels between Jeremiah's calling and Jesus' calling. Like Jeremiah, God clearly had something in mind for Jesus before he was born, but, also like Jeremiah, we know virtually nothing about Jesus' childhood. The only glimpse the Gospels give us is one little story in Luke when Jesus was twelve and traveled to Jerusalem with his family. He goes to the temple, impresses the scholars of the law, and, as sometimes happens to kids on trips with their parents, gets mistakenly left behind (Luke 2:41–50).

In this episode, the young Jesus is clearly a little different for a kid his age (engaging the scholars, interrogating his anxious parents, and talking about doing "his father's business") but not excessively so, especially when compared to the child Jesus that is depicted in the quite remarkable *Infancy Gospel of Thomas*,[3] written not too long after Luke's Gospel in the mid-second century. There little Jesus seems eerily more than human (making sparrows out of clay) and startlingly vindictive (striking dead a playmate who wrecked the little dams Jesus had made while playing in a stream). The Infancy Gospel was rejected by the church, and rightly so, for, among other things, it assumes that what is holy and extraordinary cannot arise from what is regular and ordinary. It imagines that a called life that impacts the world in a profound way must, from the start, be dramatically different in every way from any other life; effectively removing the life of Jesus from the world into which he was born and the world in which God calls him to fulfill his mission.

By contrast, after the brief story in Luke, other than noting that he went home to Nazareth with his parents "and was obedient to them" (Luke 2:51), the Bible says nothing about Jesus until, as an adult many years later, he begins his public ministry. Surely, we want to say that, if anyone did, Jesus lived a called life. But saying this need not, and should not, extract his life, especially in its early stages, from the ordinary sequences of human development. Like any other children, Jesus had a "calling" to grow and to learn,

---

3. *Infancy Gospel.*

to explore and to experiment, to be playful and curious, to take delight in just about everything, to elicit comfort and care from the older ones around him and, as he grew, to begin to make his own contributions to his family.[4] With Jesus in mind, we can say that the "vocation" of every child is to come more fully to life.

Adolescence and Young Adulthood

Now we are entering true "vocational territory" because as children move into adolescence and begin to grasp something of their own individuality and uniqueness, they naturally start asking questions such as: "What do I love? What am I good at? What can I uniquely contribute? Where do I feel most fully alive?"[5] As they change physically, mentally, and emotionally, and develop a greater sense of responsibility, adolescents find themselves "called" to many firsts: their first job, their first deep friendship, their first time falling in love, their first experience of leadership, their first sense of contributing to something bigger than themselves, and even their first serious mistakes.[6] At this stage of their journey, their world grows larger as the needs of others call them to look beyond their own needs, wants, and desires; as they do so, they begin to learn the empathy and compassion necessary for recognizing and responding to suffering and injustice. Their willingness to risk as well as their openness to questions and new possibilities inspires adolescents to devote their often considerable energy and creativity to improving life for others through greater community engagement. Perhaps most importantly, this stage of their vocational journey gives them the time and space they need to experiment, including sometimes doing foolish things, and to enjoy life with family and friends as they begin to pose to themselves the most fundamental vocational question of all: what kind of person should I become?

It is no accident that traditional societies mark the transition from adolescence to young adulthood with rites of passage, for it is here that vocation questions become more explicit and pronounced. Young adults find that with greater freedom and independence come greater expectations for responsibility. Whether they are in college or not, people continually ask what they are planning to do with the rest of their lives, not so subtly suggesting that it is time that they start supporting themselves. If young people are unsure what kind of employment or profession they plan to take up, this

4. Miller-McLemore, "Childhood."

5. Turpin, "Adolescence," 74.

6. Turpin, "Adolescence," 75.

can elicit a great deal of stress and anxiety, as well as a lingering feeling that something is wrong with them. Even though their sense of themselves, their gifts and abilities, their interests, and their moral commitments are usually much clearer than when they were adolescents, they may not yet know what they hope to do with their lives. And even if they do know, it may be hard for them to move forward in anything that they might name as a calling if the debt they amassed by going to college forces them to move back home with their parents instead of beginning life on their own.[7] This often leads to questions about self-worth, feelings that they have failed, and wondering if anything will ever work out for them. Too, even if a young adult finds a job, he may discover that what he is asked to do in it does not align well with how he thinks he might be called. Moreover, the relative impermanence of many of those jobs can make him think, as he moves from one (often low-paying) job to the next (often low-paying) job, that his life will always be in flux; in fact, it may seem that his life is really going nowhere, but is only bouncing around like an errant pinball. This constant shifting from job to job or from city to city or from relationship to relationship can be "exhausting and overwhelming," making young adults feel like "nothing is stable, settled, or secure."[8] Indeed, they may wonder if they will ever find their callings or be able to live them if they do.

In our present culture, very few young adults settle down quickly and permanently, whether in a job or with a lifelong partner. Very few, upon entering their mid-twenties, have a crystal-clear sense of who they are and what they are called to do. If that is so, perhaps young adults at this transitional time of their lives do not need to name what they are "called" to in any specific way—indeed, perhaps it is better if they do not. Rather, what they need to do is precisely to deal with the questions, the uncertainty, and the many changes that can mark their lives, and to recognize that this is normal. A change of employment, the end of a relationship, having to make one's way in a new town or city, an experience of failure, or the death of a close friend, all of these different experiences and challenges can lead to deeper self-knowledge and a better understanding of what their calling may be.

After all, most of us discover our callings not instantaneously in a sudden flash of insight, but over time and through trial and error. Even though it is difficult to change jobs often, those different experiences and challenges can lead to deeper self-knowledge and a better understanding of how we are called as well as how we are not. Too, frustration with a job, which is often felt in these earlier years of employment, while obviously not something we

7. Turpin, "Younger Adulthood," 102.
8. Turpin, "Younger Adulthood," 105.

would choose, can teach us to think about how we might be called *outside* of our employment, reminding us that our career is not the only calling of our lives and is probably not the most important one. If we don't experience our paid work as a calling, are we being called in other ways? If we find little sense of meaning and purpose in our jobs, where can we find them elsewhere in our lives?[9] Perhaps the most important lesson of this stage of the journey is to learn that we typically have to live our callings in circumstances that are less than ideal. There is no perfect job, no perfect spouse or partner, and no perfect community. This does not mean that we should not do whatever we can to improve those circumstances, but it does mean that if we wait to answer a calling until everything is perfect, until everything falls neatly into place, we never will.

No matter how difficult the transition from adolescence to young adulthood might be, it must be made if young adults are to discover and grow into their unique identity and become persons capable of making their own decisions and claiming responsibility for their lives. Remaining children for life—and this is increasingly possible, sometimes even likely, in a culture that coddles us and trains us in instant gratification—is no one's calling, for we are created to grow and mature in character and virtue. Moreover, as we noticed earlier, a call is always a call to responsibility. We need to be prepared to take something on that we will stick with and make our own. This can only happen if young adults are willing to "separate" from their parents, which Gordon Smith identifies as the most critical characteristic of this stage of one's vocational journey.[10] Even if young adults continue to live with their parents, they must gain sufficient psychological and emotional independence from them in order to discover, claim, and enter into their callings. While they surely should love and care for their parents, their primary concern should not be to please their parents but to become themselves and to gain a clearer sense of what they are called to do with their lives, which can be quite different from what their parents hope for them. Claiming this independence isn't easy—and possessive or needy parents can make it very difficult—but unless young adults do so they remain stuck in the stage of adolescence, their vocational journeys stalled, as the years continue to unfold.

Young adults are especially eager to seek their callings; propelled by a sense of responsibility and a desire to contribute, to do the work that lies ahead, they reach out toward greater involvement with society. But how and when young adults receive their callings varies. People are different, and

9. Turpin, "Younger Adulthood," 104.

10. Smith, *Courage & Calling*, 58.

God calls us differently. Some, it seems, have a clear and compelling sense of their calling early on in their lives and their stories are often the ones we tell. In 1956, Martin Luther King, Jr., then only twenty-seven years old, was already a Baptist pastor in Montgomery and was fully immersed in the civil rights struggle he would go on to lead. After a sleepless night in January, feeling drained, and frightened for the safety of his family after his home was bombed, King heard a voice telling him to "Preach the Gospel, stand up for the truth, stand up for righteousness."

King is one of those we celebrate for the clarity and singularity of his call. But his experience is relatively unique. Many of us in our mid to late twenties are yet uncertain about where life will lead us, and even less sure about the specifics of our callings. Still, we continue on our journey, hopefully gaining a clearer sense of who we are and of what we are committed to and why as we take that journey. Gradually and subtly, these commitments emerge as callings, things we know we cannot give up and still remain the children of God we are becoming. If we live into and beyond our thirties (and it is important to remember that some who are called do not, like King who was assassinated at age thirty-nine and Jesus who died even younger), we enter the stage of "middle adulthood," which runs roughly from our mid-thirties until we reach retirement age.[11]

Middle Adulthood

There are unique blessings and challenges to living vocationally in middle adulthood. These are the years when many people flourish in their personal lives and in their careers. They grow in their relationships, take pride in their families, and enjoy success and recognition in their professions. But they can also find it hard to balance the multiple callings that define their lives and the responsibilities that accompany them, callings that range from "life partnerships, parenthood, civic pursuits, religious and spiritual commitments, and caring for children or parents."[12] They feel stretched, and often conflicted, between the demands of family, work, and the larger community, and conclude that no matter how hard they try, they fall short in each of these areas of their lives. In order to succeed in their careers, it seems they must, at least occasionally, neglect their families. But the inescapable responsibilities that come with committed relationships and parenting also mean they cannot invest in their professions as much as they would like. This sense of disappointment, and even guilt, is hard to avoid because the

11. Bloom, "Middle Adulthood," 124.

12. Bloom, "Middle Adulthood," 124.

commitments middle adults make and struggle to honor effect not only their own well-being, but also the well-being of others, whether spouses or partners, one's children, colleagues at work, or one's neighbors. They make very few choices that affect only them, very few choices that do not entail obligations and responsibilities to others. Furthermore, even if they wish to, it is often difficult for middle adults to simplify their lives because many of those callings are not easily changed and bring responsibilities that extend through a good portion of their lives. No wonder that Matt Bloom, reflecting on this stage of one's vocational journey, concludes: "The ideal of a perfectly ordered life where each vocation and responsibility gets just the right amount of attention, and there is plenty of time, energy, and resources for all of life's demands, is a fiction."[13]

Beyond the challenges that arise from trying to honor all the different callings of their lives, in middle adulthood deeper questions about meaning and purpose can emerge. As each year passes, people in their forties and fifties and sixties begin to wonder about what they have made of their lives. Even if they have been successful, have they lived as they ought to have lived and loved as they ought to have loved? Have they become good persons, persons of integrity whose actions have made a beneficial difference in the lives of others? Have they become kind, just, generous, and compassionate? Will people be able to say that they were a force for good in the world?

Men and women in middle adulthood also wrestle with disappointments in their careers, strains in relationships, and a growing realization of their own limits. They may not receive the promotion they yearned for or may even lose the job they thought would always be theirs. To be in your fifties and suddenly find yourself unemployed is not only scary, but can also weaken one's sense of identity and evoke questions of self-worth. Calling implies movement towards something, but events and circumstances such as these can make us feel as if we are only spinning around. One's sense of self is also shaken when what were meant to be lifelong relationships of intimacy, love, faithfulness, and mutual support unravel and die.

Perhaps the greatest challenge of middle adulthood is acknowledging that one will not be able to do everything he or she had hoped. Some dreams will never be realized. Some plans will have to die. This is true not only because the choices we made in the past limit the options we have in the present, but also because by late middle adulthood we realize that the years that lie ahead of us are fewer than the years that are behind us.

One thing we cannot do is go back and undo the choices we made in the past, even if we regret them. We can repent of them, but we cannot

13. Bloom, "Middle Adulthood," 141.

erase them. And there's not enough time in front of us to revisit the choices we didn't make but wish we had.[14] For some people this realization leads to disillusionment about what might have been but wasn't. But others come to accept that while they may not have achieved all they had envisioned, they are grateful for the blessings they received. "Middle adulthood can often be a time to grieve the past, to reconcile oneself that what might have been—the life (or lives) one might have lived or dreamed about living—is lost forever. Middle adults must learn to live with disappointments; paths not taken, botched relationships, opportunities squandered, dreams lost."[15] Dealing with the losses, missed opportunities, and disappointments of life motivates many middle-aged adults to dig deeper into their religious and spiritual traditions; these traditions offer them a larger context for understanding their unfolding journey,[16] and a deeper, more contemplative peace.

Late and Older Adulthood

For many, the vocational journey continues into late adulthood, which is typically connected with retirement, which most people in our current culture do around the age of sixty-five.[17] The transition from one's career into retirement again reminds us that vocation cannot exclusively be about our careers. When we retire, our callings do not end; rather, they take a different form. Because life expectancy has significantly increased over the last century, today people speak of retirement more as a new beginning, even a fresh start on life, than as merely an ending. Leaving careers that may have spanned several decades can be difficult, especially in societies that closely connect personal identity and self-worth with one's professional roles and productivity. But such transitions also lead to new opportunities for volunteering and community service, for hobbies and artistic activities that could not be pursued before, for interesting projects that had to be put off for years, or more time with one's children and grandchildren. Too, late adulthood brings opportunities to address unfinished business in life, to reconnect with friends not seen in years, to reconcile broken relationships, or to make amends for things older adults wish they hadn't done or things they should have done but didn't. For people who live vocationally, retirement is not an excuse to become disengaged with life—much less to be on an endless vacation—but a call to use whatever time and energy they have

14. Brouwer, *What to Do?*, 27–29.

15. Bloom, "Middle Adulthood," 131.

16. Bloom, "Middle Adulthood," 132–34.

17. Cahalan, "Late Adulthood," 151.

to continue to do good, perhaps in ways they were not able before. Kathleen Cahalan captures well this stage of the vocational journey when she writes: "The calling in later adulthood is *to step back and step back in.*"[18]

Sometimes what those in late adulthood must "step back" into is not easy. They may find themselves having to care for elderly and infirm parents or siblings, a spouse suffering from dementia, or rescue a troubled child or raise an abandoned grandchild. Such "callings" are hardly expected and, understandably, not always welcomed. They upend the plans people had, interrupting their lives in ways they never could have foreseen, and are stressful and exhausting. Still, the example of many elderly adults witnesses that even though these callings are not sought, they can be accepted and we can grow through them. Too, if in middle adulthood we must confront the reality of limits, in late adulthood we must grapple with losses. For many, perhaps especially men, there is the loss of recognition and accomplishments that they found in their jobs. There is the loss that accompanies the steady decline in mental and physical abilities as bodily needs demand more time and attention, simple tasks become maddeningly difficult, and one must accept increased vulnerability and diminished independence. There is the grievous loss one suffers at the death of a spouse, a parent, friends, or even one's child. Is it surprising that the first thing many older persons read every morning is the obituaries? And there is the loss that comes from the unavoidable awareness of one's own mortality, so much so, Cahalan says, "that people begin to count the time to death rather than from birth."[19]

Still, if calling spans the whole of our lives, then our days of being called never end. Age and diminishment do not relieve us of having to discern how we might be called or what work we might yet have to do. If retirement is not to become an excuse for self-centeredness, one still has to determine, "What is being asked of me now?" No matter how old we may be, or how frail, we are still called to love, to be kind and considerate, to be gracious and grateful, and to find ways, however small, to do good. Gordon Smith sees a calling of older adults as not to complain or to become bitter, but to share wisdom and to bless by affirming, encouraging, listening and being present to, and taking joy in others, especially the young.[20] Cahalan adds that older adults are called to witness "how to age with dignity and honor, which includes respecting the potential and limits of one's body and mind, remaining faithful in the face of adversities, and keeping a sense of

18. Cahalan, *Stories We Live*, 43.

19. Cahalan, "Late Adulthood," 156.

20. Smith, *Courage & Calling*, 70–73. See also Brouwer, *What to Do?*, 84–85.

humor."[21] Christians, no matter how old or frail, never relinquish the call to imitate Christ, including in his suffering, to love God and neighbor, to grow in holiness, and to serve in whatever way they can. These reflections on living vocationally even through the later stages of life illustrate how callings rescue the elderly from becoming mere victims to the losses, sorrows, and occasionally painful humiliations of aging, by reminding them that they remain moral agents who can living meaningful and purposeful lives by what they witness to and do for others.[22]

We typically think of callings as inherently future oriented since through them we grow, progress, and develop, gradually becoming more than we already are.[23] But if we are given many years, in the final stage of our vocational journeys, the stage of older adulthood (which typically ranges from somewhere in one's eighties until death), what we experience is not growth and development, but ongoing decline and diminishment, often accompanied by mental and physical suffering. At this stage of our lives, as our physical and cognitive abilities continue to lessen, we become increasingly dependent on others to help us with the most basic tasks of life such as bathing, dressing, and getting around. Our world shrinks as we move from our own homes into assisted living facilities and finally into nursing homes where much of our time is spent in a single room and we find ourselves receiving care much more than giving it.[24] The experience of loss that began in late adulthood accelerates, whether the loss of skills and abilities, the loss of once familiar worlds, the loss of dignity as one's bodily needs must be attended to by others, and especially the loss of family members and friends to death. That loss of companionship is why loneliness, isolation, and depression are among the biggest challenges that the elderly face.[25]

How can seeing ourselves as called help us in the last chapter of our lives? First, elderly persons remind us that (as we have stressed many times) our most important calling is to be the person we are meant to become. As we reach the end of our lives, our wealth and possessions, our titles and achievements mean very little. What matters instead is the person we have made of ourselves and the legacy of love and goodness we leave to bless those who will live after us. Second, in societies that prize "self-sufficiency, autonomy, and individualism," the inescapable dependence and growing frailty of the elderly offer "a powerful counter-narrative" to our

---

21. Cahalan, "Late Adulthood," 166.
22. Wadell, "Call Goes On," 11–12.
23. Mercer, "Older Adulthood," 181.
24. Mercer, "Older Adulthood," 177.
25. Mercer, "Older Adulthood," 190–91.

understanding of what gives human beings dignity and value.[26] Christians should know that we matter not because of what we achieve, but because we are loved and cherished by God. Third, if one of the callings of the elderly is to graciously and gratefully receive care, in doing this they "call forth" from family, friends, and their caregivers essential human virtues such as compassion, empathy, patience, faithfulness, and generosity. Thus, precisely in their dependence and undeniable need for assistance, they help those who care for them to become better persons.[27]

Finally, one vocation common to all of the elderly is to show us what it means to die well.[28] In doing so they remind us that a good life is not measured by how *long* we have lived, but by how *well* we have lived. A good life is not one devoted to postponing the effects of aging and denying our mortality to the bitter end; rather, a good life is one in which we transcend ourselves in love and goodness to others. For Christians, a good life is one spent in friendship with God and our neighbors, a life of service to others, and a life that culminates in communion with God and the saints.[29] Callings "emerge, shift, and cease, and all callings come to an end with death."[30] Therefore, "We are called, in our dying, to let go of the things that bind us to this life," Joyce Ann Mercer writes. "Dying to this life, we hear God calling us out of the responsibilities, burdens, and sufferings of this life, and into fullness in the divine life of the resurrection," which is where all of our callings have been taking us from the beginning.[31]

The Vocational Journey—What Does It Tell Us?

What does this overview of the different stages of our vocational journey tell us about living vocationally? *First, it reveals that there is a dynamic, evolving quality to all of our callings.* Callings that stretch throughout our lives—such as the call to discipleship for Christians—are "shaped and re-shaped" by the different contexts in which we find ourselves, the changing circumstances of our lives, the people who move in and out of our lives, and the knowledge we gain from living our callings.[32] Parents are always called to be loving, caring, and responsible in raising their children, but they must grow in their

26. Mercer, "Older Adulthood," 194.
27. Mercer, "Older Adulthood," 194.
28. Mercer, "Older Adulthood," 195.
29. Wadell, "Call Goes On," 12.
30. Cahalan, "Callings Over a Lifetime," 24.
31. Mercer, "Older Adulthood," 196.
32. Cunningham, "Who's There?," 140.

understanding of what this entails, adjusting to the needs of their children as they grow. Friends are always called to seek one another's good, but their ability to do so deepens as their friendship extends over years. Couples celebrating their twentieth anniversary will vouch that saying "I do" on their wedding day began a journey that unfolded in ways they never could have anticipated. Far from being static or fixed, our callings are always in a process of further growth, change, and greater becoming.[33]

This point reminds us that just because we have discovered a calling and said yes to it doesn't mean we fully understand it. We comprehend our callings only by living into them. In answering a calling, we embark on an adventure whose meaning we grasp only as we continue to be open to what the calling may ask of us and where it may take us.[34] As we saw in chapter 3 when examining different call stories in the Bible, none of the people God called knew where the call would take them. Abraham, Moses, the prophets, and the disciples all responded to a call, but none could have predicted where it would lead or how it would change their lives. They could only understand the call by committing to it, by handing themselves over to a mystery whose meaning would only slowly be revealed to them, and by being open to possibilities, challenges, and surprises they could never foresee.

This is the nature of a journey. It is not fully charted, laid out in every detail, as we begin it. We cannot understand the journey until we walk it; and as we walk it, we learn not only about it but about ourselves and what it means for us to be journeyers. As Margaret Farley explains, "The major commitments in our lives do not carry completed blueprints, fully charted maps; they are not well constructed games or finely tuned machines for which all the options exist ahead of time." As she summarizes, "Commitments lead to genuinely new possibilities which are not foreseeable in the beginning."[35] Farley's comments illustrate why we often only understand our callings retrospectively. It is in looking back over our journey that we better comprehend both where we have been and where we are going. Things we only dimly understood when they occurred become clearer with time.

Instead of a fully woven fabric, a calling is like a "thread" that gradually emerges as we continue our vocational journeys.[36] Besides being more truthful, this way of thinking about vocation can relieve many of our anxieties. It can be a relief to recognize that we do not have to have everything figured out before we begin our journey. Instead of being immobilized by

---

33. McIntosh, "Trying to Follow," 140.
34. Pinches, "Stories of Call," 141.
35. Farley, *Personal Commitments*, 45.
36. McIntosh, "Trying to Follow," 119.

uncertainty, we can embrace it as something natural and be comfortable with it; in fact, embracing and being comfortable with uncertainty may be a necessary requirement for beginning the journey because we will never take the first step if we wait for everything to be absolutely clear. It is important to remember this when so many of us (perhaps especially college students) think everything must be squarely in place before we can begin our vocational journeys. Acknowledging that our callings are journeys that unfold over time assures us that we do not—and truthfully cannot—fully understand them before we begin to live them. Too, there's no point waiting for a huge "Aha!" moment that may never come. Sometimes the best we can do—and what at that moment we are called to do—is to take the next step, knowing that our callings will gradually become clearer to us.

Second, seeing our callings as unfolding journeys reminds us that we are moral agents who respond to our lives as they unfold, who craft our callings as we pursue and live them, and who know not only that our callings will change in what they ask of us, but also that we must change with them. Instead of thinking of vocation as an already decided and fully determined plan that God has programed for us, we should embrace the fact that as beings who are made to grow in grace and wisdom, our callings are lived out through our own freedom and action and creativity.[37] This is why we continually shape our callings and are shaped by them as we grow more fully into them. Too, that we are free means that we sometimes choose wrongly, and go astray, but it also means that, as journeyers, we can discover that we are "heading down paths that don't seem to fit,"[38] paths that clearly are not meant for us, and can change those paths.

Sometimes we worry so much about making the right choices because we believe those choices can never be revised or revisited. As Jerome Organ writes, "Our cultural setting tends to promote the idea that whatever one chooses at a relatively young age will determine one's future in a permanent way; indeed, everything about one's life seems to depend on getting this one element of life *exactly right*."[39] But that is seldom true. Many of the initial decisions we make about our futures, especially regarding potential jobs and careers, are not nearly as important as we assume.[40] People change jobs all the time, especially young adults, because as they try things and as they develop, they discover more about themselves, their interests and abilities, and what will help them live good and meaningful lives. Sometimes we are

37. Hahenberg, *Awakening Vocation*, 151.
38. Organ, "Of Doing and Being," 230.
39. Organ, "Of Doing and Being," 228.
40. Organ, "Of Doing and Being," 229.

convinced that we are perfectly suited for a particular job or career, but soon wonder what in the world we were thinking. We discover we are inept in a job where we thought we would dazzle, and miserable at something we were sure would bring us bliss.

And that's okay. Rarely is a first job a perfect fit. If it turns out to be not nearly as interesting or meaningful as we had expected, it doesn't mean we failed or made a terrible mistake, but that we learned a bit more about ourselves, which will help us better discern how we might be called in the future. If call is like a journey rather than a pre-programmed and charted course, such "mistakes" can be gathered in, helping us grasp more fully what our call might really mean. As Organ notes, typically "the first situation after college will not be the fulfillment of a dream, but simply the next step on a journey—a next step from which one will better be able to see and understand what further steps might be in store."[41] Knowing this should ease the stress and anxiety we can associate with vocational discernment. We don't have to worry about making "the perfect choice," first, because there probably isn't one and, second, because opportunities will arise that will allow us to make different and better choices as we move along our vocational journey, not so much in a straight line, but in circles—learning, redoing and choosing again.

We are all drawn to vocational success stories in which people seem always to have known what they wanted to do, always made the right choices, flourished from the start, and were happy ever after.[42] Everything proceeded so easily for them. As they took their vocational journeys, never once were there second thoughts, doubts, or moments of regret. They knew their dreams, pursued them, and perfectly fulfilled them. We are encouraged to admire such people and to aspire to be like them, but, honestly, hearing their stories can be more depressing than uplifting because most of us, more like Jayber Crow, live vocational journeys that will never be so smooth. Consequently, even though we may be intrigued by these stories, we are also somewhat skeptical. Could everything really have gone so perfectly?

Maybe we need fewer vocational success stories and more narratives of confusion, uncertainty, remorse, and even failure, stories where the journeyers meander through twists and turns, take some aimless detours, and encounter a few dead ends. Maybe we need stories where callings were missed or mistaken rather than quickly discerned and easily followed. Such stories remind us that even if we make some colossal blunders on our vocational

---

41. Organ, "Of Doing and Being," 237.
42. Mahn, "Conflicts," 53.

journeys, we are given new chances to find our way in our callings.[43] Indeed, even when we refuse, overlook, or muff a calling, things work out because there will always be another calling waiting for us.[44] This is why the most riveting—as well as the most useful—vocational narratives are not those that glisten with unblemished success, but narratives of redemption that disclose how people learn from their mistakes, live through poor choices, and only gradually come to understand how they are called. We are drawn to these stories because they correspond more closely with what we know about ourselves as people whose flaws and limitations are always with us, yet people who are made to pursue the good; thus, we struggle on towards fulfilling our call, only gradually and haltingly learning its true shape.

Third, the metaphor of journey tells us that no matter how carefully we plan, we cannot avoid—and can even welcome—vocational detours along the way. As we travel in response to callings, other callings emerge and present themselves: having to care for an elderly family member, the call to help a stranger in need, or an invitation we feel we cannot refuse no matter how much it may disrupt our lives. These callings can interrupt and redirect our vocational journeys (sometimes temporarily, other times permanently), but often they are precisely the callings we need to pursue. For instance, recently some people in the United States have taken vocational "detours" in response to the tragedies of gun violence, either as family members or close friends of innocent victims, or simply as people compelled by the stories of those who have suffered. They have felt themselves called to speak out, or organize, or act in some way to address and attempt to heal the tragedy, sorrow, and grief that have come from so many senseless shootings. Others have had their vocational paths redirected in response to callings to help refugees seeking safety for themselves and their families, to support victims of sexual misconduct or abuse, or to join organizations espousing greater care for the environment. These people did not respond to such callings because they had nothing else to do, but because these different issues stirred their consciences. It was not so much that they chose these callings, but that the particular calling thrust itself upon them with such urgency that they could not refuse; indeed, they felt morally compelled to accept the calling, so much so that if they did not they would fail themselves, those they loved, human beings in need, and perhaps even God.

These examples attest not only that our vocational journeys will be interrupted, but also that such unplanned and unforeseen interruptions are precisely the callings we should embrace even if they are costly and

43. Organ, "Of Doing and Being," 229–30.
44. Cunningham, "Who's There?," 164.

highly inconvenient. To ignore such callings when we can answer them, especially when they involve works of justice, mercy, and compassion, is to betray human beings and other creatures who are suffering. But it is also to betray ourselves and who we should be becoming. This is why not to take the detour—to continue undisturbed along the familiar and well-worn path—is to close our hearts to the very calling we most need to hear. This does not mean that we are obliged to respond to every pressing social issue; that would be impossible. But it does mean that we ought to be open and responsive to what is happening in our communities and the larger society.

And we need to be open to new possibilities and new discoveries. Vocational detours can come in many ways. We should be alert to them because they can offer us a needed change in direction and even a fresh new start. These detours remind us that sometimes it is best to let go of well-worn paths in order to take up new ones. On our vocational journeys, we come to forks in the road where we choose which path to take. We can continue on our way or we can follow another way. One path is not necessarily better than the other, but sometimes taking a vocational detour teaches us that we are renewed and reenergized when we leave the familiar for the unknown. Maybe it means leaving a job that may be financially rewarding, but is clearly not what we want or ought to do. Maybe it means becoming involved with different projects, activities, or communities because we feel we are no longer growing and developing as we should; we're in a physical, emotional, mental, or spiritual rut. Maybe it means making important but difficult changes. At a time when so much of our lives is already scripted and planned to the last detail, vocational detours can be both renewing and liberating. True, we may get lost when we follow new paths, but sometimes life is more interesting and blessed when we allow ourselves, at least occasionally, to be lost. As Barbara Brown Taylor testifies, "I have found things while I was lost that I might never have discovered if I had stayed on the path." Moreover, she adds, "God does some of God's best work with people who are truly, seriously lost."[45]

Fourth, recognizing that vocation is a journey challenges us to pay at least as much attention to where we are as where we are going. Callings tend to be "forward-looking" because they call us *from* where we are *to* where we ought or want to be.[46] The metaphor of journey acknowledges this forward-looking feature of vocation; even if it isn't always clear, there is a purpose, a meaning, and a destination to the journey. We are not just rambling along aimlessly, lazily taking in the sights, but trying to reach *someone, something,*

---

45. Taylor, *Altar*, 73.

46. Hahnenberg, *Awakening Vocation*, 152.

or *somewhere*. And yet, there is a danger in being so focused on the goal or destination of the journey that we are unable to appreciate and enjoy the journey along the way. We can devote so much time and energy to looking ahead, planning for the next thing or thinking about where we want to be, that we never look down to see where we are in order to appreciate the beauty and goodness of the present. We are so distracted by the possibilities of the future that we grow increasingly oblivious to the gifts coming our way every day. "Most of us spend so much time thinking about where we have been or where we are supposed to be going," Taylor observes, "that we have a hard time recognizing where we actually are. When someone asks us where we want to be in our lives, the last thing that occurs to us is to look down at our feet and say, 'Here, I guess, since this is where I am.'"[47]

Our capacity to live in the present time is enhanced when we think of ourselves as journeyers rather than passive recipients of life's passages. In college, for instance, students are sometimes encouraged to consider those four years as a time defined by a standard set of expectations and activities relating to the college experience. The years may involve drudgery (wading through required classes, holding down a job, the monotony of daily routines), but they are also memorable, exciting, and fun as students make friends, go to parties, maybe study abroad, and overall enjoy a newfound independence. Of course, in four years it will be over and they will move on to something else—a job, perhaps another stage of schooling, or a year of volunteer work. Knowing that those four years won't last forever can lead to occasional fits of anxiety, but these are usually shoved aside as students re-immerse themselves in the typical college life activities.

While this pattern may seem to root them in the present, in fact, it does the opposite, precisely because the terminus of college—graduating and getting a degree—allows students to orient their college years entirely in terms of this assumed future. We see evidence of this when second semester college seniors bemoan that they are about to enter the "real world," a statement that suggests that they could amble through college rather aimlessly because what truly matters will only come later. When time in college is viewed largely as a rite of passage to something much more important, it is easy to waste those years, or at least not benefit from them nearly as much as one could. By contrast, understanding ourselves as journeyers, as people on the way who are called at every stage of life, trains us to ask: What am I doing with the time I am given today? How might I be called not in the future, but now? Too, seeing ourselves as journeyers reminds us that how we are formed by the journey itself is as important as what we hope for at the end of

47. Taylor, *Altar*, 56.

the journey. Remembering this enables college students (and everyone else) not to overlook the present, but each day to attend to the people, activities, and experiences that stretch and challenge and engage us, body and soul.

Fifth, because our callings take the form of journeys, vocational discernment is a lifelong process. Even if the core callings of our lives may never change, we change as we live them. We discover more about who we are and what it means to embrace and be faithful to our callings, whether the people we are called to serve, the work we are called to do, or the person we are meant to become. Too, as we encounter different persons and different experiences, and as the circumstances of our lives change, we again have to fathom what is being asked of us. How can we better love those closest to us? What do the cries of the suffering and afflicted ask of us today? What does it mean for us to live responsibly in our own *time* and *place*? For Christians, how are we continually called to live out our baptisms in lives of faithful discipleship? Vocational discernment is inherently provisional because our callings are dynamic realities that evolve over time, along with our understanding of them. This means that vocational discernment is not something we do once, but continuously.

As already mentioned, this relieves us of the pressure of having to get everything right at the outset.[48] But it also challenges us not to become lazy or complacent in living our callings. If our callings are not to die—or we to die in them—we must regularly reflect on how we can further grow and flourish in them. Are we as responsible to our callings as we ought to be? What do we need to embrace and what do we need to leave behind? What new callings do we need to consider, and how might we have fallen into patterns of complacency or avoidance that keep us from heeding them? As Renee LaReau summarizes, "One of the biggest misconceptions about vocation is that the discovery of one's vocation is a momentary happening, an instant epiphany, or a lightning bolt that illuminates the rest of our life's path. The discovery of vocation is, rather, a process, a journey. There may be significant, discrete moments of clarity along the way, but there is always more to be discovered and discerned. On the vocational journey we never 'arrive.' We are always 'arriving.'"[49]

Conclusion

In this chapter we have explored what it means to speak of our callings as journeys. But there is one important element—and a very hopeful one—that

48. Organ, "Of Doing and Being," 233.

49. LaReau, *Getting a Life*, 143.

we did not mention: we do not take these journeys alone. Perhaps it is good to conclude with this truth not only because it is immensely reassuring, but also because we know that the presence of others brings meaning, security, hope, and even joy to our vocational journeys, no matter how difficult they may become. We have companions on the journey—parents and family members, trusted friends or strangers who will become friends, teachers, mentors, and fellow community members—who help us on our way. Some are with us throughout much of our journey, others through extended periods, and some only briefly; but no matter how long they travel with us, our debt to them is great.

These companions support and encourage us, they offer guidance and advice, understanding and consolation, and share their stories with us as we make our way in our callings. Their presence, their willingness to listen, their patience and their humor help us persevere when we aren't even sure where we are going. They help us understand our callings, embrace them, continue to believe in them, or perhaps know when we should alter or redefine them. Anyone who has ever embarked on a vocational journey knows they could never have completed it on their own. Without the help of countless people along the way, they could not have continued the journey. No wonder the Bible proclaims, "Faithful friends are a sturdy shelter: whoever finds one has found a treasure" (Sir 6:14). Hopefully, we will be such friends and companions to those we meet along our way.

CHAPTER 5

Discerning Our Callings

Talking about callings can be fascinating, invigorating, uplifting, and exciting. But determining *how* we are called, and *to what* is something altogether different. Trying to discern our callings can evoke more anxiety than reassurance, more stress than tranquility, and considerably more uncertainty than confidence. How is God calling us? What is life asking of us? Should we marry or stay single? What career should we pursue? Should we settle in one place or be prepared to go elsewhere? And, perhaps most unsettling, what if we embrace a vocation but later discover we were mistaken? These questions can fuel late-night conversations and long walks with a friend, but can also be burdensome—and even scary—when we realize that how we answer them matters for who we will become and what the future will hold for us.[1]

In this chapter we will explore how we can discover what calling or callings might be most appropriately our own. We will begin by examining three principles that provide a framework for how best to think about what it means to discern our callings. We will then outline a six-step process for discerning our vocations, paying particular attention to the importance of listening, a realistic assessment of our gifts as well as the unique circumstances of our lives, and careful consideration of how we might best use our gifts to serve others.

1. Neafsey, *Sacred Voice*, 36.

A Framework for Vocational Discernment

1. Our callings are not blueprints, but unfolding, mysterious gifts.

What principles can offer a framework to guide us in discerning our callings? What can help us think rightly about how best to understand vocational discernment? A preliminary but absolutely important consideration is to emphasize that vocational discernment should always be seen in light of God's love for us. God wants our good. It is essential to remember this in the process of discerning our callings; it is also why vocational discernment is not something to dread or be anxious about, but something to pursue in peace and with trust, confidence, and hope. God is not a trickster out to fool us, but a lover who seeks what is best for us and calls us to fullness of life. If God is loving and merciful, then even if we are uncertain about which path to pursue, God will work with us to bring about good no matter where we tread. This point was wonderfully expressed by a professor who told a student who was struggling to decide between two vocational paths, "What makes you think God wouldn't go with you to either of those places?"[2]

Remembering this should expand our understanding of what it means to be personally called by God. In *The Way of Life*, Gary Badcock recounts that when he was a child he believed that God had a single, immutable plan for every person's life. It was as if from all eternity God had envisioned one possible trajectory for our lives, a trajectory so completely determined and irreversible that there was only one correct outcome to vocational discernment.[3] Badcock compared this way of discerning vocation to "waiting for a bus, or a 'streetcar named vocation,'" and was convinced that if he "became bored and decided to wander away from the street, it would pass me by."[4] Christians have frequently been taught that God has a plan for their lives, taking this to mean "that God has a rigid, highly detailed blueprint for each life," a blueprint that must be quickly discovered and zealously pursued if one is to have any chance for happiness.[5] Viewed this way, callings are not evolving and adjustable; rather, they are absolutely specific, completely predetermined, and given once and for all. From this perspective, when it

---

2. The professor was Tom Faase, a beloved professor of sociology at St. Norbert College in De Pere, Wisconsin who died in 2010.

3. Schell, "Commitment and Community," 237.

4. Badcock, *Way of Life*, 141.

5. Schuurman, *Vocation*, 125.

comes to discerning one's calling, there are no second chances, no backup plans, and no possible options.

Not surprisingly, anyone who thinks about God's call in this way will associate vocational discernment with incredible stress and anxiety, and so will want to postpone it as long as possible. After all, the consequences of discerning incorrectly—of even only slightly misunderstanding God's call—would be immeasurable and irrevocable. If God has a blueprint for our lives that covers every detail of our existence (the career we choose, the person we marry, the causes to which we commit ourselves), then we must be absolutely sure that we get it right.

If the "blueprint" view of call is what it means to say that God has a plan for our lives, how would we advise those who, year after year, still have no sense of what that plan might be? Moreover, how could we comfort any-one who pursued what they thought was God's plan only to later discover they were mistaken? "One problem with seeking out a specific plan," Kath-leen Cahalan stresses, "is that it creates anxiety that you might miss your one chance to get it right, that figuring out your vocation is a high-stakes scavenger hunt where you are searching for one hidden treasure."[6]

Would a God who loves us make discerning our callings so impos-sibly difficult as well as morally and spiritually perilous? Would a God of love have such a completely outlined plot for our lives that if we erred in discovering it the failure would haunt us for the rest of our lives? Surely that theology is wrong, and that is why contemporary theologies of vocation stress that discerning one's vocation is not like waiting for a bus that we have only one chance to board or searching for the blueprint in which our whole life is laid out in front of us or finding that map that provides absolutely clear directions. On the contrary, as we emphasized in the previous chapter, our callings, rather than being static, linear, and immutable, are more often dynamic, and evolving. In fact, typically we only gradually come to under-stand them, and they can shift and change over time.[7]

This does not mean we should drift from one calling to another as the wind blows us. Surely there are callings, like marriage, that are lifelong. Yet the discovery of what these callings mean, as well as how they direct us to behave differently at different times, is not acknowledged by the blueprint model. If we think of our callings as blueprints, we easily conclude that once we have discovered our callings, there is nothing left to discern. But that clearly is not true since we must continually reflect on what our callings mean and how best to live them. Moreover, the blueprint model makes us

---

6. Cahalan, *Stories We Live*, 3–4.

7. Cunningham, "Who's There?," 156.

passive recipients of a plan rather than active participants in receiving, responding to, and growing in a gift. Indeed, as we live our callings we are changed by them, and in the process come to understand more deeply what they mean. Spouses and partners will tell us this, so will parents and religious community members, veterans of social justice work, lawyers and judges, doctors and nurses, plumbers and painters, or entrepreneurs about to retire.

This is true of any calling. Discernment must be ongoing—and it always remains incomplete and unfinished—because the narrative of any vocational journey testifies that "there is no point at which we have final and complete knowledge of our callings."[8] This is because vocations, far from being perfectly fixed and forever stable, are unfolding mysteries of God's love and goodness that we grow into—mysteries whose meaning we never completely comprehend. Thus, Renee LaReau says, rather than offering an exact blueprint for our lives or a perfectly outlined map, "God always invites us forward, encourages us toward growth, and promises to be persistently present" as we move along on our vocational journeys.[9]

None of this means that as we take these journeys we simply make it up as we go along, which would suggest that there is no purpose or goal to the journeys; nor does it mean that God does not care about what path we decide to take. Unquestionably, God is concerned with the direction of our lives; for Christians, this has a clear form: as disciples they are called to move closer to God by following Jesus. Too, recognizing that there is a certain fluidity in our callings does not mean they are solely our decisions, which would suggest that we are the caller as well as the called. Our callings are always first and foremost God's gifts to us.[10] But accepting a *gift* requires that we are actively involved in receiving, affirming, shaping, and living the callings that have been entrusted to us; in fact, if we aren't we can be sure that our callings will die. Too, that our callings are uniquely personal gifts bestowed on us by God and developed through our own collaboration explains why no two callings are exactly alike and why God's callings can come in a variety of ways and are lived in a variety of ways, facts that are confirmed whenever we listen to another person's vocational story. Cahalan summarizes this more personal, dynamic, and relational theology of vocation when she writes: "Perhaps a more helpful way is to say that God does not create you *with* a vocation (one single plan that God has made), but with the capacity for vocations (the ability to engage in dialogue with God and

8. Cunningham, "Who's There?," 159.

9. LaReau, *Getting a Life*, 27.

10. Newman, "Called through Relationship," 20.

others to create a plan for your life). Vocation becomes, then, a creative act, something we create with God and others, unique to each of our lives."[11]

2. As we discern, we need to distinguish among our various callings.

A second principle that provides a framework for approaching vocational discernment is that we need to distinguish among the various callings we are trying to discern. Do we want to figure out what career path might be best suited for us or are we trying to fathom how we are called to respond to the needs of our friends? Are we struggling to discover whether we are called to remain single, enter a religious community, or marry; or are we hoping to discern how we can best use the limited time we have to respond to the needs of our local community? These questions remind us that there are multiple callings in our lives and different layers of callings, some of which are clearly more consequential than others. Failing to distinguish between *primary* and *secondary* callings trivializes the process of vocational discernment by not recognizing that not every calling is equally important.

Once I am freed of the blueprint notion of calling, I can more easily recognize that not all discernment is equally significant. Whether I choose to volunteer at a local homeless shelter or a food pantry is usually not morally and spiritually crucial because either way I will be helping people who lack the most basic necessities for life. On the other hand, whether I remain single, enter a religious community, or marry requires much more careful discernment because whatever I choose could affect the rest of my life as well as the lives of others. Primary callings identify and define us, center and commit us, and indicate the future trajectory of our lives much more than secondary callings. Judgments about them, therefore, require time, prayer, and discussion with those who know us best, and whom we admire.

This does not mean that vocational discernment only pertains to major life decisions such as those dealing with careers and professions or long-term commitments such as marriage or religious life. It may be that in certain circumstances whether we help at a shelter or a food pantry does make a difference and thus is something we should carefully consider. It is also true that we have to continually discern how to fulfill the responsibilities that come with any calling. How do we honor the various obligations that we have to our friends? How do we balance the call to attend to our physical, intellectual, emotional, and moral well-being with the call to care for others? These questions illustrate not only that what discernment means

11. Cahalan, *Stories We Live*, 5.

will vary according to what we are trying to fathom, but also why vocational discernment is not something we can do only occasionally, but rather must be a regular practice of our lives.

That practice is aided, however, as we become more aware of how primary callings relate to secondary callings. A call to marriage, for instance, is helpful in discerning what other callings we should or should not pursue. Is the calling I am considering compatible with the calling of my marriage? Will it root me more fully in that calling or will it draw me away from it? Or could it be a calling that my spouse and I could do together? At the same time, we should not think that those primary callings that set the context in light of which other secondary callings can be accepted are ever discerned once and for all. As noted above, calls to marriage, community life, or the single life are deepened and renewed as we live them, come to a better understanding of them, and are called each day to again say yes to them. If callings never stop, neither does discerning what those callings might be and how we ought to follow them. As Cahalan rightly notes, "Vocation is about the whole of your life, your whole life long,"[12] and if that is true the task of discerning our callings always remains unfinished.

No matter what calling we are trying to discern, it is important to remember, as we will emphasize throughout the book, that the most important vocational question any of us has to answer is the kind of person we want to become and each day strive to become. Vocational discernment is far too narrow and shortsighted if we limit it to decisions about marriage, joining a religious community, or what career to pursue. Discernment about such matters must be preceded and accompanied by discernment about who we want to be in the world and how overall we want to live.[13] The most fundamental issue of vocational discernment is not *what we will do* but *who we will be*.[14] Obviously, what career we choose matters, but not nearly as much as how we choose to live. If in our discernment we focus first on the kind of person we want to become, we will remember that vocation is not primarily about career but rather about the whole shape of our lives. Indeed, as Jerome Organ observes, we may not always have "a great deal of choice" about what we do for a living, but we always have a choice about who we are trying to become and about how we live.[15]

12. Cahalan, *Stories We Live*, 33.
13. Mohrmann, "Vocation Is Responsibility," 39.
14. Organ, "Of Doing and Being," 225.
15. Organ, "Of Doing and Being," 239.

3. Secondary callings should always enhance the fundamental callings of our lives.

A third principle to guide vocational discernment is to remember that the secondary callings of our lives should always serve and enhance our more fundamental callings. Whether we are trying to determine a possible career, whether and whom we should marry, or if we should respond to the request of a friend, we first need to determine if what we might choose will harmonize with the deepest callings of our lives. Does a calling allow me to be true to who I am and who I most want to be? Does it open the way for me to more clearly follow Christ? If I pursue this calling, will it deepen my integrity or weaken it? If I take this job, join this community, or marry this person, will it take me away from whom I believe God is calling me to be or draw me closer to it? These questions remind us that the secondary vocations of our lives should never jeopardize, contradict, or draw us away from our most fundamental callings.

That is why we cannot discern rightly about a particular calling without seeing how it will affect our other callings. For example, if the primary vocation of every Christian is to orient their lives to God and each day to walk a path that leads to God, that needs to be at the forefront of any vocational discernment. But my faithfulness to this baptismal calling cannot be assessed simply by how I understand who I am becoming and where I am going in my life. It must also include how the church (Christians through the ages as well as those I know and admire) helps me be the person God is calling me to be. After all, the fundamental call to all Christians is to follow Christ, and we know Christ through the Scriptures, the church, and those around us who reveal him to us. So we must always, with the counsel and guidance of others, ask: If I pursue this calling, will I continue on my journey with Christ or will I wander away? Will my life remain focused on God or do I risk becoming unmindful of God? As Keith Graber Miller writes, "Christians are called to follow Christ, not to particular jobs or professions."[16] For Christians, a calling will be right only if it enables them to imitate Christ more faithfully and completely. Because there are many ways to do this, there are many callings. If we remember that our primary calling is to be faithful to the character and ways of God and that we do so by growing in likeness to Christ, we can be confident in our discernment of other callings. Any calling that frees us to love God, our neighbors, and ourselves, to follow Christ and to grow in holiness, is not only good, but sacred.

16. Miller, *Living Faith*, 33.

A Process for Discerning Our Callings

Some Preliminary Considerations

Before outlining a process for discerning our vocations, a few initial observations may be helpful. First, there is no method for vocational discernment that will always lead to perfect clarity and certainty about our callings. That may be our hope, but it doesn't always happen and we cannot always expect it. No matter how wholeheartedly we attempt to discover our callings, there is ordinarily a level of uncertainty to vocational discernment; in fact, it is typically easier to know what is not our calling—or what is not God's will for us—than what is.

Moreover, to insist on more certainty than is possible may not only result in rushed or mistaken decisions, but will also likely lead to future disappointment. There is a tentative, provisional character to most vocational discernment, which suggests that more often than not, rather than uncovering a clear and definite path for the rest of our lives, all we may be able to glimpse is the next step forward. This is why, for example, when trying to make the best possible decisions for their lives, students may talk to their parents, siblings, and friends, reach out to faculty advisors, career counselors, or mentors, and still not be completely sure. As the authors of *Listening Hearts* wisely remind us, "Discernment can be like driving an automobile at night: the headlights cast only enough light for us to see the next small bit of road immediately in front of us."[17]

Second, no matter how much effort we devote to discernment, there may be no single calling that emerges as the one we should pursue; rather, there may be several callings, each of them good, each of them equally right for us. We may be looking for *the* way that is specially marked out for us, but instead discover that there is either *a* way we can follow or perhaps *several* ways.[18] Similarly, no matter how long we discern, there is no money back guarantee that we will make the right choice. We may think a certain path is right for us, try it, and then discover we were mistaken. But that's all right, especially when we are young; leaving what we thought was a calling is surely better than forcing ourselves to remain on a path that really isn't ours. In fact, sometimes discernment includes "trial and error." In order to come to a firmer understanding of what might be our calling, we may need to experiment with several possibilities, risk new things, learn from our mistakes, and finally, knowing all that we do, make the best decision that we can.[19]

17. Farnham et al., *Listening Hearts*, 24.

18. Deane-Drummond, "Art and Science," 177.

19. Neafsey, "Psychological Dimensions," 192.

Third, while we should not rush decisions about our vocations, neither should we spend so much time probing, dissecting, analyzing, and contemplating our callings that we never decide. Vocational discernment often demands the courage to be patient and to wait, remembering that not everyone discovers their callings in the same way and at the same time. The ability to be patient is especially important if our friends seem settled in some calling while we are still fundamentally unsure about ours. However, sometimes we are tempted to wait too long, wanting to be so sure, so certain, that the process of discernment never ends. This temptation can arise from fear about making the wrong decision or anxiety about committing, and can be so strong that we talk ourselves out of every possible right decision. We endlessly explore alternatives, investigating them from every angle, wanting to know everything that we possibly can. We consult more people, pray even harder, and attend one vocation retreat after another. But instead of being more certain or confident about our calling, we find ourselves "suffering from a 'paralysis of analysis'—stuck in the process of considering various alternatives, each of which may seem comparably fulfilling (or unfulfilling)."[20] As Gregg Levoy notes, "There *is* such a thing as thinking too much about a calling," examining it so exhaustively that we find ourselves more confused than illumined.[21] In short, even though vocational discernment is important, discerning our callings should never prevent living them.

Step One: Who and where are we?

While the process of discernment does not have to follow any particular order, it is often best to start with *who* you are and *where* you are. Our callings are usually related to the distinct features and circumstances of our lives. As Cahalan puts it, "God calls you *as* the person you are in the particularities of your life."[22] If God calls us *as* the person we are, we must first be honest about ourselves, our temperaments and personalities, our strengths and our weaknesses, and our particular histories. Someone who has little interest in detail probably isn't called to be an architect any more than someone who is bored with science should be a doctor. Any valid method of discerning our callings must be rooted in *understanding* and *accepting* who we are.[23]

Similarly, the narratives and contexts of our lives shape our callings. This does not mean that our family background, social and economic

20. Organ, "Of Doing and Being," 228.

21. Levoy, *Callings*, 48.

22. Cahalan, *Stories We Live*, 29.

23. Smith, *Courage & Calling*, 47.

context, education, or the time and place in which we live completely determine our vocation, but if God calls us *where* we are, these things surely matter. It is generally not helpful to work at discerning my calling by imagining
myself as a completely different person living in a completely different place
at a completely different time. I may be able to add chapters to my story, but
I cannot completely rewrite it.

Our culture encourages us to deny the limitations that are part of every person's life. It encourages us to dream and to fantasize—urging us to
believe that we can be and do anything that we want.[24] But that obviously
is not the case. A mediocre athlete can dream all he wants about playing
professional sports, but he never will. Someone born and raised in midtown
Manhattan may flee to the country on weekends, but it is unlikely that she
will be a dairy farmer. If it is to be truthful, vocational discernment must
be based on an accurate perception of reality—the reality of who we are,
what the narrative of our life has been, and what is truly possible for us.
If God calls us as *who* we are and *where* we are, we need to be attentive to
our lives as they are now, alert to all that unfolds before us each day, and
attentive to the particular needs and challenges of our times. As Jack Fortin
affirms, "The calling of God is probably not in some faraway place, but right
in front of you."[25]

We can discover a calling that is "right in front" of us by reflecting on
the communities of which we are already a part, the causes to which we are
already committed, and the values and ideals that already inform our sense
of ourselves, our place in the world, and what we hope to do with our lives.[26]
This too is part of beginning where we are and reminds us that we may be
well on our way to living a calling before we have explicitly identified what
that calling might be. For example, during the four years of college students
typically get involved with groups, projects, and causes that help them discover the fundamental ideals, values, and convictions of their lives. Through
engagement with these local communities, they gain a clearer sense of who
they are and what is important to them as well as some understanding of
what might be a future direction for their lives.

At a time of climate change and increasing environmental crises, a crucial part of knowing where we are is to be aware of and attentive to the places
we are living in now. But, as Wendell Berry has pointed out, as the result of
our mobility in today's world as well as our dependency on technology, we

24. For further analysis see Cavanaugh, "Actually."
25. Fortin, *Centered Life*, 63.
26. Schell, "Commitment and Community," 247.

no longer know our places as well as we should.[27] And as Pope Francis and so many others have also noted, this ignorance about place has led to the denigration of local environments. We are called, all of us, to care for the earth, but we only care for what we truly know and love, which is impossible if we don't even notice where we live. Thus, knowing *where* we are demands asking: What is this place I live in? Do I know its land and its people? And what might I be able to give to contribute to the life we share?[28]

Step Two: What does our past tell us about how we might be called?

Sometimes we can only discover where we might be called in the future by recollecting our past. When we think back over our lives, do certain events, persons, and experiences stand out that might give us a sense of our callings? Are there any "signs" along the way—recurrent themes, lingering questions or concerns, possibilities that continue to appeal to us, even persistent dreams—that might point to our vocations?[29] When we look back on our life's journey, certain patterns may emerge that suggest possible callings, or perhaps eliminate other callings. One person may discover that even though he has always done well in school, looking back, what he enjoyed most was working with his hands. Another may see that, much to her surprise, the meaning she found in working with persons with disabilities brought much greater satisfaction than all her academic achievements. Still, a third might acknowledge that even though many of his peers might not understand it, he has always been drawn to a life of prayer and ministry and, as the years passed, that attraction has only grown stronger. Again, this does not mean that our past determines our future, but it does mean that we can find suggestive hints about our callings by attending to the themes, signs, and messages in our past.

Recollecting our past in order to understand how we might be called in the future can be aided by the Examen prayer of St. Ignatius of Loyola (1491–1556), founder of the Jesuit religious order. The prayer, which is ordinarily done at the end of one's day, is composed of five steps: (1) Place yourself in the presence of God and give thanks for God's love for you. (2) Pray for the grace to understand how God is acting in your life. (3) In reviewing

27. Wendell Berry explores this point both in his essays and in his novels. See Berry, *Gift of Good Land*, *Jayber Crow*, and *Hannah Coulter*.

28. For an extensive analysis of the environmental crisis and the thorough conversion it requires, see Pope Francis, *Our Common Home*.

29. Ford, *Shape of Living*, 74.

your day, recall specific moments and how you felt. (4) Reflect on what you did, said, or thought in those moments. (5) Look toward tomorrow. If we make this prayer a regular practice, it will make us much more aware of and responsive to certain patterns, events, or experiences in our lives and what paths they might be opening for us. And it will make us more aware of God's presence in our lives and how God might be calling us. The Examen prayer should not be reserved only for the times when we have to make major decisions. If we pray it regularly, not only will discerning those big decisions seem less daunting, but we will also be better equipped to see how God might be calling us each day.

Step Three: What are we hearing?

Near the beginning of *Let Your Life Speak*, Parker Palmer observes: "Vocation does not come from willfulness. It comes from listening. . . . Vocation does not mean a goal that I pursue. It means a calling that I hear."[30] The very word *vocation* suggests that our callings are not things we create or initiate on our own, but rather are things we must listen for in order to receive. But we cannot possibly hear what our callings might be unless we develop regular practices of listening, something that is not easily achieved in a culture that encourages us to constantly be busy and productive—always *doing* something—and actively discourages the silence, solitude, and recollection necessary for attentive listening. To listen we need to slow down, pull back, and sit still.

Listening becomes increasingly difficult the more we surround ourselves with endless noise and distractions. Listening requires that we learn not only to be still, but also to be quiet. And being quiet is a practice, a discipline. In fact, discerning our vocations depends on cultivating particular practices, such as regular periods of silence and attentive listening. If we have never learned to be quiet and listen, how will we hear what we need to hear when we consider the future direction of our lives?

To whom and to what should we listen? First, we surely need to listen to the desires, longings, and inclinations of our hearts. As the Jesuit Fr. James Martin observes, "God awakens our vocations primarily through our desires."[31] Of course, we must also scrutinize our desires critically, but this implies that we first must know them and cannot afford to ignore them. What do you long for more than anything else? What do you love and care for so much that you are willing to give your life to it and cannot imagine

---

30. Palmer, *Let Your Life Speak*, 4.
31. Martin, *Becoming Who You Are*, 76.

life without it? Or, as Michael Himes asks, "When you are at your best what is it that you most truly desire?"[32]

These questions disclose that callings ordinarily grow from the deepest yearnings and attractions of our lives, yearnings and attractions that not only are too strong to be silenced or ignored, but which also, when we claim them, begin to animate, shape, and guide our lives.[33] Gregg Levoy speaks of these yearnings and attractions of the heart as passions, and describes passion as "what we are most deeply curious about, most hungry for, will most hate to lose in life." Passion, he says, "is what matters most whether we're doing it or not."[34]

The philosopher Immanuel Kant taught that we should ignore our feelings, attractions, and desires—what he called "sentiments"—and instead always do our duty whether we feel like it or not. His teaching has influenced ethical, spiritual, and cultural traditions, and not without reason since there clearly are times when we must fulfill our obligations despite how we feel about them. But Kant's philosophy has had the unfortunate effect of leading people to believe that when they are faced with important decisions, they must disregard their feelings, emotions, and desires—all the messages from their hearts—since those things would likely cloud their judgment and keep them from seeing and thinking objectively.

And yet, this is not necessarily true; in fact, it is seriously misguided. Feelings may not always be trustworthy, but they can illumine our judgments and guide us to a better understanding of what we ought to do. Isn't it true that we sometimes know something in our hearts long before we are able to give a carefully reasoned argument to support it? Even more, isn't it highly unlikely that we are called to something for which we have absolutely no desire, no attraction, no depth of feeling? We cannot give ourselves wholeheartedly to a calling, no matter how good it is, unless it is something we genuinely desire. Callings demand commitment, they are built on promises. But we cannot promise ourselves to something unless we see it as truly promising; and we won't see it as truly promising unless it is something our hearts really want. This is why attention to our feelings and desires—to what goes on in our hearts—should inform any process of vocational discernment from beginning to end.

To be sure, just because we desire or are attracted to something does not mean we should pursue it, much less that it is our calling. Not everything we desire is necessarily good; and even if it is good, we can still pursue it in

32. Himes, *Doing the Truth*, 56.

33. Furey, *Road to You*, 3.

34. Levoy, *Callings*, 69.

unhealthy and self-defeating ways. Thus, we need to distinguish between "ego-centered" desires and inclinations and "God-centered" desires and inclinations. Any true calling summons us out of ourselves in love and service to others, but ego-centered desires turn us in on ourselves, closing us off from others and making us indifferent to their needs. Ego-centered desires are "self-serving, self-promoting, self-protective ways of feeling and thinking that incline us toward ways of living that are out of tune with the call of God," Neafsey writes. "If we follow them, we are likely to get caught up in the kind of empty, superficial, inauthentic, self-centered ways of living that have traditionally been known as sin."[35] By contrast, God-centered desires and inclinations "draw us into deeper, authentic, loving connection with God, others, and ourselves,"[36] which is what every genuine calling should enable us to achieve.

This is why as we "listen to our hearts" we must also be listening to God, which we do through prayer. Prayer is an indispensable element to discerning our callings. St. Teresa of Avila described prayer as "nothing else than an intimate sharing between friends; it means taking time frequently to be alone with Him who we know loves us."[37] Friends want what is best for one another and are devoted to one another's good, which, as we suggested, is eminently true of God's relationship with us. Thus, we can trust that God will not mislead us as we discern our callings. Friends also support and encourage one another and help one another persevere through struggles. If God is a friend who wants our good and who supports us, bringing any apprehension about a calling to God in prayer can not only help us deal with our fears, but can also give us a sense of peace and reassurance and a better understanding of how we might be called.

Genuine friends not only support and encourage us, they also are willing to challenge us and be truthful with us precisely because they care for us and want our good. What we receive from God in prayer may be a word of consolation and reassurance; but it can also be a word we don't especially want to hear. This is one reason people often avoid prayer; it's not, as they might say, that they are too busy to find time for prayer, but that they don't want to get too close to a God who might confront them with an uncomfortable truth. Prayer keeps us honest, especially if we stop talking long enough to allow God to speak.

Most of us are experts at self-deception. Like the biblical Jonah who knew he was called to preach to Nineveh, but instead ran in the other

35. Neafsey, *Sacred Voice*, 42.

36. Neafsey, *Sacred Voice*, 42.

37. Ryan, "Foundations and Dynamics," 48.

direction, we may know how we are called, but have become skilled in offering all kinds of reasons to talk ourselves out of it. Maybe we have been telling ourselves lies—and lies always hurt, perhaps especially when we tell them to ourselves. No true friend would allow us to hurt ourselves this way. Listening to God in prayer enables us to hear something other than our own misgivings, excuses, rationalizations, and fears. It opens us to hear a word that, even when it challenges us with truths we have worked hard to avoid, always comes to us in love.

Third, we need to listen to others. Discerning our calling is intensely personal, but we cannot—and should not—do it all on our own. In fact, call is much too important to be left entirely to ourselves, especially because we can be wrong about how we might be called. We need the counsel, guidance, wisdom, and expertise of others. We need "companions in discernment." They can be family members (parents, grandparents, siblings, aunts, uncles, and even our children), close friends, teachers, academic advisors and career counselors, pastors and ministers, and all the other unofficial mentors of our lives. Who are people you trust and admire? Who inspires you? Who truly knows you, and loves and cares for you enough to give their honest assessment of how they think you might be called? Who is willing to really listen to you and to ask the right questions in response, including the hard questions you may have been avoiding?

People close to us often know us better than we know ourselves; sometimes they can see us more clearly and insightfully than we see ourselves. This does not mean we should always follow their advice, and it certainly doesn't mean that we let them decide for us. Similarly, we must be careful not to let their hopes and expectations talk us out of a calling that really is ours or pressure us into one that clearly isn't. But listening to others invites the people most dear to us into our discernment process. This not only relieves us of the burden of trying to discern our callings alone, but also allows people who love us and truly want to help us to do so.

Step Four: What do we do well?

An important fourth step in vocational discernment is an honest assessment of our gifts and abilities. What do we do well? What talents have others affirmed in us? And what don't we do well? Where are we competent and where are we limited? These are important questions because it makes little sense to pursue a vocation for which we have little aptitude or ability. To do so would set ourselves up for endless frustration and failure. This does not mean that we shouldn't challenge ourselves, trying different things that seem daunting because we are uncertain we have what it takes to do them. We all know instances where people who were less talented in certain areas surpassed their more gifted colleagues because they worked harder, were more deeply motivated, and refused to give up. Nonetheless, even if they were *less* gifted than their peers, they were still *sufficiently* gifted to succeed at their callings. As Margaret Mohrmann notes, "But it is surely the case that we are not *called* to undertake a task or a career for which we possess no such capacities and at which we can only fail, or that will stunt us personally or lead to a lifetime of tedious desperation."[38]

To pursue a calling for which, given our lack of talent, we could not possibly succeed would also be terribly irresponsible because it would prevent us from being able to do good for others; in fact, we could harm them. Someone who has no aptitude for teaching should not be entrusted with the education of students any more than someone who is woefully tone-deaf should be giving voice lessons. This does not deny that God can call us in ways that don't—at least initially—seem to correspond exactly with our gifts. But, all things considered, "God usually works with, not against, our abilities and aptitudes."[39] After all, God gave us particular talents and abilities precisely so that we could use them on behalf of others.

An adage you can find posted on the walls of certain church basements reads: "God doesn't call the qualified, He qualifies the called." It is true that sometimes it is only through answering a call that we discover the skills and abilities we need to fulfill it. We saw this in our analysis of call stories from the Bible in chapter three. Many of the people God called initially felt unfit for the call because they believed they lacked whatever gifts the call required. In answering the call, they discovered gifts of which they were previously unaware. Students experience this all the time. They say yes to something that is asked of them and by accepting the invitation discover a gift. That discovery often brings a better understanding of how they might be called.

Christians believe the Holy Spirit equips each of us to serve the church. As St. Paul tells the Christian community at Corinth, God has entrusted everyone with a distinctive gift or charism. There is no one in the community that has not been gifted, no one who has not been blessed with a particular talent or skill (1 Cor 12:7). Paul is clear that we do not give ourselves these gifts: "All these are activated by one and the same Spirit, who allots to each one individually just as the Spirit chooses" (12:11). Since all our gifts come to us from God, we should not be jealous or envious of others' gifts, but

38. Mohrmann, "Vocation Is Responsibility," 31.
39. Schuurman, *Vocation*, 143.

appreciate how both they and we have been gifted. Moreover, the fact that God is the source of these gifts again underscores that our callings are "not ultimately about us as individuals," but much more about what God accomplishes through us communally.[40]

Our gifts are the very personal and distinctive ways each of us serves the common good; in fact, when we know our gifts we also know how God will most effectively use us to serve others.[41] "So each of these gifts is God's way of ministering to the vast variety of human needs through those who are being charismed or gifted," John Haughey explains. "Each charismed or gifted-by-the-Spirit person . . . adds a distinctively new note to the symphony of God's love that all are meant to hear in the course of their lives on earth."[42] To discern our calling is to discover what gifts God has given us so we can sound the "distinctively new note" that we are meant to play in God's symphony of love.

Step Five: Where are we needed?

Where are we needed? How should we serve? The fact that our gifts are to be used to benefit others and to contribute to the common good indicates that a very important dimension of discovering our callings is to consider the needs of the world; or, in what is perhaps the most often quoted statement about vocation, what Frederick Buechner calls "the world's deep hunger." As he puts it, "The place God calls you to is the place where your deep gladness and the world's deep hunger meet."[43] If discernment goes no further than the first part of this statement, focusing only on what brings us satisfaction and joy, it becomes dangerously self-centered. If discernment consists only in *turning inward* to discover what we want, and never *turns outward* to consider how we might address the pain and brokenness, the sorrow, tears, and sufferings of the world, living vocationally will increase injustice rather than stem it. Vocational discernment should always open our eyes to others, especially to the needs and sufferings of our sisters and brothers as well as all created beings. It should evoke greater generosity and compassion in us and enable us to widen our circle of concern. Any genuine process of vocational discernment must ask whether a particular calling "would be of any real help or service to people in the real world. Would it usefully address

---

40. Newman, "Called through Relationship," 23.

41. Cahalan, *Stories We Live*, 65.

42. Haughey, "Three Conversions," 10.

43. Buechner, *Wishful Thinking*, 95.

a human need or make a helpful contribution to the world in any way?"[44]
If we cannot answer yes to those questions, we should discern some more.

The fact that vocational discernment must be attentive to the needs
of the world indicates that our callings come from outside us as much or
more than from within us. Indeed, a chance encounter with another human
being can even lead to a call. Someone presents us with a need, asks if we
would help, and we say yes. An example is Sr. Helen Prejean, a Catholic nun
famous for being an outspoken critic of the death penalty. She undoubtedly
sees her work as a calling. But she arrived at this awareness not by carefully
scrutinizing her gifts or by recognizing her deepest passion, but because
one day she was asked if she would write to some prisoners on death row
at the Louisiana State Penitentiary.[45] She was asked to do something she
had never considered doing and said yes. That calling, which she neither
expected nor prepared for, redirected the course of her life.

Sr. Prejean's story exemplifies how many callings are best understood
not as things we choose, but as needs that present themselves, needs that
evoke in us a sense of responsibility from which we cannot turn away. We
cannot respond to every need and must learn sometimes to be content with
what we can do rather than rush after all we would like to do; however, such
a realistic assessment of our limitations should never be an excuse for doing
nothing at all. As Darby Ray comments: "A key question for the individual
who is in discernment is not only 'What do I want to do with my life?' but
also 'What does the world offer or ask of me?'"[46]

Step Six: What brings us joy?

If something is truly our calling, living it should bring a sense of joy or,
in Buechner's words, a "deep gladness." Who would be attracted to living
vocationally if it did not promise some amount of happiness, contentment,
and peace? If it did not bring some sense of wholeness and completion to
our lives? But here again we must be careful. Living vocationally does lead
to a flourishing and good life; however, any genuine and substantive calling
makes demands on us. Our callings will bring joy and meaning to our lives,
but they will also bring moments of tremendous challenge, exasperation,
frustration, and exhaustion. Indeed, there are times when being faithful to
a calling will not make us happy. Doctors and nurses certainly aren't happy
when their patients die any more than parents are happy when their children

44. Neafsey, *Sacred Voice*, 45.
45. Prejean, *Dead Man Walking*.
46. Ray, "Self, World," 315.

deeply disappoint them or teachers when a class goes poorly. Yet, doctors, nurses, parents, teachers, and all the rest of us, pursue and remain in our vocations even when it would be easier to flee them because our vocations allow us to combine our passions with our gifts so we can offer our lives as a truthful sacrifice to others and to God. Only this can bring deep gladness, a joy that abounds.

This sixth dimension of discernment may seem to be of less use to us as we begin a process of discernment because joy comes not before we take up a calling, but as we live it. This joy is far deeper and more resilient than a momentary pleasure that comes and goes. The joy that ensues from entering fully into our callings is a grace that confirms that the callings we have given ourselves to are indeed the right ones. Joy flows from lives that, however difficult, are full of meaning and purpose. Joy assures us that how we are living matters. Joy keeps us from doubting or continually second guessing our vocations. LaReau describes it as "the inner conviction that what I'm doing is good even if it does not make me happy or content one hundred percent of the time." Joy is one of the great consolations of living vocationally because even when being faithful to our callings is not easy, we still are blessed "with a profound sense of conviction that this is a good way to live a life."[47]

But there is a way that a sense of joy, or at least an intuition of joy, can be experienced prior to living a calling. This is suggested by two practices, both based on the *Spiritual Exercises* of Ignatius of Loyola. First, if you are unsure how you might be called because you feel drawn to several different callings, try to imagine where following a certain calling will lead in the long run. What would your life be like if you took this path? What would it make of you? Would you be happy with that life or disappointed? Or consider living with a particular choice for three days. Over those three days, how did you feel? What did you experience? Did the call feel genuine? As you lived it, were you able to say: "This is really me!" After three days, do the same with another calling, then compare the experiences. Or, in a slightly different approach, imagine yourself on your deathbed looking back at your life. From that perspective, see if one path emerges more clearly and urgently than another. On your deathbed, would there be a calling you would regret never having chosen?

Second, Ignatius thought we could test certain decisions by considering the feelings we have as we imagine making them, first one way, then the other. If you imagine making a decision or following a path in life, and this is accompanied by a sense of peace, joy, contentment, and clarity—what

---

47. LaReau, *Getting a Life*, 41.

Ignatius called feelings of "consolation"—that is a strong indication to follow it.[48] Ignatius believed that such consolation foreshadowed the joy that would come from living out a calling. Whatever joy we experienced in contemplating a calling was an inkling of the joy that would bless us as we lived those callings. By contrast, if when you imagine acting or deciding in a certain way you feel troubled, agitated, unsettled, depressed, and even more confused—which Ignatius called feelings of "desolation"—that is an equally strong indication that it is not the right way to go.[49] Ignatius recognized, as we emphasized in step three of the process of discernment, that we must take the feelings we experience seriously in every stage of vocational discernment.

Conclusion

Vocational discernment is serious business that should not be taken lightly; but neither should it be paralyzing, overwhelming, and burdensome. So it may be good to end this chapter with some reassuring wisdom. In *An Altar in the World*, Barbara Brown Taylor reminisces about her own process of vocational discernment. Like many of us, early in her life Taylor believed "there was one particular thing I was supposed to do with my life. I thought that God had a purpose for me and my main job was to discover what it was,"[50] she recalls. "So I began asking God to tell me what I was supposed to do. What was my designated purpose on this earth? How could I discover the vocation that had my name on it?"[51] Almost nightly, Taylor climbed a fire escape and prayed, beseeching God for an answer. "Then one night when my whole heart was open to hearing from God what I was supposed to do with my life," she recounts, "God said, 'Anything that pleases you.'"[52]

What Taylor discovered that evening on a fire escape was both reassuring and liberating. That auspicious discovery should guide our efforts of figuring out our callings and safeguard us from being overly anxious and stressed. After all, if God loves us and wants our good—and will work with us no matter what we finally decide—there is every reason to imagine God saying those same words to us.

48. Neafsey, "Psychological Dimensions," 174.

49. Harman, "Vocation," 113.

50. Taylor, *Altar*, 108.

51. Taylor, *Altar*, 109.

52. Taylor, *Altar*, 110.

CHAPTER 6

Living the Called Life— Dangers and Warnings

"ACTUALLY, YOU CAN'T BE anything you want—and it's a good thing too." That's the title of a recent provocative article on vocation by William Cavanaugh. Cavanaugh is getting us to think about call in a different way from how we are trained to think in our culture. We often hear all about how you can be anything you want to be; but as Cavanaugh argues, it's not true!—and we need to recognize this if we are to make headway in thinking about call. Borrowing from Luke Epplin's interesting article in *The Atlantic*, Cavanaugh notices that this idea is the unspoken premise of almost every kids' movie on the market. A young hero wants or hopes for something that seems far above and beyond him. In pursuit of his dream the young hero encounters a little difficulty, maybe faces down a villain, but in the end he wins the race or the contest or the affirmation of all the people. He gets to be whatever he wanted to be.

Harmless fun? Perhaps. But buried underneath are some strong ideas that can affect how we see our lives. There is the implication that our path in life is guided mainly by our desires and choices. Find out what you want to do, and choose it! Also, according to these movies, it is pretty easy to become really good at just about anything. You just have to believe. For instance, on Epplin's analysis, two such young movie heroes, Turbo and Dusty, "don't need to hone their craft for years in minor league circuits . . . It's enough for them simply to show up with no experience at the world's most competitive races, dig deep within themselves, and out-believe their opponents."[1] Dream big, struggle just a little, hardly practice, just keep believing—and, suddenly, you've made it! You've achieved whatever you wanted to!

1. Epplin, "You Can Do *Anything*," quoted in Cavanaugh, "Actually," 25.

What happens to our ideas about vocation when they get run through a culture that surrounds us with messages like this? What if, contrary to the messages, we don't always get what we want in our callings, or don't get to choose them? Or what if the struggle is ongoing, or if it turns out that we were wrong about what God was calling us to be or do? In this chapter we want to consider some prevalent ideas of our time that might mislead us about call—which we will put in terms of dangers and warnings along our vocational journey.

Call and Choice

Choice plays a prominent role in how we are taught to think of our lives. "Being anything you want" frees us from constraints that might determine our wants or limit our choices. This sounds like a liberation, but is it? Not so clearly for the prodigal son Jesus tells a story about in the Gospel of Luke. He acted on what he thought he wanted, cut loose from his family, squandered his inheritance on "riotous living," and ended up destitute (Luke 15:11–32). We can choose badly; if we choose anything we want, we might choose something that can destroy us. Sometimes we need to be saved from our wants and choices.

Moreover, the idea that we can be anything we want to be can make us lonely and anxious, especially as young adults. As Cavanaugh notes, young adults, especially those emerging from college, "are often told not only that they can and must *choose* their life, but that they must maximize that choice and choose their *best* life . . . [But] do they really *know* what they want? How does anyone really know what kind of life one wants? Can people choose what sorts of lives are right for them before they have lived enough to know? The whole exercise of *choosing* one's vocation becomes fraught with anxiety."[2]

It is also true that choice, especially "unlimited choice," accompanies luxury. The idea that a child from rural Africa, for instance, can be anything he or she wants to be is absurd, and something of an insult, since the idea that my life is not full unless I can get just what I want assumes that those who cannot choose in this way are consigned to diminished lives. A key problem with telling anyone they can be whatever they want to be is that it tempts us to think that we make ourselves solely through our choices. Yet it is God who created us and continues to create us by calling us. If "call" is to offer us anything more than getting the life we choose, it must begin with this fundamental point. We do not choose ourselves.

2. Cavanaugh, "Actually," 26.

Douglas Schuurman notes that our modern emphasis on freedom "masks the ways in which we are not free, but are being formed by powers beyond our control." In fact, even if it seems like we have unlimited choice, we do not; we receive our lives far more than we choose them from circumstances and powers that set their context. But, adds Schuurman, "Christian faith perceives these powers to be ultimately in the hands of a merciful, provident God."[3] Standing on its own, choice puts us in charge—but this is not only not comforting, it is frightening. By contrast, call holds out the promise that there is one who knows us, goes before us and beckons us toward a higher good. This conviction, that we are in the hands of a merciful, provident God, will need support—many us may find it difficult to believe. Yet if we open to the possibility that we are called, we begin to consider that it might be true. Even the dawning of this openness can revolutionize our lives, especially in this time when we are propagandized to believe that we are in charge of choosing ourselves, of forming our lives into whatever shape we happen to want.

As Cavanaugh points out, our modern affinity for choice has a history. "[T]he notion of 'choosing' one's line of work was not simply a brainstorm that occurred between the ears of Puritan thinkers [who were among the first to claim we must a choose a calling]; it marked a major shift in the economic reality of developing capitalist economies."[4] With the industrial revolution, families left their farms and moved into urban areas to go to work at the burgeoning factories. This was not really their choice; it was forced by the "market," since in this time it became increasingly difficult to survive as subsistence farmers. To be sure, the industrial revolution eventually made way for the many choices we have today. Yet the outcome also has displaced us, and increased our anxiety. As Cavanaugh notes, "As efficiency has replaced self-sufficiency, people entering the market feel increasingly at the mercy of larger forces that are beyond their comprehension and control. People seeking employment must try to conform to the ever-shifting demands of the job market . . . Individuals who have successfully negotiated the educational system are thrust out onto the job market with the expectation that they must invent their own lives without traditional markers of identity and custom."[5]

The irony of our modern accent on choice is that it has put us in a desperate position, for we have to choose a meaningful life in a world where the only meaning we can find is based on our choosing it. In this context, we

3. Schuurman, *Vocation*, 121.

4. Cavanaugh, "Actually," 28.

5. Cavanaugh, "Actually," 33.

will be tempted to use "call" as a way of providing the meaning we think we need to make a choice. Having a vocation might seem to promise us salvation from the tyranny of choice. But it cannot be only this. Or, better put, if in the midst of our many, confusing choices we begin desperately wishing to hear a voice from God that breaks in to tell us which choice to make, we might just as well throw dice. Call cannot substitute for choices that we have grown tired of having to think through.

On the other hand, as just mentioned, openness to call can encourage us to consider whether there might be someone else who knows more than we do about how our lives might be better lived. This in turn encourages us to become less fixed on our present wants and desires, and more attuned to how we might need to grow to become people who want better things. And we can begin to notice how our lives depend on others' gifts, gifts that constrain us in the sense that they hold us fast by ties of love and connection.

We need to be opened to call, not simply by desperation about our choices, but by a willingness to receive a gift and put our lives in the hands of another. Christians believe that God comes to us in this way; as he does, we must be prepared to discern how best to respond to the gift—with others' help, of course. Once discerned, our calls will be something we can say yes to; to choose, not as a way of inventing ourselves but as a way of handing ourselves over. There is discovery in this, a discovery not so much in terms of my wants or even my perceived talents, but rather in the context of the gifts and circumstances I have been given. As we discover this, and begin to live toward it, we will also be better able to choose it, daily.

To summarize about the dangers of choice:

> *One warning sign along the vocational journey helps us navigate through the roundabout of choice. We do not choose our lives, nor our callings; and a call is not the same thing as a choice. Understandably, we look for a call when there are too many choices; yet call requires a readiness to notice what we have been given, and so to be prepared to give ourselves over to the will of another, who knows what we need and want better than we know ourselves. The choice to do this is ours; as we live into our callings, we will be given the grace to make it, daily.*

Call and Struggle

When they are learning to ice skate, nobody wants, or chooses, to slip and fall on the ice. It hurts! It might be nice if we could just lace on a pair of skates and, on our first try, glide gracefully around the rink. But of course slipping and falling is an essential part of learning to skate; and those who state well—effortlessly, perfectly—can do so only because they have fallen countless times, and learned from this. Mind you, we don't always want to learn, since it requires change. Our reluctance about getting hurt can combine with our preference to keep things the way things are, and so we refuse to begin something new that might change us for the better.

Call requires both falling and being changed. Like ice skating, we get better at following our callings after we fall, or fail. We tend to think of our callings exclusively as the work we do in the world, some job or task or service to someone. Callings can be that, but this is only half the story. For call is always also "reflexive," which means it is about us and how we need to change and grow. Our callings never leave us alone. They will challenge us and demand things from us, things we are not always eager to give.

As we have noticed, choice in our modern world typically relates to the things we want and plan to get. But call takes us somewhere we had not really planned on going. As it does this, it requires a change in us, and this can be painful. For Christians, the call comes from Jesus and always involves discipleship: following him. Yet the story of Jesus, the path his life takes, leads to the cross. How do we choose that? Dietrich Bonhoeffer, who followed the call all the way to death in a Nazi prison, believed that "No man can choose such a life for himself. No man can call himself to such a destiny . . . The gulf between a voluntary offer to follow and genuine discipleship is clear."[6]

Not everyone who faithfully follows Jesus dies for it, like Bonhoeffer did. Rather, what Bonhoeffer's point reveals, and his life shows, is that from its beginning the call to discipleship does not come to us loaded with incentives that appeal to our appetites. In fact, when the call first arrives it can shock us; at the very least, it demands our full attention. We can't respond to just a little bit; it is not a "halfway" call. Becoming a disciple of Jesus is not like walking through a cafeteria line, picking and choosing what we like best.

It is interesting that in the stories the Gospels tell of people setting off to follow Jesus, we get no account of their choosing to do this: they just follow. Of the fishermen brothers, Simon Peter and Andrew, we are told that after Jesus calls, "Immediately they left their nets and followed him" (Matt 4:20). By contrast, when the Gospels talk about someone deliberating about whether to follow Jesus, they often do not actually do it. For instance, we hear of a man who says to Jesus, "I will follow you, Lord; but let me first say farewell to those at my home." To which Jesus replies, "No one who puts a hand to the plow and looks back is fit for the kingdom of God" (Luke 9:62).

6. Bonhoeffer, "Cost," 391.

The clearest example of a person deciding *not* to follow Jesus is the rich young man who comes to Jesus asking, "Good master, what shall I do to inherit eternal life?" Jesus treats him a little roughly at first, asking him why he calls him "good," then tells him to do the obvious: keep the commandments—don't steal, don't lie, honor your parents. The young man, who seems very eager and likable, answers that he has done all this from a young age. But here is how the story ends: "Jesus, looking at him, loved him and said, 'You lack one thing; go, sell what you own, and give the money to the poor, and you will have treasure in heaven; then come, follow me.' When he heard this, he was shocked and went away grieving, for he had many possessions" (Mark 10:21–22).

This story shows we can refuse a call; we can consider it, recognize what it will require of us, and say "no thanks." How does this happen? As Bonhoeffer observes, this man "wants to follow, but feels obliged to insist on his own terms."[7] He is eager, but prepared to receive the call only within a range of what he has already set for himself as acceptable. He wants to do something for God, but remain the same. Bonhoeffer suggests the rich young man is primarily interested in an academic answer; he wants to talk about religion with Jesus, not about himself. "He had hoped to avoid committing himself to any definite moral obligations by forcing Jesus to discuss his spiritual problems. He hoped Jesus would offer him a solution for his moral difficulties. But instead he finds Jesus attacking not his question but himself."[8]

Cardinal John Henry Newman relates this episode to Jesus' command in the Sermon on the Mount: "Be perfect, therefore, as your heavenly Father is perfect" (Matt 5: 48). The rich young man finds this a "hard saying."[9] We all resist the idea of perfection, for who can be perfect—and who wants to try? But the trajectory of Jesus's sermon, and the exchange here with the rich man, suggest that perfection is the endgame for anyone God calls. Here we can see the "reflexivity" of all God's callings. We are called to work in the world, yes, but doing such work will also change and reform us, strengthening us for the journey. Not unlike ice skating, by entering our callings we begin to do things that train us, including falling frequently. This is not always pleasant. It is a struggle, and at the start there is a very long way to go, not only in the path we have to travel or the things we must do, but in the changes that call will bring in us. Reluctance to be changed is one of many

---

7. Bonhoeffer, "Cost," 392.
8. Bonhoeffer, "Cost," 397.
9. Newman, "Divine Calls," 345.

reasons not to follow, but—as Peter and Andrew did, and the young rich man could not—we need to simply open ourselves and begin.

The reflexive feature in call is, in a way, its most difficult. We are aware, perhaps, that God's call will demand that we do some difficult things . . . but to be changed within ourselves?—this seems like too much. We are tempted to think of a call as the gateway to smooth traveling. In a time of so many complicated choices, we can even hope that "call" will provide us a sure way of knowing what we are supposed to be doing. But if our calls are always reflexive, this means that they will always want something from us; they will work a change in our souls. Since we usually don't want to be changed, this will make call extra difficult. And we will surely have times of doubt and confusion within ourselves.

Christians, especially Evangelical Christians, can be tempted to offer call as a way out of confusion. This is what we earlier spoke of as an already decided and fully determined plan that God has for us—like a blueprint or roadmap. This view of call says: God has a plan for you, and you need to get with it. You need to read the signs to find the plan; once you know, mainly what you need to do is stick with it and it will take you through the obstacle course of life unscathed. So long as you live according to God's plan you will prosper, spiritually and perhaps even materially.

A difficultly with thinking of call as "plan" lies in how it conceives of God. God is the great civil engineer in the sky who has drawn out in detail the roads he expects his human creatures to travel. Rather than as the destination of our lives, or the one who accompanies us on the human journey, this God is like a mastermind who knows what we are supposed to be doing—that we should go to this school, or move to that city, or buy that house—but is revealing this to us only in little bits. By contrast, when Jesus says, "Come, follow me," he calls us into a relationship; we are following a person, which means not just tracking his movements, like Daniel Boone tracking a bear through the woods, but learning to walk with him, and be like him.

To say God is our destination is not to say that God is like a coordinate we might reach by following our GPS. Rather, as C. S. Lewis describes the Trinity, "God is not a static thing . . . but a dynamic, pulsating activity, a life, almost a kind of drama . . . [even] a kind of dance."[10] What we can know is that because we have been called to participate in this life, to join the dance, we will be given opportunities to grow into it—to become daily more conformed to Christ's perfect life, and perfect relation to his Father. Thinking about call as following out a life plan provides little room for this.

10 Lewis, *Mere Christianity*, 175.

The "plan" idea of call borrows its assumptions from our consumer society. We buy a device, follow the instructions about how to set it up properly, turn it on, and we are good to go. A little work and struggle up front, but it is worth it for the ease it brings in the long run—so long as everything continues to function as it should. And, if it turns out that things aren't going quite right, we can take it back and ask for a new device, or plan. We look for a new sign from God that we should turn here or adjust there so we can get back on the track God has planned out for us.

The reminder that call is always reflexive can keep us from the theological puzzles in the "plan" view, and also prepare us better for the struggle that accompanies the called life. If call is not only about tasks undertaken and successfully completed, or about the road traveled from point A to B, but about what happens within us who are called, how we change and grow towards "perfection," then we can be a little less anxious as we receive it. Call is less about determining which school to go to, or profession to enter, or spouse to marry, and more about what happens to us after as we find ourselves living into the shape of the commitments we make. This means that if we decide to go to University #1, when we arrive, we do not need to worry so much about whether we are "in God's plan"—wondering perhaps if God was really telling us to go to University #2 and we just somehow misheard him. We can, rather, get right down to the work of being a student there, to struggle at this—and learning will be a struggle if we are really to grow in it. To be sure, under certain circumstances we might later decide to move to another university; universities are for learning, and if we find we can't learn at a particular one, we should stop and go to another. There might be other good reasons to move, like our responsibilities to other callings. Whatever the specific case, the reminder that our call is always reflexive, that it includes our growth into God's life, helps orient our thinking about such details.

The Gospel story of the rich young man catches our attention because it is about someone refusing a call. It makes clear that we can and do sometimes miss our callings. When we read that the young man "went away sad," this means that he lost an opportunity. The opportunity was not just for the poor who could have received a helping hand from his money (no small thing), but for him: he misses a chance to enter a relationship that will change and transform him. This is sobering, for the same might happen to us. But it ought not to be disabling, for the story is transparent: we can see clearly why the call was refused. The young man is held back not by some mysterious force, or failure to follow the clues to the complicated blueprint of God's plan, but because of his attachment to other lesser things and his reluctance to change. It leads to a simple question: Are we similarly hampered? What smaller desires might be holding us back? In what parts of ourselves are we especially resistant to change? We will find these difficult questions, not because they require complicated algorithms about the inscrutable plan of God, but because we so often deceive ourselves and get pulled down by our petty desires. And, in fact, the attachments we human beings develop towards these lesser things follow patterns. Like this man, we like money and the security it brings and the way it helps us live as we desire.

Remembering that our callings are about us and our transformation and, as well, that there are certain attachments that typically keep us from consenting to this transformation, should help us avoid the nervous guessing game that talk about "finding your vocation" can lead to. The struggle of our callings remains, even deepens; but the struggle is with ourselves and our resistance to genuine growth rather than with the nagging "what ifs" of a plan that didn't work out as we thought.

Thinking in this way, when it is combined with the Christian conviction that God is gracious and merciful, is also consoling in another way. For it means that the train we missed last time will always loop back around. As Cardinal Newman concludes his comments on the story of the rich young man, he says, "all through our life Christ is calling us. He called us first in Baptism; but afterwards also; whether we obey His voice or not, He graciously calls us still."[11] The implication is that, even if we never hear about him again in the Bible, it is not over for the rich young man. The text tells us, "Jesus looking on him, loved him." This means Jesus will not abandon this man who refuses his call; he will not leave him alone. For, after all, the man and his transformation is the main target of the call. As the Gospel story of the good shepherd implies, if one sheep out of a flock of 100 wanders off, the shepherd will not leave it behind, but rather pursue it relentlessly (Matt 18:12).

The consolation that comes with this commitment on the shepherd's part not to leave us does not mean the struggle is lifted. In fact, as we resist, it grows. The rich young man is in for a difficult time, more difficult after he goes away than when he first comes running to Jesus. But sometimes, even often, a response to a call on its second or third or fourth iteration can deepen precisely because of the struggle and suffering that came as a result of the earlier refusals. *New York Times* columnist David Brooks calls our attention to "second mountain people," those who set their sights on a first mountain of success or achievement yet end up empty after climbing it. Perhaps they suffer grief over a death, or someone betrays them, or they simply feel lost and alone. Yet rather than breaking them, they find

11. Newman, "Divine Calls," 346.

themselves "broken open. They have been reminded that they are not just the parts of themselves that they put on display. There is another layer to them they have been neglecting, a substrate where the dark wounds and most powerful yearnings live."[12] And so they can set about to climb a second, different mountain; they can embark on a larger journey that is not about all they can accomplish or what race they can win, but rather what they can give themselves to.

Struggles and sufferings come to us all in life. To heed a call does not eliminate or reduce our struggles; in fact, it will likely increase them. Yet if we understand that responding to a call also changes us to become better people, more like the God who calls us, we will be equipped to respond well to these struggles as they come, not simply fighting against them, but seeing them as essentially connected to our callings. In this context, Cardinal Newman helps us when he refers to the "accidents of life," which come as "sudden and unexpected" trials. "A man is going on as usual; he comes home one day and finds a letter, or a message, or a person, whereby a sudden trial comes on him, which, if met religiously, will be the means of advancing him to a higher state of religious excellence." We need not think that God, the master planner, placed this trial, like a landmine, in our path to make us change to another way. To Newman, these are really accidents. Yet as he goes on to say, while it may take years, as we respond to the accident and the shape of our life changes, we can come to see God's coaxing towards a deeper and more perfect life. "We through grace [respond] in a way we never did before; and in the course of years, when we look back on our life, we find that that sad event has brought us into a new state of faith and judgement, and that we are as though other men from what we were."[13]

Such "accidents" in our lives often involve suffering and struggle. But as we have been suggesting in this section, call and struggle go together. Again, this is not just because the work we are called to do in the world is difficult—we know it sometimes will be since, after all, the kingdom that Christ calls us to work for in the world is built upon the cross. But it is also because we ourselves are in need of reconstruction: as we follow God's call we will be changed, and the change is sometimes painful. But as we have also been suggesting, it brings us to a fullness and joy that could not come otherwise, to a transforming of the self to share God's life, and so to all the more fully and effectively join in God's work in the world.

To summarize about the dangers of struggle:

12. Brooks, *Second Mountain*, xii.
13. Newman, "Divine Calls," 347.

A second warning sign along our vocational journey reminds us not to think that all we need is a road map, as if our callings, once we find them, will open to a smooth and easy passage through life. In fact, call will always challenge us, and demand that we struggle and change. Call is reflexive, always also about us and our transformation toward "perfection," since our destination is to join in God's perfect life. Yet we can be assured that while we will sometimes turn away, we will be called again, by Christ who walks with us and will not leave us alone.

Call and Limits

David Cunningham has recently described the word *vocation* as "capacious, dynamic and elastic." Wisely, he has added, "a word can become so capacious and so dynamic and so elastic that it means nothing at all."[14] Taken together, his comments imply that, first, there is room in our talk about vocation for a variety of different perspectives and, second, that we also need to be careful, since we cannot use the term however we like.

Among the things Cunningham identifies as part of the "capaciousness" of call is that it accommodates "a variety of theological perspectives." This seems an important point for Christians to affirm. "Call" has been accented by Christians, and it might appear that they wish to monopolize the language. Yet Christians believe that God calls each one of us as the particular human beings we are, which means a person's call is to a unique relation between God and that person. Further, the call is to a certain kind of work that relates to that person's unique gifts as well as her or his specific time and place, a work that builds the kingdom or reign of God, which is wide and expansive.

Christians don't need to theorize about whether others besides Christians receive God's call. They can see this right in front of them. For instance, the life of Mahatma Gandhi, a devout Hindu, followed the shape of the kingdom of God as Jesus describes it much more clearly than most Christian lives. Christians should tell the story of Gandhi along with other stories of God's call, learning from his wisdom and virtue, noticing especially his resolve to live always according to *ahimsa* (non-violence), which requires "utter selflessness."[15] One reason we are writing this book is that we believe that all of us can learn in our vocational journeys from the stories of how others have lived out their called lives. We have concentrated on

14. Cunningham, "Hearing and Being Heard," 9.
15. Gandhi, *Non-Violent Resistance*, 40–42.

the Christian tradition, for it is ours; but it has no corner on the market of called lives—which means that many other stories are worthy of telling and hearing.

Yet in his discussion of the capaciousness of call David Cunningham makes another comment that might mislead. Speaking about how others outside of the Christian faith might regard call, he says: "If one's vocation is narrowly defined as the human response to the specific call of God, and if *God* is understood in specifically Christian terms, why would a follower of another faith tradition or philosophical perspective be the least bit interested in having a 'vocation'?"[16] This comment makes it appear that "vocation" is something that might be marketed from one tradition to another—and if it is too Christian, who else besides Christians will buy it? Yet as we have noted, vocation is not really something we choose to have; it is a gift we receive. If people share the belief, whether they are Hindus or Christians or Jews or Muslims or none of the above, that each human being in his or her distinct situation can receive the gift of call, that each human being is offered the chance to rise above the narrow, animal concerns of our daily wants and needs to live a more challenging and worthy life, then shouldn't all these people be listening for such a call? If we listen for it and believe we hear it, this should be enough to take a further look into what it might actually means for us to follow it.

If someone is open in this way, we don't really need to worry too much about convincing her that she is called. The much more important matter will involve how one changes one's life in response to the call that comes to them. How will we know the shape of the life we are being called to? Won't we need to inquire about the one whose voice we believe we might be hearing? If we begin to do this, we will be taken to a consideration of some religious tradition.

Religious traditions of all sorts turn our attention to the transcendent as it intersects with mundane human life, directing it towards something higher. As *Nostra Aetate* puts it, all major religious traditions address the "unsolved mysteries of the human condition," including questions arising within the essential human journey regarding "whence do we come, and where are we going."[17] These sorts of questions bring anyone who asks them to consider something like what we have been calling our vocational journey. Call serves as an invitation to consider what we are living for; it starts things. After receiving the invitation, those who are called will need to ask how their vocation fits within a larger communal understanding of what the

16. Cunningham, "Hearing and Being Heard," 11.
17. Flannery, ed., "Declaration."

called life is. Since the call is understood to be of divine origin, the called one will need to know more about who God really is—and for this she will need help. If a person believes the God who calls me is simply "my god" and nobody else's, then there is no check or limit on what he might believe he is "called" to do and be. If call has no limit, it has, in Cunningham's words, become so capacious and elastic as to "mean nothing at all."

The point is this: we need religious traditions to interpret our calls, for they convey to us knowledge and wisdom about the God who is calling. Anyone who believes she is called will need to talk with the people of the tradition she claims. While they can always agree that she is called by God, because they have experience with the God who calls, they can't always affirm what she thinks she heard from God. This is why it does not make sense to make call less Christian (or Jewish or Muslim). Religious traditions set limits on what we can be called to do with our lives; we need these limits or call will mean nothing at all. So, for instance, the Christian tradition will say: "Whatever you thought you heard, the God Christians know did *not* call you to be an abortionist, neither did this God call you to bomb abortion clinics." Or, "*No*, the God we know in Christ does not call people to spend their lives accumulating wealth; if you want to follow this God, that cannot be your calling."

Douglas Schuurman relates the disturbing story of Barend Strydom, a young, white Afrikaner, who in 1989 murdered eight black South Africans in cold blood. At his trial his father testified that he was a devout Christian. Before he went on his killing spree, he "had spent three days and nights alone meditating and praying to ensure that he was doing God's will."[18] Christians will know that Strydom was *not* following God's call for his life. And since he claimed the Christian God, they will also want to ask how he could think he was. What went so terribly wrong? The question will no doubt relate to Strydom's mental health. Yet the key word in his father's description of how he prepared himself is "alone."

Religious communities give space for God's call of particular individuals to a particular life, but they also limit this space. They hold the person who believes he is called accountable. We need these traditions to speak within themselves about their limits, providing reasons that are rooted in genuinely communal theological understanding. As an example, a statement issued almost immediately after the terrorism of September 11, 2001 by Sheikh Yusuf al-Qaradawi, chairman of the Sunna and Sira Council, Qatar, included these words: "Our hearts bleed for the attacks that have targeted the World Trade Center [WTC] . . . Islam, the religion of tolerance,

18. Schuurman, *Vocation*, 77.

holds the human soul in high esteem, and considers the attack against innocent human beings a grave sin . . . 'Who so ever kills a human being [as
punishment] for [crimes] other than manslaughter or [sowing] corruption
in the earth, it shall be as if he has killed all mankind' (Al-Ma'idah:32)."[19]
Sheikh Yusaf does not offer a general condemnation of the terrorists' actions; rather, he shows how Allah, the God the terrorists thought was calling
them to target the WTC, could not have done so.

In the historic Protestant Christian tradition, such limits were set by
placing any "particular calling" a Christian might have under the gover-
nance of the "general calling" to follow Christ. William Perkins, the six-
teenth-century Puritan thinker, puts it this way: "A particular calling must
give place to the general calling of a Christian when they cannot both stand
together . . . because we are bound unto God in the first place and unto man,
under God."[20] Indeed, Perkins believed certain "professions" were excluded
from the repertoire of Christian "vocations"—for instance, usury or running gambling houses. The earliest Christian churches also did this in the
context of the professions of the Roman Empire.[21] That Perkins followed
them in a more modern setting rightly challenges a tendency within some
forms of Christianity to baptize roles (or "stations," as Martin Luther called
them) within a civic order, turning them all into callings.

A critical theological perspective rooted in a particular faith tradition
prevents "calling" from simply merging with the reigning social and political vision, which easily happens if the God who called is "my god" and nobody else's, or simply the god of civil religion—like the god of the American
way. This is important so that Christians (or Muslims, or Jews, etc.) entering
society in some working capacity will ask whether they can identify whatever work or profession they plan to take up as a call. For instance, following
Perkins about usury, can I be called by the Christian God to work within the
financial structures of my time and place?

This critical perspective within religious traditions on the content of
callings allows also for strong affirmation of many patterns of life and work.
It can even help define these patterns. Medicine provides an excellent example. In Western culture the association of medicine with the sacred is partly
due to the fact that the Christian story helped form culture. Jesus is often
described as "the great physician," and "care for the sick" is a corporal work
of mercy in the Christian tradition, but the vision of medicine as a sacred

19. "Sheikh Yusaf."

20. Perkins, *Works*, 457, quoted in Schuurman, *Vocation*, 78.

21. See for instance *Canons of Hippolytus*.

calling[22] also predated Christianity, as is demonstrated in the Hippocratic oath (circa 350 BCE), wherein those entering the profession swore before Apollo, Asclepius, and all the other Greek gods, to "in purity and according to divine law carry out my life and my art."

Accepting the responsibility to work "for the benefit of the sick," as the oath puts it, also means to accept the *limits* of this sacred calling. Such limitations are not simply imposed from outside, but grow up from within. In the original Hippocratic oath these included that physicians should not perform abortions, seduce their patients, or break patient confidentiality. Hippocratic doctors also pledged always to place their patients' interests above their own. These limitations actually create community around the service of an essential human good—here, the benefit of the sick. If medicine is more than just a set of ordered tasks to get some job done on a human body, if it is, rather, a sacred calling to care for the sick, then doctors who enter it are limited in how they can conduct themselves and still meaningfully claim they are following this call.

Many codes of professional conduct, extending beyond medicine, relate to something like this vision and understanding. The term *calling* can easily stretch to include these—like the calling to be a teacher or a civil servant. Such codes limit what one can do and still be legitimately considered as acting with that calling or profession. Unfortunately, "professions" in our time, including the profession of medicine, are susceptible to a kind of heroism of achievement that can also strain at the limits that "calling" implies. The high demands of technical skill within many of our professions today, perhaps especially medicine, require that anyone who wishes to become an excellent practitioner discipline herself, internalizing the knowledge and methods and techniques of her craft. These do equip her, if we continue to use medicine as our example, to "save more lives." But they also can tempt her to push beyond the limits of her calling, imagining she is almost godlike in her knowledge and skill. Here the high calling that a profession like medicine presumes becomes its foil. Participating in God's work without the constant reminder of what the privilege of participation involves, and how it includes the limits of not being God, can easily lead to mistaking ourselves for God.

What remains necessary, always, is a broader understanding of who we are and where we are headed as human creatures of God. On the pattern Perkins laid out, the "general calling" (for Christians, to follow Christ) always guides and limits a "particular calling," such as a call to practice medicine. As well, it reminds us that allegiance to a profession, even one

22. For a short history, see Laurel, "Medicine."

that helps us do the work of God's kingdom, is not our highest allegiance. The meaning of our lives and the long path they take as we follow out our vocational journeys can be enhanced by what we do in our work lives, but they are by no means determined by it.

To summarize about the dangers of no limits for our callings:

> *A third sign along our vocational journey cautions us not to imagine we are the sole arbiters of the individualized callings we think we have received from God. If God's voice becomes merely the echo of our own individual voice, "calling" has lost its meaning. In any religious tradition, and particularly in Christianity, God has a character, and this limits what can count as a call from this God. Such limits can challenge how a given social order thinks about its way of life and its work, although we also can discover congruence, as in particular callings such as medicine that have their own internal moral limits. Even still, those limits are secure only if they remain encased within a larger understanding of what human life is for, and how it is rightly lived out in relation to the God who calls us.*

The Called Life of Dr. Paul Kalanithi

We began this book about the "called life" with high praise: it is the best sort of life human beings can have, we said. But this chapter has been filled with warnings about call, how it will set limits upon us, or entail great struggle, or often involve something quite different from what we might choose. How can these pictures be fit together?

Yet when we look closely at the called lives we most admire, those filled with great beauty, compassion, and grace, we often discover elements that relate to the points we have been discussing. A called life is not always the life we would choose, if we could choose. Nor is a called life an easy life. And a called life will set limits on us, and require us to live within certain strictures, for only as we do this will we be able to locate our lives within the larger spheres of human work and community that provide the full context for their meaning.

The life of Dr. Paul Kalanithi, a brilliant neurosurgeon whose life was cut short by cancer at the young age of thirty-seven, is an example of these points, and illustrates well how a called life can be difficult, unchosen, limited—and also inspiring and beautiful. Paul wrote out the story of his life in the months just before he died. It was subsequently published as

When Breath Becomes Air, reaching number one on the *New York Times* best seller list.

While a number of Paul Kalanithi's Indian-American relatives were medical doctors, he grew up certain he would never become one. As an undergrad at Stanford, Paul studied literature and philosophy, but also nursed an interest in science, even if he did not expect it to lead to any sort of career. During his senior year his neuroscience professor took the class to visit a home for people who suffered from brain injuries. As they walked through the wards Paul's attention became fixed on a young woman, roughly his age, who stared blankly off into space. Paul approached her bed, took her hand and, looking into her eyes, smiled. "She gurgled," Paul reports, "and, looking right at me, smiled." The hopelessness he felt walking through the wards lifted, for a moment—until the attendant and his professor suggested that what Paul thought was a smile was little more than a neurological tic. Was his effort to connect with a fellow human being simply wishful thinking? In philosophy class he had learned how the brain gives rise to capacities that make our lives truly human, including especially the capacity to form relationships. But on this field trip he encountered a stubborn fact about brains: "sometimes they break."[23]

As he neared graduation from Stanford, Paul experienced a call. "Walking home from a football game one afternoon, the autumn breeze blowing, I let my mind wander. Augustine's voice in the garden commanded, 'Take up and read,' but the voice I heard commanded the opposite. 'Set aside the books and practice medicine.'" Paul suddenly saw that medicine was a place where "biology, morality, literature and philosophy intersect."[24] Moreover, the fact that his father, uncle and his elder brother had all become physicians did not need to keep him from a similar path; in fact, it provided a good reason to follow it.

In quoting St. Augustine, Paul places himself among those few who actually hear a call. Yet the voice Paul heard did not come from nowhere; he was long prepared for it by his family history, his interest and talent in science, and by experiences like his encounter with the girl in the neurology ward. A child of relative privilege, studying at one of the most highly touted universities in the United States, Paul was one of the lucky ones whose life could have followed many paths. In this moment after the football game, this one was named for him—although in a sense he also discerned it. From among the various possibilities, this one emerged. As he says in retrospect:

23. Kalanithi, *Breath*, 38.
24. Kalanithi, *Breath*, 41.

"Suddenly it all seemed obvious."[25] Rather than choosing a path, it is more accurate to say that Paul in this moment receives his life; it comes to him as both gift and call.

Paul excelled in the study of medicine at Yale. The science interested him; yet he found that the most important things he learned related to medicine's fundamentally human aspects: the awareness of the sacred presence of a human corpse in the cadaver lab; the joy of a birth for an anxiously awaiting family; the pain of death after surgeons had tried mightily, but failed. He became aware that medicine was not simply a body of knowledge one needed to understand and remember but a practice that required "taking action, with its concomitant responsibility."[26] This action always involved making judgments, many of them involving life or death. "How could I ever learn to make, and live with, such judgment calls . . . ? Surely intelligence wasn't enough; moral clarity was needed as well."[27]

Paul was learning the demands of call, and the necessary involvement of our whole person in answering it. As his class neared graduation, Paul noticed how many of his young colleagues chose what were casually referred to a "lifestyle specialties"—those with "more humane hours, higher salaries and lower pressures."[28] He was also surprised at a movement among his classmates to remove the language in the oath they were to take at graduation which required that they "place our patients' interests above our own." This perspective was "reasonable" in one sense, yet Paul judged it antithetical to medicine. As he notes, "lifestyle" factors are "how 99 percent of people select their jobs: pay, work environment, hours. But that's the point. Putting lifestyle first is how you find a job—not a calling."[29]

As his fellow students at Yale demonstrated, Paul's understanding of medicine is not universally held. It can slip away amid lifestyle considerations or concern exclusively for technical competence. Fortunately, Paul was surrounded by others who remembered the point of medicine. One was Lucy, a fellow student he fell in love with at Yale and subsequently married. Paul describes a scene that occurred one night as Lucy, a medical student at the time, was sitting in his apartment studying "the reams of wavy lines that make up EKGs." Pausing on one, "she puzzled over, then correctly identified a fatal arrhythmia. All at once, it dawned on her and she began to cry:

25. Kalanithi, *Breath*, 41.

26. Kalanithi, *Breath*, 63.

27. Kalanithi, *Breath*, 66.

28. Kalanithi, *Breath*, 68.

29. Kalanithi, *Breath*, 68–69.

wherever this 'practice EKG' had come from, the patient had not survived."[30] For Lucy in this moment, the essential humanity of the profession she was entering, filled up as it increasingly is with all sorts of fancy techniques and machines, became crystal clear.

To retain this humanity, Paul learned that the singular importance of the relationship between doctor and patient is maintained by trust, and trust is developed not principally by technique or expertise, but by words, and the attitudes they reveal. "When there's no place for the scalpel, words are the surgeon's only tool."[31] Neurosurgery seems glamorous because of the miracles we hear it works, but far more often the news is not good, and the surgeon must speak sincerely and truthfully to the dying one and his or her family. Paul tells often of mentors who did this well, conveying support and concern in the midst of great pain and sadness.

Bearing this pain continually, one case after the next, is perhaps the greatest struggle and challenge of a physician's calling. As Paul describes, "the weight of it all became palpable. It was in the air, the stress and the misery. Normally, you breathed it in, without noticing it. But some days, like a humid muggy day, it had a suffocating weight of its own. Some days, this is how it felt when I was in the hospital: trapped in an endless jungle summer, wet with sweat, the rain of tears of the families of the dying pouring down."[32] This sheer weight of responsibility and sorrow keeps many from shouldering it—and who would wish to bear it? A sense of calling is indispensable. Paul had it, remaining aware throughout not only of the good of what he was doing, but also its sacredness. "I don't think I ever spent a minute of any day wondering why I did the work, or whether it was worth it. The call to protect life—and not merely life but another's identity; it is perhaps not too much to say another's soul—was obvious in its sacredness."[33]

This reference to something deeper, something sacred and holy, reminds us that the calling of medicine, indeed, all our callings, derives its force from beyond itself. It is rooted in the mystery of the human being and, as Christians will add, in the mystery of the God who embraces each human life. While raised a Christian, in this period of his life Paul had little to do with church. Nevertheless, as he understood it even then, the physician's role is a pastoral one.[34] At the heart of medicine lies a sacred relationship between one human being and the other.

---

30. Kalanithi, *Breath*, 51.

31. Kalanithi, *Breath*, 87.

32. Kalanithi, *Breath*, 78.

33. Kalanithi, *Breath*, 97–98.

34. Kalanithi, *Breath*, 88.

With other neurosurgeons, Paul was sometimes tempted to another vision of the doctor as heroic savior. "Concomitant with the enormous responsibilities they shouldered, neurosurgeons were also masters of many fields . . . Not only would I have to train my mind and hands, I realized; I'd have to train my eyes, and perhaps other organs as well. The idea was overwhelming and intoxicating: perhaps I, too, could join the ranks of those polymaths who strode into the densest thicket of emotional, scientific, and spiritual problems and found, or carved, ways out."[35] While exciting, in time this idea of medicine will yield the God-Doctor: the mighty one who knows all and can do all, saving us from death. This may seem a high calling, but it so easily topples. Paul discovers, for instance, a resident with whom he was paired who was simply incapable of admitting a mistake, of saying, "I'm sorry." Instinctively, Paul knew this young man could never survive as a neurosurgeon.[36] More poignantly, somewhat later in his residency Paul received a jolting phone call about his good friend Jeff who was just finishing a surgical fellowship in the Midwest. Jeff had a "difficult complication" in surgery and his patient died. As the phone call continued, "Last night he climbed onto the roof of a building and jumped off."[37]

Maintaining this vision of medicine as a sacred trust between doctor and patient is especially difficult when things are going well. Emerging from ten years of rigorous training, Paul heard from his director at Stanford that he was "the number one candidate of any job." At age thirty-six Paul felt he "had reached the mountaintop. I could see the Promised Land."[38] Yet, at the same time he began to feel a tension, a nagging pain in his back. He ignored it at first, but became more aware as he began to lose weight. One day while sitting together in the park, Lucy noticed that Paul had been searching "cancer in thirty-year-olds" on his cell phone. She confronted Paul: why had he not shared his concern with her? Why wasn't he confiding in her?

For Lucy, Paul's reluctance to share was a sign of a growing isolation in their marriage. In pressing to reach the mountaintop of his profession, Paul had forgotten to care fully for his wife. Lucy decided to move out for a week to consider the state of their marriage. Looking back on this time, Paul tells us how he felt: "Fine, I said [to myself]. If she decided to leave, then I would assume the relationship was over. If it turned out that I had cancer, I wouldn't tell her—she'd be free to live whatever life she chose."[39]

35. Kalanithi, *Breath*, 72.
36. Kalanithi, *Breath*, 79.
37. Kalanithi, *Breath*, 114.
38. Kalanithi, *Breath*, 7.
39. Kalanithi, *Breath*, 10.

This response reminds us that Paul and Lucy's story takes place in modern America where "choosing whatever we want" is the go-to good. Earlier Paul had recognized that if medicine is a call, it cannot yield to "lifestyle," the kind of life I want, that is comfortable and flows on smoothly, all according to plan. Nevertheless, here in his marriage, also a calling, Paul returns to the default view: Let us each have the life we choose—and if I can't have mine, let her have hers.

Fortunately, this attitude is short lived. Paul soon discovers for certain that he has cancer and shares this with Lucy. As Paul reports, "She leaned her head on my shoulder, and the distance between us vanished. 'I need you,' I whispered. 'I will never leave you,' she said."[40] In this moment, after contemplating the possible end of their marriage, both are given the grace to see what it really involves as a shared calling. And so a new chapter, indeed, a new series of calls, entirely unexpected, terribly difficult and filled with suffering, but also surprisingly infused with strengthened love and much joy, begins for Paul and Lucy together.

One very difficult thing was for Paul to surrender up the plan he thought his called life would follow. And, without the security of the plan, how was he to go on?

> My carefully planned and hard-won future no longer existed. Death, so familiar to me in my work, was now paying me a visit. Here we were, finally face-to-face, and yet nothing about it seemed recognizable. Standing at the crossroads where I should have been able to see and follow the foot-prints of the countless patients I had treated over the years, I saw only a blank, a harsh, vacant, gleaming white desert, as if a sandstorm had erased all trace of familiarity.[41]

In his hospital bed, he stared often at "a photo of Lucy and me from medical school, dancing and laughing; it was so sad, these two, planning a life together, unaware, never suspecting their own fragility."[42] False hope or melancholy, these seemed at the time the only two possibilities. "What was the alternative story?"[43]

Paul was graced with a skillful and attentive doctor, Emma, who followed carefully through the medical options for addressing his disease. In consultation together they settled on a drug, Tarceva, as the best course of treatment. It paid off, at least initially, and Paul began to regain his strength.

40. Kalanithi, *Breath*, 15–16.

41. Kalanithi, *Breath*, 120–21.

42. Kalanithi, *Breath*, 126.

43. Kalanithi, *Breath*, 127.

Remarkably, with much effort Paul was able to return for a time to practicing neurosurgery. His sense of sacred call pushed him in this direction.
"People often ask if it [neurosurgery] is a calling, and my answer is always
yes. You can't see it as a job, because if it's a job, it's one of the worst jobs there
is . . . [Furthermore] I was making the decision to do this work because this
work, to me, was a sacred thing."[44]

While Paul was briefly able to once again perform the grueling and
technically demanding features of neurosurgery, he also became increasingly aware that the calling of medicine is best described not in terms of
saving patients from death but rather helping them stand up to honestly
face both life and death. Physicians "take into our arms a patient and family
whose lives have disintegrated and work until they can stand back up and
face, and make sense of, their own existence."[45] This is a high calling indeed,
but it is also temporary. Emma had done this for Paul, and now it was time
for him to stand up, and fully consider the meaning of his existence.

In Paul's weakness, Lucy and Paul's marriage strengthened. They
talked openly about their hopes and fears, including the possibility of having a child. Both had wanted children, but in their current state, was this
wise? "Will having a newborn distract from the time we have together?"
Lucy asked. "Don't you think saying goodbye to your child will make your
death *more* painful?" Almost surprising himself, Paul replied, "Wouldn't it
be great if it did?"[46] Together they had discovered that life is not about
avoiding suffering. If we think it is, we will be completely unable to respond
to a call, to begin a new vocational journey. And so Paul and Lucy opened
their lives to a child, to the calling of parenthood.

They also began going to church. As Paul explains, "I returned to the
central values of Christianity—sacrifice, redemption, forgiveness—because
I found them so compelling."[47] What returned faith seems to bring to Paul
is a sense of how his life fit within a larger company of lives, each differently
called, to pursue truth and care for one another and God's world. At worship
one Sunday Paul is struck by a passage from the Gospel of John where Jesus
tells his disciples, "the sower and reaper can rejoice together. For here the
saying is verified that 'One sows and another reaps.' I sent you to reap what
you have not worked for; others have done the work, and you are sharing
the fruits of their work."[48] It suggested to Paul that, while his life's work was

44. Kalanithi, *Breath*, 151.

45. Kalanithi, *Breath*, 166.

46. Kalanithi, *Breath*, 143.

47. Kalanithi, *Breath*, 171.

48. Kalanithi, *Breath*, 173. The passage quoted is John 4:36–37.

and had been important, he was not responsible for the whole business. Others had borne him up; together they shared the fruits. We receive the gift of our lives from God and others. For these gifts, we can together rejoice and be glad.

And then . . . the cancer returned in full force. Paul realized clearly and with finality that he could no longer practice medicine. Emma recommended chemotherapy and it was especially hard on Paul's weakened body. Paul knew that his time was limited. Discussions of a renewed career and a five-year plan dwindled. What took over instead, just then, just at the time of Paul's acceptance of the fact that he was beginning to die, was the arrival of a daughter, born on July 4, 2014. And, no longer a practicing physician, Paul took up his pen. A father and a storyteller, working to leave behind the truths of his life, for his daughter Cady later to know, but also for us all to share. An unexpected calling, but a high one nonetheless.

Lucy remembers Paul's final months as a time for savoring married love. "We each joked to close friends that the secret to saving a relationship is for one person to become terminally ill. Conversely, we knew that one trick to managing terminal illness is to be deeply in love—to be vulnerable, kind, generous, grateful." She recalls with conviction a time earlier, not long after Paul's diagnosis, when they stood together in a church pew, singing "The Servant Song." "I will share your joy and sorrow / Till we've seen this journey through."[49]

In his last weeks, Paul especially relishes the gift of Cady, his newborn daughter, whose father dies before she reached a year. His last words are written to her.

> When you come to one of the many moments in life where you must give an account of yourself, provide a ledger of what you have been, and done, and meant to the world, do not, I pray, discount that you filled a dying man's days with a sated joy, a joy unknown to me in all my prior years, a joy that does not hunger for more and more but rests, satisfied. In this time, right now, that is an enormous thing.[50]

Conclusion

Paul Kalanithi was a person of extraordinary intelligence and talent who dedicated his life to gaining the skill and virtue he needed to minister to

49. Kalanithi, "Epilogue," 216–17.
50. Kalanithi, *Breath*, 199.

those suffering from brain injuries and illnesses. It is immensely sad that so profound a mind and spirit would succumb to death just as he was entering the full flower of his medical career—or, as he would emphatically put it, his *call* to medicine, received as a surprise on his way home from a football game. In his practice of it, he learned that following the call that is medicine is also to recognize the limits it imposes on us.

As we have argued in this chapter, accepting the limits of our callings is necessary if we are to fulfill them well. As a neurosurgeon Paul sometimes worked wonders; yet learning to speak to his patients and their families when there was nothing more medically to be done taught him more about what his calling to medicine really meant. Call can tempt us to heroism; yet none of our callings makes us invulnerable. If we believe we are destined to set all wrongs right, we will fail—and become dangerous as we do. Professions like medicine can teach us about these limits, and religious communities also remind us that we are not God and that call does not come to us alone but to many who go with us and before us. Only in awareness of our dependency can we, like the sower and the reaper, rejoice together when the work is done.

Our limits are also placed clearly before us by our mortality. As embodied creatures we are subject not only to death but also suffering; pain or grief or disappointment can quickly turn our lives into stories of struggle. Yet as we have argued, struggle is part of call. As Paul Kalanithi knew, to accept a call is not to make a lifestyle choice; the called life is not an easy life. As his story also illustrates, what Newman called the "accidents of life," its sudden and unexpected trials, can place us on a new path, bring a new calling, that changes and transforms us so that, by grace, we become better people. While we do choose to receive our callings, the called life never takes the shape we might initially desire—a good thing, since we need to be changed and transformed in our lives. God's call does for us what we could not do for ourselves.

As we have suggested throughout this chapter, choice, the avoidance of suffering and struggle, and of limits, are highly touted in our present culture. To live the called life well, we need to be aware of these messages, and be open to a different way of thinking and being.

PART III

Virtues for the Journey

CHAPTER 7

Virtues for Beginning the Journey—
Attentiveness, Humility,
and Gratitude

OUR CALLINGS ARE GIFTS because they put us in touch with the unique way that God loves us and beckons us to life. They are gifts because they enable us to live with integrity and authenticity, and to transcend ourselves in love and goodness to others. But they can also be threats because the callings of our lives demand a lot of us, sometimes more than we think we can possibly give. They can be energizing, and true pathways in hope; but they can also be burdensome, exhausting, confusing, and sometimes even frightening, leaving us more unsettled than comforted and reassured. As anyone who has embraced a vocation knows, there are seasons to living our callings. Sometimes it is spring where life abounds and everything looks fresh and promising. Other times we find ourselves deep in the bleak landscape of winter, where there is more darkness than light and signs of life are scarce.

Many people begin a vocational journey with enthusiasm, confidence, and joy. The journey might be beginning college, entering into a friendship, committing to marriage or community life, or taking up a profession that seems exactly right. But these initial blessings are sometimes later over-shadowed by doubt and disillusionment, by setbacks and difficulties, and perhaps even intense suffering and disappointment—or simply the malaise and boredom that can creep into the relationships and routines of our lives. In such times we experience our callings as burdens rather than blessings. We question the choices we made and mourn the choices we didn't. We feel trapped in the things that once brought us life and look for ways to escape them, so much so that we find ourselves resenting the persons, communities, projects, and professions we once loved. Unless we deal with these challenges and find ways to work through them, we will grow increasingly disenchanted with our callings, and eventually walk away from a gift.

This is why we need the virtues. Virtues are characteristic ways of being and acting that make both *who we are* and *what we do* good.[1] They are the enduring qualities of character—attitudes, affections, dispositions, beliefs, and habits—that help us grow and develop in all the right ways for a human being and help us deal successfully with all that life might throw at us. This is why we can think of them as liberating ways of being and acting. Virtues such as justice, courage, prudence, generosity, patience, and forgiveness don't repress us but form us into exactly the kind of people we need to become in order to do well in life. Indeed, the virtues make our lives as a whole promising and good, and thus lead to genuine flourishing for others as well as ourselves. Put simply, the virtues enable us to live wisely and well in all the various circumstances and shifting situations of life.

It is no surprise then that living and growing in our callings is impossible without the virtues. A vocation is a living thing, and like any living thing it cannot be taken for granted but has to be cared for and nurtured. The virtues help us do this. Virtues such as fidelity and courage help us remain engaged with and committed to the most important projects and goals of our lives, such as growing in a sometimes difficult friendship or not giving up during a particularly trying semester. Virtues such as hope and patience are absolutely essential if we are not to be overwhelmed, or even defeated, by the unavoidable challenges and hardships that can imperil any vocational journey.

The virtues help us live according to what is real. And the reality is that human life and human relationships—and therefore human callings—all require work, not the least because we ourselves require work. We need to be willing to grow and to change. We need to be honest about our shortcomings and weaknesses, but also about the bad habits we may possess that will undermine our ability to succeed in our callings if we are not willing to address those bad habits and do what we can to overcome them. This is why, for example, the most successful marriages are not ones that have escaped hardships and challenges (for no such marriage exists), but ones in which the spouses, rather than surrendering to those hardships and challenges, developed the virtues that enabled them to work through them and overcome them. With the virtues we do more than simply endure the commitments that define and guide our lives; rather, we find ways to continually grow

---

1. Much of this brief overview of the virtues is taken from Wadell, *Happiness*, 90–94.

and flourish in them—and even know joy in them—amid the struggle and uncertainty that inevitably mark any vocational journey.

We cannot embrace, remain committed to, and flourish in our callings without many virtues. In this chapter, we consider three that are related— and especially important ones with which to begin the journey of living vocationally. These are attention, humility, and gratitude. Let us call these the "situating virtues" because they root us in a time and place, and remind us of who we really are. In this way, they help us settle into our callings, and help us to hear them and know them, which also means knowing ourselves in relation to others and to God. We need to be equipped with these virtues as we begin the journey that comes with our callings. But we not only want to begin the journey, we want to be able to continue it no matter what we might encounter as we make our way, and so we need virtues that steady and protect us, virtues that enable us to deal wisely and well with whatever awaits us. That is what fidelity, justice, and courage do. We will consider these three virtues in the next chapter. And because we want to complete the journey that begins with our callings, we need virtues such as hope and patience, which we will examine in the final chapter.

Attention

A most basic calling is to *pay attention*, to open our eyes and our hearts to what God, other people, our communities, the world, or life itself might be asking of us each day. In this respect, the virtue of attentiveness is akin to the virtue of prudence because both teach us to *see* and to *act* according to what is real. Apart from an accurate perception of reality, we cannot possibly know how we are called every day of our lives. To pay attention is to see what truly matters.[2] It is to be attuned not to some imaginary world but to the world in which we find ourselves. Instead of the thoughtlessness or indifference by which we turn in on ourselves and become carelessly disengaged with life, the virtue of attention forms us into persons who are fully present to life. Calling on the insights of Simone Weil, Steven Garber notes: "All day, every day, there are both wounds and wonders at the very heart of life, if we have eyes to see. And seeing—what Weil called learning to know, to pay attention—is where vocations begin."[3]

This is why we have suggested that to restrict calling or vocation to a profession or career, or to a particular state of life such as marriage, is to think of it much too narrowly. If I think living vocationally can only happen

2. Garber, *Visions of Vocation*, 26.
3. Garber, *Visions of Vocation*, 35.

when I've settled into a career or made a lifelong commitment such as marriage, I am woefully oblivious to how life calls to me and makes demands on me every day. If I am a student, the virtue of attention summons me not only to show up for class, but also to be actively engaged with it and to approach it with the openness and intellectual humility without which education is a waste of time and money. It requires me not to sleepwalk through life, dazed to all that is around me, but to be conscious of the time and place in which I find myself now, and especially conscious of the people who make up my life each day, particularly those around me who are most frequently overlooked and neglected. As this example illustrates, the virtue of attentiveness helps us settle into our callings whatever they may be and wherever we may be at any stage of our lives.

With the virtue of attention, we let the world speak to us and draw us out of ourselves for the sake of others, rather than bend the world to our own interests and often conflicting needs. Attention enables the self-transcendence that is necessary if we are to live for something more than our own cravings and cluttered desires. It pries us free from a self-centered view of existence so that we can awaken morally and spiritually in order to love the people who comprise our lives, even the strangers we may never see again, rather than apprising them only in terms of what they can do for us. "The purpose and end of attention," A. J. Conyers writes, "is a transformation in which reality awakens within us, pushing aside the unreal and selfish dreams which had kept us subdued in unwakefulness."[4]

Like any virtue, attention changes us for the good. Instead of being mired in a life that extends no further than ourselves, attention draws us out of ourselves and thus more fully into life. Our lives become more challenging and complex, likely messier and sometimes more uncertain, but also infinitely more interesting and hopeful. A life characterized by attentiveness is a life without regrets because attentive people, rather than being nostalgic about a past that will never return or captive to a future that may never arrive, are alert to the surprising graces that are right in front of them. Those surprising graces happen all the time. It may be seeing something special in someone we had previously barely noticed or perhaps even disliked. It may be seizing opportunities for kindness that were always right in front of us but that before we never were able to see. It may be recognizing the promise and beauty and goodness in the ordinary circumstances of our lives. Or it may be the life-saving grace of recognizing how sad it is to pass up any opportunity to love. The moral and spiritual awakening elicited by the virtue of attentiveness explains why it can fittingly be described as prayer. As Barbara

4. Conyers, *Listening Heart*, 121.

Brown Taylor observes, "Prayer, according to Brother David, is waking up to the presence of God no matter where I am or what I am doing. When I am fully alert to whatever or whoever is right in front of me; when I am electrically aware of the tremendous gift of being alive; when I am able to give myself wholly to the moment I am in, then I am in prayer."[5]

Why Paying Attention Matters

Vocation means "to be called," but unless we cultivate the habit of attentiveness, we have no idea who or what might be calling us. This is why attentiveness is an essential virtue as we begin our vocational journeys. When we earlier examined different ways to think about vocation and different ways we might be called, we noted that some have maintained that a fundamental and inescapable calling of every human being is to be responsible. A responsible human being is someone who responds reliably and fittingly to the different dimensions of ordinary life, particularly other persons. Such a person realizes that to be human is to be obliged and accountable, and knows that these obligations are entailed "not just by one's career or job, but also by one's very existence as a person—who is necessarily in relation with other persons and with the world."[6]

This is why responsibility is woven through every calling of our lives, including not only the most momentous and long-lasting callings, but also the most immediate and temporary ones. At the basis of every calling, whether a friendship, a career, or being patient with a stranger, is a summons to responsibility; however, we cannot be responsible without an accurate perception of reality, and we cannot accurately perceive reality without growing in attentiveness. Moreover, we cannot answer that summons to responsibility, much less hear it, without the virtue of attentiveness. Attentiveness enables the "deep listening" by which we open ourselves to others and gain a better sense of the world as it really is and, therefore, a better sense of to whom and how we are responsible.[7] And it enables us to be a force for good in the world because deep listening forms us into persons who can "listen to the voices we too often fail to hear, to see the truths and ask the questions we might otherwise neglect."[8]

The habit of attention also matters because, as we have noted, we never finish discerning what our callings mean and what they ask of us. Because

5. Taylor, *Altar*, 178.

6. Mohrmann, "Vocation Is Responsibility," 23.

7. Ray, "Self, World," 313.

8. Ray, "Self, World," 313.

the contours of our callings change, we must continually fathom what it means to grow in them and be faithful to them. Consider the fundamental calling to love. If the love we have for parents, siblings, spouses, partners, or friends is effective, we must regularly think about what it means to love them well as they grow, change, and move through the shifting circumstances of their lives; in other words, we must pay attention. Similarly, though the vocation of teachers might not change, their students do; consequently, even if they often teach the same courses, to be faithful to their calling they must be steadfastly attuned to the unique gifts, struggles, needs, and challenges of those they teach. Teaching must never become so mechanical and routine that they neglect the attentiveness that real love requires. People formed in the virtue of attention know that they must regularly consider, "What is being asked of me now? What do I need to see and hear today?"

Why Paying Attention Is Difficult

And yet, some of the reasons why attention is indispensable for faithfully engaging our callings are also why it can be a very difficult virtue to acquire. Instead of cultivating the virtue of attention, we often find ourselves growing in inattentiveness, a vice that will make it impossible to settle into our callings because we will be habitually oblivious of *when* and *where* we truly are. Today this inattentiveness is fed by a cascade of distractions. It is not just that our lives are increasingly full of distractions but also, more seriously, that we have become comfortable succumbing to them; in fact, most of us find it far easier to be distracted than attentive. We are used to being distracted, it is our normal way of being, so much so that it is hard for us to imagine any other way of living. Consequently, our lives can be endlessly cluttered with so much noise and so much busyness that we do not hear what we need to hear and miss what we need to see. This is why Conyers not only says, "To be modern is to exist increasingly in a state of distraction," but also, "To be modern is not only to find ourselves thus distracted, but to justify that life of distraction."[9] If that is the case, we cannot live vocationally because we will never be truly situated in our callings. We'll live everywhere but where we are.

Technology, obviously, has been quite effective in both nurturing and encouraging distraction; indeed, the very companies that never tire of coming up with new products that they promise will keep us "connected" are arguably intent on destroying the attentiveness that true friendship and intimacy require. Their desire is not for us to occasionally put down our

9. Conyers, *Listening Heart*, 55.

phones or stop sending or searching for messages, but for us to become so addicted to those activities that we gradually (and quite obediently) train ourselves *not to hear* and *not to see*. Having become experts at inattentiveness, we never allow ourselves the silence and solitude necessary to hear any call at all, perhaps especially the call of our own famished spirits. As Darby Ray observes, "Like a hungry hummingbird, screen-focused minds are often frenetically mobile, always on the lookout for the next tweet, text, status update, or image. Flitting almost involuntarily from message to message, post to post, or image to image, the mind eventually loses its ability to dwell contentedly in one place for any length of time. Unless counteracted by disciplines of attentiveness, this habit portends a life of distraction and superficiality."[10]

There is a scene in Walker Percy's novel *Love in the Ruins* that captures how the voices we truly need to hear—God, family, friends, acquaintances and strangers, those who are suffering, other creatures—are drowned out by the noisy distractions that intrude on our lives. It is Sunday morning at St. Michael's parish and Fr. Rinaldo Smith steps into the pulpit to give his sermon. But instead of saying anything, he remains absolutely silent for thirty seconds. As Percy comments, "Thirty seconds is a very long silence. Nothing is more uncomfortable than silence when speech is expected." The parishioners, wondering what has happened to their pastor, "began to cough and shift around in the pews." The tension is finally broken when Fr. Smith taps on the microphone and announces, "'Excuse me, . . . but the channels are jammed and the word is not getting through.'"[11] The congregation is momentarily relieved because they conclude there must be a problem not with their priest but with the sound system—and probably because there would be no sermon that Sunday. But their relief vanishes when their enigmatic pastor exits the sanctuary and returns to the rectory without finishing the mass.

The scene from *Love in the Ruins* is a metaphor for our lives. Sometimes the "channels" of our lives can be so jammed that nothing worth hearing, nothing that truly matters, gets through to us. We become "hard of hearing," "deaf" to what we need to hear. Or, if we're honest, we might admit that we jam the channels of our lives deliberately because we don't want to hear what we know we need to hear. Our "hearing" becomes strategically selective because we fear what might be asked of us or where true listening might lead us. This often happens when trying to discern our callings. We

10. Ray, "Self, World," 312.
11. Percy, *Love in the Ruins*, 175.

say we want to know how we might be called, but continually find ways to distract ourselves from what is calling us.

A second reason it can be difficult to cultivate the virtue of attention is that we live in a culture that makes an idol out of busyness. Even if we don't have much to do, we at least want to appear to be busy because we have been taught to measure our worth by how exhaustingly full our lives are. Our complaining about how busy we are is often a clever way of boasting about our packed schedules. We do this because our society, which puts so much emphasis on activity and productiveness, preaches that a successful life is a relentlessly busy one. And so we believe there is something wrong with us—some embarrassing deficit to our lives—if we are not continually busy. "If you are very busy, then you must be fine. If you have more to do than you can do, and the list never gets done but only longer, then you must be very fine," Taylor writes, "because . . . successful people are very busy people. . . . For millions and millions of people, busyness is The Way of Life."[12]

But busyness as a way of life impairs our ability to live, to grow in, and to be responsive to our callings because it undermines the attentiveness necessary to be attuned to them. If we are perpetually busy, how can we ever be aware of the world around us and the people who make up that world? If we are perpetually busy, how can we really settle into our callings? We need to find ways to counter the distractions and busyness, and instead cultivate the virtue of attention. There are many things we can do, but three seem essential.

Cultivating the Virtue of Attention

To grow in the virtue of attention we need, first, regular times for silence and solitude. This won't be easy since in our distracted, frenetic lives silence and solitude at first will seem strange, even unnatural. Quiet time by ourselves may make us feel anxious and uncomfortable. But if we commit to practicing silence and solitude, we will eventually experience them as healing and renewing. We will realize how out of balance our lives have been. We may discover that in being so busy and distracted that we lost touch with ourselves, especially with what our hearts most need. We may see that the kind of life our society tells us to pursue is actually physically, psychologically, emotionally, morally, and spiritually damaging. During these times of silence we may pray, opening our hearts to listen to God. We may meditate. We may sit quietly to recollect ourselves. No matter what we do, we might be startled to realize how unaware we had become, and how out of touch we

---

12. Taylor, *Altar*, 123. See also Smith, *Courage & Calling*, 19.

were with callings that come from both within us and outside us, perhaps especially the call to love, care for, and be present to those closest to us. As Renee LaReau shares, "Silence unclutters our minds, allowing us to pay attention to new details, freeing up mental space for new insights and reflections. Silence makes our souls beautiful over time."[13] Silence and solitude must become a regular practice in living vocationally.

Second, in a busy and distracted culture, growing in the virtue of attention requires setting aside time for relaxation and leisure, which also must become a regular practice as we live our callings. We need time to slow down and rest. We need time to be renewed and refreshed. Instead of being crushed by the tyranny of busyness, we need time to celebrate, time for conversations so rich and captivating that we lose ourselves in them. We need time to love, enjoy, and cherish the people we've been given, especially our families, friends, and community members. By committing to regular practices of rest and leisure, we are gradually pried free from the wearying effects of distraction and busyness and thus see, as if for the first time, the world that has been there all along.

Jews and Christians spoke of this as "keeping the Sabbath holy." Interestingly, God didn't *suggest* that the Sabbath be kept holy, God *commanded* it. Like all of God's commandments, it's for our own good. Like God who rested on the Sabbath, when we "keep the Sabbath holy" we learn that our work, no matter how important and meaningful it might be, should not overly define our lives. A life comprised solely of work and busyness is not a good life, is not a truly human way to live. Keeping the Sabbath holy reminds us of who we really are and what truly matters. By keeping the Sabbath holy, Jews and Christians learned that they had worth and value and dignity not because of how much they produced or earned or achieved; rather, they had worth and value and dignity because they were loved and cherished by God. This was liberating. Keeping the Sabbath holy brought a wholly different perspective to life. If we commit to keeping the Sabbath holy we will learn, as Taylor writes, "that you are worth more than what you can produce—that even if you spent one whole day being good for nothing you would still be precious in God's sight . . ."[14]

Knowing that frees us to live differently. It certainly frees us from seeing ourselves as nothing more than producers and consumers. If we remember that our ultimate identity comes not from *what we do* but from *who we are*, children of God who are loved by God and who come to life in loving God and all that God loves, then we are free to set aside time when we can step

---

13. LaReau, *Getting A Life*, 148.

14. Taylor, *Altar*, 139.

back from our ordinary routines to listen for what will truly bring us life. Without time for rest and leisure—without practicing the Sabbath—we lose touch with what really matters, and thus also lose touch with ourselves.[15]

Third, we can grow in the virtue of attention through community or civic engagement. This may seem at odds with the practices of silence and solitude, rest and leisure. Yet sometimes the only way we can hear the calls we need to hear is by stepping outside of our usual world.[16] A danger of living an overly distracted and busy life is that my world becomes too small, too untroubled and secure. And it is a world in which I am too often in control. I hear what I want to hear and see what I want to see, what satisfies and reassures me; but not what might draw me out of my self and more deeply into relationship with others, particularly those whose lives might be very different from my own. I allow the distractions and activities of my life to let me escape the world—to live selfishly rather than justly and compassionately. I insulate myself from the cries of the poor and the sorrows of the suffering; from all the people who are regularly shut out of the very things I take for granted. Community engagement cracks open my world by putting me in contact with people whose lives, precisely in their differences, can save me from myself; so it too should be a regular part of our vocational journey.

If we were asked what virtues we would need to settle into and embrace our callings, attention would not come first to mind. But, as happens when we lack any virtue, the absence of this virtue in our lives will cost us. People who develop the virtue of attention discover that being attuned and responsive to their everyday lives—living fully in the present—keeps all their different callings fresh. We don't get tired of our friends, but see them kindly and compassionately. We don't allow the routines of our lives to lead to the malaise that takes the joy out of any calling; rather, we look for ways to renew our callings by attending to how we might respond to them in more hopeful and creative ways. And, perhaps most reassuringly, if we let ourselves be awakened to all the ordinary goodness and beauty that surround us even when life is hard, we may see glimmers of light where we thought there was nothing but darkness.

Humility

When was the last time you thought about the virtue of humility? Have you recently heard anybody say, "I want to become humbler?" Humility rarely makes anyone's list of the most important virtues. We hear a lot about love

15. Smith, *Courage & Calling*, 93.

16. Ray, "Self, World," 312–13.

and justice, mercy and compassion, honesty and loyalty, or courage and perseverance, but hardly a whisper about humility. As the philosopher Robert
Roberts concedes, the "virtue of humility has fallen on hard times."[17]

Perhaps we don't appreciate humility because we think that if we grow
in this virtue we will never get ahead. We may feel that in the kind of world
we have today, humble people will be stepped on, shoved aside, and permanently left behind. That's understandable. We live in a society that celebrates
competitiveness, that encourages self-assertion and an exaggerated sense of
one's importance. We typically affirm self-esteem, not humility, as an essential character trait. In a world that often suggests that we must all look after
ourselves because nobody else will, to seek to be humble seems not only
foolish, but also downright dangerous. As LaReau notes, "Humility does not
fit neatly into a culture that values being in charge and controlling your own
destiny, your own self-improvement."[18]

And yet, perhaps we are squeamish about humility because we too
easily confuse real humility with its counterfeit versions. Humility is not
insufficient self-regard or an unhealthy lack of confidence. And it certainly
has nothing to do with denying one's dignity, worth, and sacredness as a
human being. Humble people do not tiptoe through life with a chronically
low opinion of themselves. Neither does genuine humility have anything to
do with self-loathing and diminishment, much less a lack of self-respect.
Those qualities are vices, not virtues, because they reflect a lack of appreciation for our preciousness as persons who are imbued with, and called to
bring to life, some unique expression of the love, goodness, and beauty of
God. Moreover, a humble person is not someone who tiresomely denies his
gifts; rather, to be truly humble is to know our gifts, to be grateful for them,
and to use them generously on behalf of others. After all, how can we live
our callings, much less be useful to anyone, if we never affirm how we have
been blessed? Similarly, humility does not require that we deny our achievements. As LaReau says, "There is nothing wrong with celebrating and being
excited about the things we do well. That kind of pride, good pride, does not
preclude humility."[19]

In fact, a person who has little regard for herself, who continually sees
herself as inferior to others, and who doesn't speak up when she is manipulated or mistreated, is actually not humble at all. Humility is not humili-
ation. Jesus was humble, but he was also utterly confident in who he was
and in the vocation given him by God. Jesus was humble, but he knew his

17. Roberts, *Spiritual Emotions*, 78.

18. LaReau, *Getting a Life*, 66.

19. LaReau, *Getting a Life*, 66.

gifts and he embraced his calling. Jesus was humble, but he was also bold and fearless in speaking out against what he knew was wrong. Jesus was humble, but nobody pushed him around. To let ourselves be manipulated, mistreated, bullied or pushed around is never virtuous, but a tragic inability to love and care for ourselves.

What Humility Is and Why It Matters

Humility is clarity of vision about our self and our place in the world. It is a realistic understanding of who we are and can be. It is unflinching honesty about our gifts and our potential, as well as our limitations, and thus about the unique ways we are called to do good. Humility is an essential virtue for settling into and beginning to live our callings because without it we never see clearly who we are—we never really *know* or *accept* ourselves—and thus fail to appreciate what we have to offer. If we think of humility in this way, we can see how it protects, serves, and is connected to the virtue of attentiveness. Humility bestows on us the moral and spiritual vision that enables us to live attentively because it protects us from immersing ourselves in self-absorbed and self-promoting fantasies that would prevent us from accurately perceiving reality, especially about ourselves.

Lacking humility, we can spend much of our lives trying to be someone we aren't, chasing after "calls" never meant for us. With humility, we don't hide behind masks, we don't pretend that we are somebody we are not, and we don't let ourselves be manipulated by the wishes, expectations, and desires of others. This is because we know who we are and are secure in God's love for us. The security humility gives us guards us from living falsely and from succumbing to inflated and distorted understandings of ourselves. In this way, humility and genuine self-confidence, rather than being at odds, are intimately connected; in fact, Timothy Radcliffe notes, the theologian Jean-Louis Bruges "wrote that humility is the Christian name for self-esteem. 'Thanks to humility I rest in myself,' content to be who I am."[20]

The word humility is derived from the Latin *humus*, which means "ground" or "soil" or "of the earth." A humble person is a well-grounded person, a person who is rooted and centered in a secure and insightful assessment of who he or she is. Consequently, not only can they appreciate their own gifts and callings, but they can also appreciate the gifts and callings of others. With humility, instead of envying the gifts and callings that may not be our own, we are grateful for them and realize we can be blessed and enriched by them. Instead of comparing our callings to someone else's, with

20. Radcliffe, *What is the Point?*, 133.

humility we recognize that every calling has value and makes an important contribution. With humility, instead of being threatened by how God works in other people's lives, we celebrate and give thanks for this, acknowledging that life is better when all of us faithfully and creatively live out our callings and support one another in doing so. With this perspective, we can be friends and companions rather than rivals or enemies on our vocational journeys. As Gordon Smith summarizes, "Humility is the acceptance of who we are—the grace to embrace our own identity and calling rather than to live by pretense. And this, of course, means that we refuse to envy others. Humility frees us to celebrate the gifts and abilities of others rather than to feel diminished by them."[21]

With humility we resist the temptation to think of ourselves as more important than we really are, and thus are willing to admit our imperfections and limits, as well as our need for others, both of which are essential for living vocationally, but perhaps especially as we begin to live our callings.[22] Without humility, we think too highly of ourselves but not highly enough of others; thus, our estimation of ourselves as well as our estimation of others is distorted. Pride, the vice that directly opposes humility, distorts our view of ourselves because it prevents us from acknowledging who we really are: gifted but also limited, blessed but also incomplete, capable but also dependent on others. Lacking humility, I will stubbornly refuse to acknowledge that I don't know everything and therefore need to learn from others who may well know more than I do. Lacking humility, I'll never admit that I cannot succeed in any of my callings unless I am open to being helped by others. Lacking humility, I won't be able to cooperate with others, which is something any calling requires. And I'll likely never admit that I am wrong, which I must be willing to do if I am to grow in my callings. As LaReau writes, "The presence or absence of humility within our persona has major ramifications for how we deal with others. If we expect ourselves to be perfect, or think of ourselves as perfect, we will have that same unreasonable expectation of others. If we are overly impatient with our own shortcomings, then we will have very little patience for the shortcomings of others. We owe it to others to be humble just as much as we owe it to ourselves."[23]

21. Smith, *Courage & Calling*, 119.
22. Pinches, "Stories of Call," 129.
23. LaReau, *Getting a Life*, 67.

Why It Pays to be Humble

Several things can be gleaned from this analysis of humility, but four seem most important for situating us in our callings. First, humble people have richer lives because they are not afraid to let other people into them. Humility provides the openness and vulnerability we need to love and to be loved, to bless and to be blessed, to help and to be helped. Second, humility gives us the freedom to fail, which is a wonderful freedom to have because somewhere along our vocational journeys we will fail. Just because a particular calling may be absolutely right for us doesn't mean we will always succeed at it. Even the most gifted athletes can play poorly, just as on some days even the best teachers fall woefully short. Similarly, parents soon discover how easy it is, despite their best intentions, to make mistakes with their children just as students who may be very good in their majors inevitably learn that doesn't mean they'll do well on every exam. Humility teaches us how to deal with failures wisely and well. Humble people don't let momentary failures lessen their zeal for their callings; rather, they learn from them. Too, humility lessens the sting of failure because humble people are able to laugh at themselves; indeed, humor helps them move beyond failure more quickly. Third, humility gives us a healthy and absolutely necessary sense of limits. We cannot respond to every calling. We'll never be able to answer every need. We do the best we can wherever we are, recognizing we will always leave many good things undone. In this respect, humility keeps us from spreading ourselves too thin or burning out from saying "yes" when we should have said "no."

Finally, people formed in the virtue of humility know that no matter how long they have lived their callings, there is always room for growth, deepening, and transformation, a truth that is important to acknowledge as we begin to live our callings. We never "master" our callings or achieve such expertise in them that there is nothing more for us to learn. "Humility means we never 'arrive.' Humility means we are always 'arriving,'" LaReau explains. "To be humble is to acknowledge that one spends a lifetime in the discovery of a vocation. To be humble is to recognize that we can always, always change for the better. We can always improve who we are. We can always be more true to the person that God is calling us to be."[24] This is precisely why humility keeps our callings fresh and appealing, and guards against them becoming stale or uninteresting.

---

24. LaReau, *Getting a Life*, 66.

Gratitude

If we were to gather together everybody who has ever accepted a calling, and asked each person to share what they had most learned in living their vocations, it wouldn't be surprising if all of them at some point said, "It's been much harder than I ever imagined!" Even if they were grateful for their callings—the small as well as the big ones—and declared that they didn't regret any calling that came their way, would we expect them to say that living their callings had been easy? Each of our callings, from the briefest and most easily accomplished to the ones that stretch most of our lives, requires deep and abiding generosity. That's because every calling involves the ongoing expending of ourselves for the sake of something good and because every calling draws us out of ourselves and more deeply into relationship with others, even if only momentarily.

Callings live on generosity, and it's hard to be generous, hard to give of ourselves in friendships and families and communities, in service to others, or in kindness and thoughtfulness, every day. But it is much easier to be generous when we are grateful, much easier to find the generosity all of our callings require when we are persons of grateful spirit, persons who every day find reasons to give thanks. This is why gratitude is another virtue that helps us settle into our callings as we begin the journey of living vocationally. Put more strongly, gratitude is an essential virtue in living vocationally because we won't get far on the journey without it.

Gratitude has always been recognized as a core characteristic of the Christian life. In Ephesians 5:20, the members of that early Christian community are exhorted to give "thanks to God the Father at all times and for everything in the name of our Lord Jesus Christ." They were not to give thanks occasionally or sporadically or selectively, but every day. They were instructed to see goodness and giftedness everywhere, not because they closed their eyes to the sufferings and hardships of life, but because they were seized with gratitude for God's goodness toward them, for God's endless blessings and unbreakable love. In fact, the New Testament suggests that gratitude should be the most natural virtue of all for Christians—their lives should pulse with it—because Christians know everything they have is a gift. They know they live from the never-ending love, goodness, and generosity of God. They know that in Christ they have found a hope they could never have given themselves and a mercy that will never be denied them. They know that gifts surround them every day: the gift of God's good creation, the gift of the beauty of nature, the gifts that come their way in every person. No wonder that the great twentieth-century Reformed theologian, Karl Barth, said that gratitude is not only the very center of the Christian life, but a Christian's true identity. Christianity, Barth suggested, is a life of continually saying thanks; it is to make one's life a great song of thanksgiving.[25]

But gratitude is not just for Christians, it's for everybody. Gratitude helps us resist the deep inclination to put ourselves first, to secure our interests, needs, and well-being over the interests, needs, and well-being of others, dispositions that will sabotage any calling. Gratitude fights the temptation to pull back, to become calculating, or to harden ourselves to the needs of others. Moreover, gratitude fortifies us against resentment, complaining, cynicism, and negativity, each of which is toxic for the relationships and healthy communities that help sustain us in our vocations. "These forms of ingratitude are deadly: they kill community by chipping away at it until participants long to be just about anywhere else," Christine Pohl writes. "While gratitude gives life to communities, ingratitude that has become established sucks out everything good, until life itself shrivels and discouragement and discontent take over."[26]

Where there is gratitude, there is life. Gratitude opens our eyes to see the beauty and goodness of life. The virtue of gratitude teaches us to look for what is there instead of what is missing, which is why gratitude, like humility, is connected to the virtue of attentiveness and strengthens us in that virtue. Gratitude serves attentiveness because it is easier to attend to the world around us and to be fully present to life when we are grateful. So much of our perspective on life depends on what we notice or fail to notice. Grateful people notice; they attend. And so they see what others overlook. This doesn't mean they are oblivious to the sufferings of life or to the bleak periods that occasionally visit all of us; in fact, grateful people are typically more aware and responsive to the misfortunes around them than people who seldom give thanks for anything. People formed in the virtue of gratitude recognize that life, even when it is hard and even when it seems blatantly unfair, is still filled with gifts. Grateful people know that life doesn't always give us what we want, but it does often give us unexpected goods and pleasures, as well as blessings we never knew would come our way. As Pohl summarizes, "When our lives are shaped by gratitude, we're more likely to notice the goodness and beauty in everyday things. We are content; we feel blessed and are eager to confer blessings. We are able to delight in the very existence of another human being."[27]

In many respects today, gratitude, like humility, is decidedly counter-cultural. In a society that encourages "a well-developed sense of entitlement,"

25. Pohl, *Living into Community*, 17.

26. Pohl, *Living into Community*, 18.

27. Pohl, *Living into Community*, 22.

a society that convinces us that we deserve everything that we have, and that teaches us to say "mine" much more than "ours," gratitude can quickly become a forgotten part of our vocabulary.[28] This is especially true in a culture of consumerism that tells us we should always be dissatisfied and discontented with where we are and what we have. But if I'm always grabbing for more, will I ever be grateful for anything? Will I ever realize how much my life rests on the generosity and goodness of others? And if I am forever dissatisfied and discontented, how can I truly settle into any calling? How can I take the first step on the vocational journey if I'm griping before I've even begun? Gratitude roots us in our callings because it protects us from the envy and resentment that make us think everybody has it so much better than we do.

Without gratitude, we complain rather than say thanks and feel cheated much more than blessed. But what does this do to our spirits and how does it impact our lives together? There is nothing worse—nothing more dispiriting—than being around people who constantly complain, who always feel slighted, and who are chronically bitter about something they think they deserved. Try having a party with them! (Although, if we're honest, there probably have been times when people were complaining and we readily joined them. And we likely have been to parties where people came together to complain!) Moreover, gratitude fades quickly in a culture that touts independence and individual achievement, teaching us that whatever success we've garnered we owe it all to ourselves. In such a culture, Pohl writes, gratitude is "an uncomfortable reminder that we need other people and that our lives are dependent on their gifts and generosity."[29]

Growing in Gratitude

In order to settle in, remain committed to, and ultimately flourish in our callings, we need to be habituated in gratitude. How can we grow in this virtue? What can we do to acquire it? For Christians, the Eucharist (in some denominations, the Lord's Supper or communion) is the center of a grateful life and the primary context for growing in gratitude. In the Eucharist, which means, "to give thanks," Christians celebrate and remember God's abundant and abiding goodness to them; such continual remembering helps shape them into persons and communities of gratitude. Regular practices of prayer also deepen dispositions to gratitude because prayer quiets and centers us in a way that makes us more attuned to the blessings and graces of our

28. Pohl, *Living into Community*, 27.
29. Pohl, *Living into Community*, 28.

lives, including those in the past that we didn't recognize at the time. Prayer teaches us to remember not regretfully or begrudgingly, but gratefully, and such grateful remembering enables us not only to live more gratefully in the present, "noticing the goodness, beauty, and grace around us,"[30] but also to be more alert to the gifts and blessings of the future. "By remembering gratefully—whether special moments or overall trajectories—we see more clearly the ways in which we've been blessed," Pohl explains. "In this sense, gratitude is often a backward-looking practice—but it also shapes the future in that it allows us to build on the past in hope and confidence."[31]

In *Getting A Life: How to Find Your True Vocation*, Renee LaReau offers the very practical suggestion of ending every day by jotting down three to five things for which we are grateful: a word of encouragement from a friend, the unexpected kindness of a stranger, an uplifting conversation, a chance to do good for others. Doing this not only opened LaReau's eyes to blessings she had overlooked or taken for granted, but also led her to begin each day "as if I were on the lookout for the good things instead of waiting until the end of the day to find them."[32] LaReau's suggestion reminds us of St. Ignatius's Examen prayer, which we described in chapter 5 when considering ways to discern our callings. The Examen is a very helpful practice for alerting us to how God is present to us and blesses us every day of our lives.

Finally, an especially important way to grow in gratitude is to thank the people who have loved us, supported us, helped us, taught us, challenged us, and even cared enough about us to correct us. Becoming experts in saying thanks opens our eyes to how much we are indebted to all the persons who come in and out of our lives. Too, giving thanks is not only a poignant reminder of the procession of people who have blessed us, but also makes us much more likely to ask: Who am I called to bless today? That is a calling we can always answer and gratitude teaches us how to do it well.

Conclusion

In *An Altar in the World*, Barbara Brown Taylor, a woman of many callings (college professor, author, priest of the Episcopal church), declares: "Call me a romantic, but I think most people want to be good for something. I think they want to do something that matters, to be part of something bigger than themselves, to give themselves to something that is meaningful instead of

---

30. Pohl, *Living into Community*, 51.

31. Pohl, *Living into Community*, 43.

32. LaReau, *Getting a Life*, 95.

meaningless."[33] Anyone who lives vocationally will completely agree. To see ourselves as called, as persons summoned to make a unique contribution to the world, means that we not only want to be good *at* something, but also *for* something. Instead of just drifting through life aimlessly, bouncing from one thing to the next, we "want to do something that matters," want "to be part of something bigger" than ourselves, and want "to give ourselves to something that is meaningful instead of meaningless."

But we cannot aspire to anything that Taylor holds out to us without the virtues because the virtues endow us with the characteristics, habits, practices, and skills necessary to excel in life. In this chapter we explored the crucial importance of the virtues in living our callings by focusing on three that are especially significant as we take up the journey that every calling is. Attention, humility, and gratitude aid us as we begin the journey because they help root us in our callings by keeping us mindful of the time and place in which we find ourselves. Additional virtues will be examined in the next two chapters, but it should already be clear that living vocationally and the virtues go hand in hand. We cannot get far in thinking about our callings without considering the virtues because the virtues form us into persons who recognize that our callings are gifts, but gifts that can never be taken for granted. With the virtues, instead of letting our callings weaken, wither, and die, we are vigilant about nurturing and caring for them. With the virtues, we do not let hardship, adversity, suffering, disappointment or disillusionment deny us the blessings in which we find ourselves and come more fully to life. Aided by the virtues, our vocational journeys, no matter how challenging and arduous, remain itineraries of hope.

33. Taylor, *Altar*, 113.

CHAPTER 8

Virtues for Continuing the Journey— Fidelity, Justice, and Courage

CALLINGS DON'T TAKE CARE of themselves. It is tempting to think that once we have discerned our callings the hard work is done. But that isn't so. It is much more challenging to live our callings than it is to discover them, and this is true, perhaps surprisingly, for the callings with which we have most invested our lives. If this were not the case, marriages would never die, friendships would never be abandoned, communities would never lose members, and promises would never be broken. Unfortunately, those things happen all the time. They happen because it is easy to take our callings for granted, assuming that because we have given our hearts to them that we can never lose them. We might not consciously or intentionally neglect a calling, but we can become complacent, even careless, in living our callings, unaware that we are gradually slipping away from the persons, communities, and projects to which we have promised ourselves.

Other times callings die not because we take them for granted but because we don't know how to manage the challenges and frustrations that are part of living vocationally. We learn that living our callings requires more energy, attention, and commitment than we realized. We discover that the persons we fell in love with aren't always lovable (anymore than we are), that even our best friends can be tiresome, or that the communities in which we were sure we would always find life are not, even at their best, the vestibule of heaven. We still care for the persons or communities to whom we committed ourselves, but something is missing. We have changed and they have changed. Where once we were zealous and enthusiastic, now we are listless and indifferent; increasingly detached from the things that once wholly engaged us. No longer single-hearted, we find ourselves split by conflicting desires and haunted by unchosen possibilities we thought we had left behind. The callings that at first were liberating and uplifting are now suffocating because they restrict us in ways we had not envisioned. Taking more life from us than giving it, we scheme for ways to escape the vocations we thought we would never question. At these moments of disillusionment—and they always come—we imagine life anywhere else as better than the life that is ours. If we do not find ways to rediscover the promise in our callings and to once more affirm their goodness, they will die, leaving us wondering how something once so promising could be forever lost.

Callings don't take care of themselves. If we are to continue on our vocational journeys, we need virtues to steady and protect us as we make our way. One of the most essential virtues for helping us continue on the journey is fidelity. Fidelity is a ruggedly realistic virtue because people skilled in fidelity recognize that callings are gifts that cannot be taken for granted. They know that living vocationally is not easy. They know the future holds challenges, trials, and difficulties they can never fully anticipate. And they know themselves well enough to admit that even though they love the different callings that comprise their lives, they can be fickle, selfish, and halfhearted, qualities, that if not confronted and overcome, will eventually suck the life out of any calling. Fidelity may not be the most important virtue, but for anyone who seeks to grow and flourish in the different callings of their lives rather than just stumble through them or, much worse, simply endure them, fidelity is indispensable. If each of the virtues helps us live wisely and well, fidelity does so by teaching us how to deal with the inevitable challenges that accompany any calling so that we remain continually engaged by, and faithful to, the persons, communities, and projects with which we have aligned our lives. Fidelity reminds us of what we love and do not want to lose. It protects us from the harm that will come, both to ourselves and to others, if we casually walk away from the callings that once were, and still can be, paths to life for us.

This chapter will focus principally on the virtue of fidelity. We will begin by considering what fidelity is, why we need it, and how fidelity works to safeguard our callings. Second, we'll look at justice, a virtue closely linked to fidelity because in responding to a calling we promise something of ourselves to others and those promises create obligations and responsibilities that cannot be neglected or relinquished without considerable harm to others. Nonetheless, because the different callings of our lives have inherent value but not necessarily absolute value, we'll also examine why it can sometimes be justified to be released from a particular calling. And because our responsibilities extend beyond those most closely associated with us (spouses, partners, friends, local communities), we'll think about how justice summons us to help create the social, economic, and political conditions that would allow every person, not just the privileged, to pursue truly life-giving callings. Finally, we'll turn to courage, a virtue in the service of fidelity, because courage gives us the resolve, determination, stamina, and insight necessary to persevere through, and hopefully overcome, the challenges and hardships that are part of any vocational journey. Courage is the virtue that protects us from abandoning the most blessed and promising callings of our lives when being faithful to them seems not only overwhelming, but also downright impossible. Our analysis will reveal that fidelity, justice, and courage are virtues that steady and protect us as we make our way in our callings lest we be overcome by the struggles that lie ahead of us. This is why, in addition to attentiveness, humility, and gratitude, we need them for our vocational journeys.

Fidelity

Perhaps the best way to begin thinking about the meaning of fidelity is to consider a conventional symbol of faithfulness: a wedding ring. A special part of every wedding ceremony is the blessing and exchange of rings. Each of the soon-to-be spouses gives the other a ring as a sign of their enduring love and a pledge of their faithfulness. They wear those rings "till death do us part" as a daily reminder of what they have promised and of their mutual intention to care for the gift of their marriage from that day forward. No matter what else may be swirling around them and no matter what may lie ahead of them, the rings testify that nothing will draw them away from one another and that nothing will diminish the love that has been entrusted to them. Even though they cannot predict the future, their fidelity creates a way of life—a true way of being—so that the love that joins them together on the day they marry will unite them even more deeply in the years ahead. And even though they will age as the years unfold, those rings signal that because of their shared faithfulness, their love will remain fresh, vital, and promising; indeed, the fidelity that exists between them will continually rejuvenate their love.

And so we can describe fidelity as the virtue by which we remain centered and focused on the multiple callings of our lives (our core relationships, communities, and projects) so that rather than forsaking them, we grow more deeply into them. Fidelity maintains a strong and vibrant relationship between our callings and ourselves by guiding and shaping our freedom so that it works on behalf of our callings rather than against them. As noted in the last chapter, virtues are the habits and qualities of character we need in order to live truly good lives. They are the habits and qualities of character we must develop if we are not to end up with lives that are little more than a chronicle of wrong choices, misguided priorities, wasted opportunities, and endless regrets. In this respect, the special work of fidelity is to stabilize and solidify our relationship to the various callings of our lives so that we grow and flourish in those callings rather than drift away from them. Fidelity sustains us in living our callings so that we come to know their full promise, something that cannot happen if we neglect them, grow complacent with them, or allow ourselves to be lured away from them.

This does not mean that every calling demands the same degree of fidelity, because not every calling of our lives is equally important. Some callings are quite weighty and substantial (such as callings connected with vows) while others are relatively minor (such as helping a friend through a difficult week). Some callings span the whole of our lives (such as the calling that comes with baptism) while others may be quickly fulfilled and quite temporary (such as promising to have lunch with a colleague). Still, even though some callings are clearly more important than others, even lesser callings are morally important because every calling in some way grows from a promise made to others.

Why We Need Fidelity

Arthur Miller's play *After the Fall* tells the story of Quentin, a New York lawyer uncertain about the future of his relationship with Holga because he is haunted by memories of broken relationships, especially the dissolution of his marriages, first to Louise and then to Maggie. The play takes place in Quentin's mind as he recollects his past and the recent history of the world, a world in which everything seems to be falling apart, a world of lost innocence and broken promises, a world in which people who should be friends grow increasingly separate and alone. As the title of the play indicates, it is a world far removed from the paradise of Eden. Nonetheless, at the end of Act One, Quentin says, "It's that the evidence is bad for promises. But how else do you touch the world—except with a promise?"[1]

In a world littered with broken promises and at a time when betrayal and infidelity can seem much more common than faithfulness, there is no doubt "that the evidence is bad for promises." People break promises all the time, so much so that it is almost expected that at some point in our lives we will either betray or be betrayed. Moreover, if broken promises and failed commitments are more the norm than fidelity, it can seem foolish to be

---

1. Miller, *After the Fall*, 86.

faithful. If everybody is hurting everybody else through infidelity, why risk the pain fidelity is bound to bring?

But Quentin is right. Even though the evidence for promises and faith-fulness may be lousy, there really is no other way for us to "touch the world," no other way for us to connect with life than by promising ourselves to persons, communities, and projects worthy of our selves. A very important first reason that fidelity is indispensable for living our callings is that we come to life only through promising and come more fully to life only by being faithful to promises. When we say yes to a calling we are recognizing and responding to the goods (persons, communities, projects) by which we choose to be known, identified, and defined as persons, the goods through which we step into existence and begin to be. Thus, just as prior to cre-ation everything was a "formless void," a "wasteland," so too do we remain formless and undefined—a mere batch of possibilities rather than anything actual and real—if we spend our lives in a permanent state of indecision and faithlessness.[2]

This is why even when betrayal and infidelity seem normal that we still feel a natural affinity with fidelity. Even if we have broken promises and betrayed commitments ourselves, we know some kind of fidelity is abso-lutely essential for life. Personhood requires promising and promises live through fidelity. We grow as persons and acquire a substantive and endur-ing identity only by being faithful to the promises by which we embrace, enter into, and live our callings. We gain character and depth in our lives, we find purpose and meaning, not by avoiding commitments but by faithfully giving ourselves to them. Even though a prevalent cultural script suggests that being faithful to commitments keeps us from living fully and freely, the truth is that if we never find something promising to which to be faithful, we will never find our self. Without fidelity we become chronic bystanders to life, not active participants, perpetual adolescents who dabble with life rather than live it.[3]

A second reason that fidelity is essential for living and flourishing in our callings is that the full meaning of our callings always lies ahead of us. We cannot understand our callings without saying yes to them, but even when we assent to a calling there is still a sizable gap between that initial yes and a greater comprehension of its value and meaning. This is true whether the calling is a friendship, a profession, joining a community, or trying to grasp the value of a good and holy life. We don't appreciate the meaning and promise of any calling instantaneously, but only as we grow more fully into

2. Haughey, *Should Anyone Say Forever?*, 22.
3. Haughey, *Should Anyone Say Forever?*, 62.

it, and that is impossible without fidelity. Fidelity provides the stability and permanence we need to live into our callings long enough to sufficiently understand and appreciate them. It protects us from abandoning our callings before we have lived them long enough to have tasted their particular goodness, and thus helps us appreciate what we will lose if we forsake those callings; in this respect, fidelity protects us from ourselves. Too, because we are temporal beings, no matter how fully invested we might be in a calling, no single moment of our lives, no matter how intensely memorable, cherished, or significant, can completely capture the whole promise of any calling. Couples realize this when they celebrate anniversaries and friends too when they mark special moments in their relationships. Those special moments are milestones on the journey, milestones that look back on what they have already shared, but that also look forward to a greater realization of the unique goodness of their calling. Fidelity assures that we not only have a past to remember with our callings, but also a future to eagerly anticipate.

A third reason we need fidelity for living vocationally is that so many things threaten our callings—perhaps especially ourselves. Human beings are fickle creatures with weakened wills and wayward hearts. There would be no need for fidelity if our wills were unwaveringly steadfast and our hearts absolutely undivided, but they aren't. We can be trustworthy and reliable, but we can also be irresponsible and unpredictable, people who make promises one day, fully intending to keep them, but who conveniently forget them when something more alluring comes along. We are complex, puzzling creatures who, despite our best efforts, are subject to conflicting desires and attractions, creatures who sometimes find themselves pulled in directions not entirely compatible with their callings. Our feelings vacillate, our minds change, and our once sturdy intentions grow frail. Margaret Farley captured well the multiple contradictions that can beset us when she observed, "I experience myself as fragmented and conflicted, conditioned as well as self-determining, 'swept away' as well as 'self-possessed.'"[4] It is precisely because of these unsettling facts about us that living vocationally is impossible without fidelity. As Farley elaborated: "We need and want a way to be held to the word of our deepest self, a way to prevent ourselves from destroying everything in the inevitable moments when we are less than this."[5] The special excellence of fidelity is that it provides a way for us "to be held to the word of our deepest self" lest we destroy everything promising about our callings and, in doing so, also diminish ourselves, along with those most closely connected to our callings.

4. Farley, *Personal Commitments*, 33.
5. Farley, *Personal Commitments*, 34.

Sometimes we can only appreciate a virtue's importance when we grasp the consequences of not having it, and this is certainly true with fidelity. Without fidelity, instead of actively resisting, we passively surrender to all the elements of our personality and character that weaken commitment to our callings. That commitment can erode because of selfishness—the need to always get our way and to always put ourselves first. It can weaken due to the insecurity, anxiety, and fear that can occasionally be elicited by any calling. We can turn away from our own callings if we are jealous and envious of another's calling, if we find ourselves bored and restless in our callings, or simply by discovering that we are not as settled in our vocations as we thought. So many things can leave us increasingly alienated from our callings so that we become strangers to the very things we swore we would never doubt, even to the point that we can no longer touch—or be touched by—what was once so promising to us. With all zeal for a calling dissipated, we find ourselves not only distant and detached from a calling that once engaged us completely, but also dead to it. Even if we remain in the calling, and do our best to appear that all is well, instead of truly living a life, we just inhabit one. It's as if we are taking up space in our own life. Farley captures well this frightening condition from which fidelity can protect us when she writes: "The most frantic of activities do not change the fact that we are observers of our committed lives, not participants. Sooner or later it is not just boring for us, or empty, or like a strange dream; it is oppressive and intolerable."[6]

Fourth, we need fidelity because every choice we make carries within it a reminder of what we did not choose, and this is especially true when our choices take the form of promises. To promise ourselves to a calling is to intend our lives in a certain way. That promise signifies that we decide to invest our lives (to focus our minds and our hearts, our talents and our time) in certain possibilities, but in doing so explicitly rule out other possibilities, either because they are incompatible with our promise or simply because we cannot pursue all possible goods. A commitment to a particular calling is done for the sake of certain goods with which we choose to align our lives, but choosing those goods means turning away from other goods. The root meaning of *decision* is to cut or to separate; thus, when we decide to give ourselves to a particular calling we simultaneously separate ourselves from other possible callings.

This is never easy because it means that we always live "at the expense" of other possibilities. Every calling we say yes to opens up certain possibilities but closes off other possibilities. We can't be friends with everyone. We

6. Farley, *Personal Commitments*, 52.

can't marry every person we love. We can't join every community that appeals to us. And we can't say yes to every promising major or career. There are multiple renunciations at the heart of every promise because the only way we can turn toward any possible calling is by turning away from other possible callings, perhaps all of them equally good. We make promises because we need to locate our lives in relation to certain possibilities in order to make good on anything at all; in other words, without committing ourselves to something, we remain potentially many things, but actually nothing.

But it can be difficult to keep those promises and to be faithful to those commitments because the ruled out possibilities still inhabit our world and, perhaps in ways we do not suspect, sometimes our hearts. We feel secure in our callings only to be awakened by the appeal of ruled-out possibilities. We think we are firmly settled in our vocations, but unexpectedly find ourselves haunted by something (another person, another way of life) we were sure we had left behind. Those unchosen possibilities can revisit us with amazing freshness and vitality, as if they had always been inside our minds, our memories, and our hearts, just waiting to reassert themselves. Thus, it is not surprising that we can experience our wills as conflicted. It is as if within us live both the desire to be faithful and the temptation to betray. This is when we most need fidelity to steady and protect us in our callings.

How Fidelity Works

These reflections remind us that we cannot be naïve when it comes to living and growing in our vocations. We need to be prepared for the challenges that come with any calling, knowing how to respond to them and overcome them, which is what fidelity enables us to do. With fidelity, instead of being lured away by rival callings, we give the benefit of the doubt to the callings we have chosen. With fidelity, instead of becoming cynical and disenchanted with our callings, we commit to rediscovering their goodness, the goodness that first enabled us to say yes to them. With fidelity, instead of fantasizing about other possibilities or losing ourselves in dreams about "what might have been," we recommit to the callings that have been specially entrusted to us. Fidelity is the virtue by which we fortify our intention to love, grow, flourish in, and be grateful for, our callings. With fidelity we say *yes* not just once, but again and again.

How then does fidelity safeguard our callings? First, fidelity organizes our life in service to our callings. Fidelity unfolds in a way of living in which everything works on behalf of our callings rather than against them. People habituated in fidelity do not allow anything to become more important than their callings. Fidelity gives them the ingenuity necessary not only to protect their callings, but also to strengthen them by continually growing more fully in those callings. Too, as we saw in chapter one, if one of the keenest challenges of living vocationally is knowing how to address the conflicts and tensions that can exist among our many callings, fidelity helps us discern how our different callings should be ordered and prioritized so that each receives the attention it deserves. If I find myself giving excessive attention to my work but deficient attention to my spouse and family, fidelity awakens me to the imbalance, motivates me to change, and helps me discern how best to be responsible to all of my callings. If students find themselves juggling the responsibilities of academics, relationships, social life, and work, with fidelity they find ways to keep their lives centered, integrated, and as balanced as possible.

Fidelity is like a rudder on a ship guiding our behavior, influencing our decisions, keeping our lives on course so that we can continue the journeys we have set for our lives and eventually complete them, whether the destination we aspire to reach is graduation, success in a profession, a good and happy life, or the reign of God. If we find ourselves wandering into treacherous waters, fidelity pulls us to safety, reminding us of the commitments we made, why we made them, and what we risk in abandoning them. Fidelity is the virtue that enables us to continue on the journey undeterred by creating a way of being designed to safeguard the key commitments of our lives and by making some options, some possibilities, and some choices truly unimaginable. The French philosopher Gabriel Marcel expresses well this dimension of fidelity when he writes: "The fact is that when I commit myself, I grant in principle that the commitment will not again be put in question. And it is clear that this active volition not to question something again, intervenes as an essential element in the determination of what in fact will be the case. It at once bars a certain number of possibilities, it bids me invent a certain *modus vivendi* which I would otherwise be precluded from envisaging."[7]

Marcel's comments indicate why, in one sense, a virtuous person has fewer choices than an unvirtuous person. Someone habituated in fidelity does not have to decide day after day whether or not she will be faithful because if she truly possesses the virtue of fidelity, the decision has already been made for her. She will be faithful to her callings because by living and acting faithfully she has become a faithful person and thus does not have to choose to be faithful at the start of every day. By intending to be faithful from the beginning and verifying that intention by acquiring the virtue of fidelity,

7. Marcel, *Creative Fidelity*, 162.

she has declared, as Marcel said, "that the commitment will not again be put in question." Formed in the virtue of fidelity and guided by it day by day, she can be sure that what she promised would be the case in the beginning will continue to be the case as she lives more deeply into her calling.

This has to happen because there are so many other things that clamor for our attention, most of them good. People formed in fidelity do not deny the goodness of other possibilities; to the contrary, they are astute enough to know that precisely because these other possibilities are good that they can, if they give them more attention than they deserve, supplant their callings. This is why they rightly see them not as possible options to pursue, but as temptations to avoid. Anything that threatens the callings to which we have given ourselves must be seen as a temptation. We may shy away from calling something good a temptation, but the language is important because it lets us know what place something can or cannot have in our lives. If something is a temptation, we cannot entertain its possibility without risk to our callings. The language of temptation reminds us that there are some things to which we ought not be open, some things we should not choose, not because they are necessarily evil, but because choosing them would jeopardize the callings with which we have most deeply identified ourselves.

For many people today hardly anything counts as a temptation, but that is only because they have never surmised what is lost to us if we never learn to safeguard what we love. If we genuinely cherish our callings, we will not hesitate to name some things temptations because we know that if we do not, we can begin to imagine their possibility. If this happens, instead of redirecting our attention, we allow ourselves to linger with these possibilities until we no longer realize that they are incompatible with our callings. People schooled in fidelity know that most betrayals begin not with grand acts of defiance, but by giving temptations undue attention, contemplating them until what once was unthinkable now seems not only plausible, but also acceptable and perhaps even inevitable. This is why betrayal is typically less a single act and more a series of inappropriate yeses that culminates in a tragic act of unfaithfulness. Anyone who has betrayed a lover, a partner, or a spouse can testify that this is true. As Farley reflects, with fidelity I recognize "that there are certain ways I cannot allow myself to *think*." With fidelity, when faced with anything that might turn me away from what I have promised in my callings, I "'stop' long enough to hear the voice within me that is most truly mine. If, halting there, I understand that I do not want to lose what I have pledged myself to and I do not want to betray what I have chosen to love, then I cannot, not even in my imagination, play games that will threaten that bond. I must not begin what will lead where I do not ultimately want to go."[8]

Second, fidelity sustains and strengthens us in our callings because genuine fidelity is always *creative*. Fidelity entails both permanence and change. What is permanent is the value and goodness of our callings, but what changes is both our relationship with those callings and how life experiences, both positive and negative, impact them. Marcel claimed that given the historical character of our lives, fidelity must be flexible and supple enough to help us deal wisely and well with change; not only the changes that we and the people to whom we promised undergo, but also changes that come with the unexpected, with surprises and obstacles, and with pretty much everything life might throw at us. To speak of fidelity as creative means that true fidelity must be thoughtful, insightful, and imaginative enough to recognize what we must do to keep ourselves fully engaged with our callings in order to continue to grow in them. Consequently, genuine fidelity should never be associated with rigidity or sterile immutability; in fact, if that's how we approach our callings, we aren't being faithful, we're being stubborn and lazy and irresponsible because we are allowing them to grow stale. As Marcel insisted, "an effective fidelity can and should be a creative fidelity."[9]

We can appreciate the importance of creative fidelity if we contrast it, as Marcel did, with constancy. Marcel described constancy as "the rational skeleton of fidelity"[10] or as "only a semblance"[11] of fidelity to indicate that while constancy may, at first glance, appear to be the core element of what it means to be faithful to our commitments, it is, at best, a deficient form of fidelity. To be "constant" in my callings, Marcel suggests, implies that I fulfill my commitments, but without any hint of enthusiasm or eagerness. I show constancy in friendship, for example, when I fulfill my obligations to a friend, but more from duty than love. I do what I ought to do, but there is no joy in my actions, no energy. No one could excuse me of being explicitly unfaithful to my friend, but she could hardly be faulted for expecting more of me. I might, strictly speaking, fulfill my duty to my friend, but if I can't put my heart into what I do, am I really being faithful? Am I truly present to her? It is true that during times of stress, exhaustion, difficulty, and disappointment constancy may be all we are able to achieve in our callings, and that should not be dismissed. By remaining constant when we experience

8. Farley, *Personal Commitments*, 48.

9. Marcel, *Creative Fidelity*, 152.

10. Marcel, *Creative Fidelity*, 153.

11. Marcel, *Creative Fidelity*, 154.

our callings more as burdens than as gifts, we show that we haven't given up on them and are doing our best to remain in them, and that counts for something. Constancy may be the bare minimum for fidelity, but sometimes it may be the best we can do.[12]

Still, true fidelity can never be satisfied with sheer constancy. Marcel distinguishes constancy from genuine fidelity—a truly vital and creative fidelity—by noting a difference between *perseverance* and *presence*.[13] With constancy, I persevere in my commitments, but am not fully present to the persons or communities to whom I made those commitments. Moreover, Marcel argues, if I reduce fidelity to constancy, I can easily switch the focus to myself from the person or community to whom I pledged fidelity. My utmost concern is not for the other, but for myself and my sense of myself; particularly for the idea I have formed of myself, namely that I am someone who fulfills his duty and thus acts with integrity.[14] In my own eyes, Marcel says, "my conduct has been irreproachable,"[15] but is that how it looks to the person or persons to whom I pledged to be faithful? This is why he says I may be able to judge whether I have been constant in my promises, but only those to whom I promised can assess whether I have been truly faithful.[16] When fidelity is reduced to constancy, those to whom I promised will quickly experience the difference.

Marcel's insistence that true fidelity is always *creative fidelity* emphasizes that it takes skill, insight, imagination, flexibility, and even spontaneity to keep the different callings of our lives fresh and engaging. People formed in the virtue of creative fidelity know that being faithful does not mean doing the same thing in the same way over and over again. That isn't being faithful; it's being stuck in a rut. Creative fidelity teaches us that being faithful to our callings means so much more than just "staying put," for we can "stay put" and be very unfaithful, especially if we are physically present to others, but emotionally, psychologically, and spiritually distant. The people to whom we have committed ourselves deserve more than our physical presence; they deserve our *wholehearted* presence.[17] A person of genuinely creative fidelity learns how to remain fully engaged and enlivened by the different callings of her life in a way that is challenging and healthy for her, but also for the sake of those to whom she promised. She recognizes when something needs to

---

12. Farley, *Personal Commitments*, 46.

13. Marcel, *Creative Fidelity*, 153.

14. Marcel, *Creative Fidelity*, 154.

15. Marcel, *Creative Fidelity*, 155.

16. Marcel, *Creative Fidelity*, 155.

17. Marcel, *Creative Fidelity*, 153.

change or when she should try something new, something different, so that her callings remain life giving and promising. Friends know this, married couples surely do, and so do communities. Without creative fidelity, life ekes out of our callings, often so slowly and quietly that we don't even notice. But at some point we recognize that we've lost touch with the original promise of our callings. We may "stay put," but we're only going through the motions, play acting at something that once had won our hearts.

Third, fidelity protects our callings by giving us a certain control over time. When we make a promise we are declaring something about our future. We are stating that we will do all that we reasonably can so that the future will know the fullness of what we promised. Whether that promise extends only for an afternoon, a few weeks and months, or the rest of our lives, it signifies what we *intend* to do with our time and what we want our future to be. With that promise we assert that we will do our best to make sure that the future, however murky and uncertain, serves our callings. This is certainly the case when couples say, "I do," when religious profess vows, or when we commit to any person or project, especially over an extended period of time. In each instance we declare that the future will be what we have promised it will be. Thus, with fidelity, we shape the future in favor of our callings by connecting the *present* reality of our callings to their *future* fulfillment. This obviously does not mean we can predict everything that will come our way; in fact, we need fidelity exactly because we don't know everything that will come our way. But it does mean that with fidelity we don't pass the time or simply suffer it; rather, we guide and shape time so that we will be who we have promised to be and do what we have promised to do. With fidelity, we do not hand ourselves over to any possible future, but take responsibility for it. This is why the future we intend, commit to, and hope for is contained in the promise we have made and will unfold from it.

And yet, is this really possible? Given all the things that undermine and imperil our commitments (social and cultural dynamics, our own weaknesses and limitations, the frailties of other people), can we, even with the best of intentions, promise to be faithful? How do we know that our feelings will not change? Can we be confident about any calling if we are honest about ourselves, honest about human nature and the world in which we live, and honest about how little control we have over life? Is fidelity a fool's errand?

Left to our own resources, fidelity, especially fidelity for the rest of one's life, seems questionable at best. But is it all up to us? Do we have to confront the challenges of being faithful completely by ourselves? Here a Christian understanding of fidelity can help us. A Christian theology of fidelity argues that we must see our promises to be faithful in light of a higher faithfulness—the faithfulness of God. From a Christian perspective, when we promise we never promise all on our own, but always in partnership with God. Our pledge to be faithful is rooted in, connected to, suspended from, and continuously dependent on the absolute faithfulness of God. God's fidelity is primary, our fidelity is always secondary. In this respect, our commitments constitute an appeal to God to help us do what we know we cannot do ourselves. When we promise we acknowledge our radical insufficiency by calling on God to give us the ongoing grace we need to be faithful. For Christians, the virtue of fidelity never means, "counting on oneself" alone, but relying always on the unsurpassable fidelity of God to guarantee the commitments we cannot guarantee on our own.[18] Fidelity flows from faith and is possible only with faith: the faith that God accompanies us, the faith that God will help us, the faith that God's love, mercy, and goodness are always at hand. If fidelity steadies and protects us as we live out our callings, ultimately that is primarily due not to our own abilities and will power, but to God's undying faithfulness to us.

Justice

Justice is the virtue that guides our relationships with others (including other creatures and species) by teaching us to recognize and respect their dignity and to give them their due. Minimally, justice is about fairness. People formed in the virtue of justice know that they have obligations and responsibilities to others they ought not to ignore. Moreover, because a virtue is a characteristic way of being and acting, just people don't occasionally work for the good of others, but do so consistently, willingly, and even joyfully. Just persons live with others in mind—those who came before them, those who are part of their world now, and those who will come after them. The needs of others are at the forefront of their consciousness, not in the background. In short, justice is all about being in "right relationship" with others, and truly just persons know how to do that in all of the different relationships that comprise their lives; again, whether in the past, the present, or the future.[19]

18. Marcel, *Creative Fidelity*, 167.

19. For an extended analysis of the virtue of justice see Wadell, *Happiness*, 237–61.

Why Fidelity Is a Matter of Justice

How can justice give us a fuller understanding of fidelity? How can it steady us when our commitment to our callings grows wobbly and weak? More basically, what does justice have to do with fidelity? Callings make our lives a tapestry of promises. Parents promise to help one another and to be there for one another, and to love, care for, and be responsible in raising their children. Students who register for a class implicitly promise to show up, do the work, and contribute just as their professors promise to be prepared, to devote time and energy to the class, to care for their students, and to be fair. When we start a job we promise to be responsible and dependable, to cooperate with others, to give our best, to be open to criticism and to be willing to learn. If we commit ourselves to a project, we promise to give ourselves generously to it and not to abandon it except for serious reasons.

Here a qualification may be important. Even though we are focusing on the responsibilities that flow from promising, not every obligation does. For example, each of us is born indebted not only to our parents and the family members who preceded us, but also to countless others who made our life possible; therefore, we have responsibilities in justice to them, responsibilities that ought to be embraced in gratitude. Even though we did not choose our parents or our siblings or our extended family, we were born into a web of relationships, relationships that create commitments and bring countless obligations we should honor. Similarly, we have obligations to other human beings, particularly the poor and vulnerable members of society, because of the bond that exists among all human beings, a bond that justice teaches us to recognize and respond to regularly. These examples testify that fidelity extends beyond relationships created by promises. Moreover, it is by being faithful to these "unchosen" relationships and the commitments that arise from them that we learn the rudiments of fidelity and are thus better prepared to undertake other commitments and promises.

Those promises create obligations and responsibilities. They create an "ought" because as soon as I make a promise I owe something to the person or persons to whom that promise has been made and am obliged in justice to do all that I can to fulfill it. Promising signals an important change in a relationship because it creates another moral bond between myself and the persons to whom I have promised, one that goes beyond the fundamental bond that already exists between us as human beings. Because of what I have promised—and because I have identified myself with the promise—I have responsibilities in justice to them and they have justified expectations of me that did not exist prior to the promise. "If I, in and through commitment, give someone a claim over me, then it is a matter of 'justice' that

I honor the claim," Farley explains. "Something now is 'due' that person. What I have given to her is a new 'right' in relation to me."[20]

Promises change the moral meaning of a relationship because in making them we extend something of ourselves—and sometimes our entire selves—to others and give them the right to hold us accountable to what we have promised. An obvious example is marriage. Marriage may not create a completely new relationship because spouses knew one another prior to getting married. But marriage does give a significantly new meaning to the relationship because through their mutual promise each gives their self over to the other as a pledge of who they will be and what they will do for the other. Through their marriage vow they attest that each can count on the other in ways they could not expect of each other before they promised. As Farley elaborates, "To give my word is to 'place' a part of myself, or something that belongs to me, into another person's 'keeping.' It is to give the other person a claim over me, a claim to perform the action that I have committed myself to perform."[21]

These reflections on what is at stake in making a promise underscore that one reason fidelity is a matter of justice—even a demand of justice—is because of the terrible cost of infidelity. When we promise we give another our word that they can count on us and, as is the case with marriage, deep friendships, or religious life, entrust themselves to us, fully confident that we will not go back on our word. We declare that we will be *for* them and *with* them, so much so that they can place themselves in our hands, knowing that we will receive their life as a gift to care for and cherish. That kind of love is what all of us hope for and what all of us need. When we experience that love we come more fully to life because we are known and accepted, affirmed and cherished, for the unique human being we are. At the same time, the utter vulnerability required to experience that love is what makes infidelity so treacherous. Our society may treat infidelity lightly, but no one who has been a victim of infidelity does. People who have been betrayed by those they thought they could trust (friends, lovers, partners, spouses, fellow community members) know that infidelity wounds deeply, often leaving permanent scars. They know that even slight betrayals bruise while deep betrayals leave one shattered and broken, wondering if they can ever risk trusting and loving again. Betrayal wounds deeply because if we tell someone they can place their lives in our hands, to go back on our word is to let go of them at exactly the point that their trust for us leaves them most unprotected. To call that unjust is accurate, but hardly seems adequate.

20. Farley, *Personal Commitments*, 71.
21. Farley, *Personal Commitments*, 16–17.

There is another way that fidelity is a matter of justice that is often overlooked: It is hard for us to be faithful to our promises when other people are unfaithful to theirs. When we make promises we accept obligations and responsibilities to others, but what is sometimes forgotten is that in receiving our promise they accept obligations and responsibilities toward us. Fidelity typically must be mutual and reciprocal—one faithfulness is met by another faithfulness. We can see in each of the examples sketched above how one person's ability to be faithful to a calling is conditioned by others' faithfulness to their own calling. The most dedicated and gifted teachers will find it hard to fulfill their callings if they regularly encounter lazy and indifferent students just as the most zealous and responsible students will unlikely remain engaged if each day they are met with inept, indifferent, and uninspiring professors. Similarly, a man or woman may wholeheartedly commit to a religious community, but they cannot live their calling with any joy, hope, or promise unless each member of the community also promises to be wholly committed to their own callings so that all of them together can flourish. Whether a friendship, a marriage, or a community, each of us depends on the fidelity of those to whom we have committed ourselves in order to live our callings. This is one reason Marcel said that the most essential characteristic of creative fidelity is *presence*. Presence means that each partner to the promise, whether an individual or a community, communicates through their attitudes and actions that they are wholly available to the other and do not wish to be anywhere else. Through mutual presence, each person knows that they stand together and can count on one another. Most of all, through presence I know that the other is "*with* me."[22]

Can We Be Released from a Calling? Should Promises Ever Be Broken?

Are there times when we ought to be released from the callings to which we have committed ourselves? Are there conditions in which, however regrettable, promises can, and perhaps even ought, to be broken? Or, extending our analysis of the link between fidelity and justice, if justice demands that we ought to remain in our callings and keep our promises, could it ever require that we leave a particular calling or be released from a particular promise? Obviously, everything we have said about the pivotal importance of fidelity argues that neither callings nor promises should ever be abandoned for selfish or trivial reasons; in fact, our initial assumption must always be to honor both the calling and the promise. But does this assumption always hold?

22. Marcel, *Creative Fidelity*, 154.

Farley says no. While she consistently emphasizes the moral serious-
ness of our commitments, she identifies three situations in which those
commitments are no longer binding, two of which are particularly pertinent to our analysis of living vocationally. The first situation is when it is no
longer possible to fulfill the conditions of the promise or commitment.[23]
We can only promise what is possible; consequently, if there is no way we
can reasonably fulfill what we have promised, the promise no longer makes
sense and, therefore, no longer binds. Farley gives the example of a marriage
that has so thoroughly deteriorated that it truly is beyond repair. "What was
once love is now so mixed with bitterness and hate that they simply cannot
remain together without the utter destruction of themselves and the loss of
even what Theodore Mackin calls 'the most detached and cold wishing the
best' for one another."[24] The alienation between the partners is so pervasive
and unyielding that not only is any shared life between them impossible,
but reconciliation is likewise unimaginable. In such dire situations, there
is no hope for restoring a relationship that is unquestionably dead and has
been dead for a long time, and, therefore, no way the spouses can fulfill
the conditions of their original promise. Farley does not want us to reach
these conclusions quickly or prematurely, but she does say there is a "threshold of impossibility" beyond which commitments no longer hold.[25] That
"threshold of impossibility" is crossed when relationships and situations
have grown so intolerable that they are no longer psychologically, emotionally, morally, or spiritually healthy; they may also have become physically
unhealthy, even dangerous. In these circumstances, we should be released
from our callings because to remain would be destructive to ourselves and
to others.[26] As Farley observes, "while we may sacrifice everything we have,
we may not sacrifice everything we are."[27]

The second situation when a commitment can end is if by keeping it
we can no longer fulfill "the purposes of the larger and more basic commitment that it was meant to serve . . ."[28] As Farley explains, our callings are
not ends in themselves, but means for achieving higher goods and larger
purposes. We marry, join communities, and commit ourselves to projects
and purposes for the sake of something else, whether happiness, a sense of
meaning and purpose, or a life of contentment and peace. As a Christian,

23. Farley, *Personal Commitments*, 85.

24. Farley, *Personal Commitments*, 85–86.

25. Farley, *Personal Commitments*, 87.

26. Farley, *Personal Commitments*, 88.

27. Farley, *Personal Commitments*, 106.

28. Farley, *Personal Commitments*, 92.

Farley identifies that higher good and larger purpose as continually growing in love of God, our neighbors, and ourselves. Each of the callings to
which we give ourselves should deepen our capacity to love. When instead
of aiding our growth in love, a calling seems to increasingly hinder it so
that it works against its most fundamental purpose, then, Farley suggests,
our commitment to the calling no longer binds. From a Christian perspective, the callings of our lives are *relative* goods meant to help us achieve
the truly *absolute* good of growing in love for God, others, and ourselves.
When it is abundantly clear that this is no longer possible with a specific
calling—indeed, the specific calling may prevent us from achieving the
higher calling—we must abandon it for the sake of being faithful to a greater
good and purpose.

How Justice Extends the Responsibilities of Fidelity

Several times in *Visions of Vocation* Steven Garber zeroes in on what he
believes is a key vocational question for every human being, a question that
was noted in chapter 2: *"Knowing what I know, what will I do?"*[29] Sometimes
conversations about callings focus so much on personal fulfillment and happiness that they quickly become a self-absorbed exercise of the privileged.
Vocation becomes the exclusive domain of those with sufficient resources,
status, freedom, and opportunities to plan promising pathways for their
lives, leaving those not as fortunate permanently shut out of the conversation. But any understanding of vocation that is informed by a substantive
account of justice vigorously rejects the idea that vocation is all about me
and what is good for me. It is not enough to care about the prosperity and
flourishing of ourselves and those closest to us because, as Garber's question
underscores and Christian social teaching affirms, we cannot separate our
well-being from the well-being of others or our flourishing from the possibility of other human beings (and other creatures) to flourish at all. When
vocation is "exclusively or primarily focused on the self," the world becomes
"a convenient backdrop for one's personal odyssey."[30] But the virtue of justice reminds me that the world is not a backdrop for me to do whatever I
want. No, justice—particularly a truly social understanding of justice—calls
me to make things better for others. It summons me to open my eyes to
the sufferings and afflictions of others, to see the blatant contrast between
what the world is and what it can and ought to be, and especially to respond
to the cries of all who are beaten down by injustice. Justice demands that

29. Garber, *Visions of Vocation*, 52.
30. Ray, "Self, World," 320.

we extend the parameters and responsibilities of fidelity beyond those most closely associated with us to consider how we are called to help create the social, economic, political, and religious conditions that would allow every person to pursue life-giving callings.

Thinking rightly about vocation should naturally lead to matters of social justice for no other reason than it is much more plausible to think about discerning and answering a calling when the social, economic, and political conditions in which a person finds herself make doing so a real possibility. It is much easier to encourage someone to consider how she might be called when her fundamental needs are met, when she has access to good schools and good careers, and when she is treated justly enough to know that a hopeful future is a real possibility for her. But people for whom every day is a question of survival; people who are told both subtly and blatantly that they will never matter as much as others and will never truly belong; and people who know from the start that doors that will open for others will never open for them, might rightly scoff at the invitation to think about their callings. Who could blame them?

If thinking of ourselves as called is a meaningful and hopeful way to envision our lives, then it should be genuinely possible for everyone, not just a lucky few. That cannot happen when patterns of exclusion become normal. It cannot happen when racism, sexism, bigotry and prejudice, or any other ideology becomes so prevalent that they are invisible to all but those who suffer from them. Those of us fortunate enough to have access to the resources and opportunities that make thinking and living vocationally not only appealing, but also plausible, must regularly ask: "What can I do to make a calling possible for someone else?" "How can I help create the social, political, economic, and religious conditions that would allow everyone to discover and respond to their callings?"

Catholic social teaching roots this broader and more extensive understanding of the responsibility that we have to all members of the global community in its emphasis on *solidarity* and the *option for the poor*. In his 1961 social encyclical *Mater et Magistra* ("Christianity and Social Progress"), Pope John XXIII captured the essence of solidarity when he wrote that we are all "members of one and the same household."[31] He saw that human beings are inherently social beings, creatures who are inescapably bound together and, therefore, responsible for one another. John suggested that to ignore the needs of another human being—to treat him or her unjustly in any way—was like betraying a member of our family. Years later, Pope John Paul II developed the meaning of solidarity by describing it as "a *firm*

---

31. John XXIII, *Mater et Magistra*, 157.

and persevering determination to commit oneself to the *common good*; that is to say to the good of all and of each individual, because we are *all* really responsible *for all*."[32]

Similarly, the option for the poor insists that when the poor are regularly shut out of sharing in the resources, benefits, and opportunities of society—when they are regularly excluded from the very things that make pursuing a calling feasible—then their needs demand primary consideration. David Hollenbach outlines well the practical implications of the option for the poor in three principles, principles that are important to remember when we want everyone to have the opportunity to live vocationally: "(1) The needs of the poor take priority over the wants of the rich. (2) The freedom of the dominated takes priority over the liberty of the powerful. (3) The participation of marginalized groups takes priority over the preservation of an order that excludes them."[33]

Both the principle of solidarity and the principle of the option for the poor illumine why an understanding of fidelity that is informed by justice challenges us to rethink who we are responsible to and why. Yes, we are called to be faithful to those with whom we are most closely committed, but our vision of fidelity is inexcusably shortsighted if it extends no further. This point is powerfully made in the parable of the Last Judgment (Matt 25:31–46), where Jesus makes it absolutely clear that the final and definitive assessment of our lives will be determined by whether or not we showed compassion and justice to the most needy, vulnerable, desperate, and forgotten members of society.

Courage

Several years ago one of us participated in a retreat that focused on vocation. On the morning of the final day of the retreat, a Native American woman who was on the retreat said she had a gift to share with all of us. She was holding a brown paper bag and asked each of us to take one of what was in the bag. We were soon holding in our hands a small colored pouch filled with herbs and spices. The woman explained that in her tribe you were given this pouch any time you needed "to be brave."

Those tiny pouches should come with every calling. Young adults need to be brave when they leave home for college and must deal with the understandable fears that accompany what for many is the first major transition of their lives. Couples who say "I do" on the joyous day of their wedding

---

32. John Paul II, *Sollicitudo Rei Socialis*, 38.

33. Hollenbach, *Claims in Conflict*, 204.

can scarcely foresee the extent to which they may need to be brave in the years ahead. What happens to their commitment if they face severe financial stress due to unemployment? What if the child they fiercely love fiercely disappoints them? What if they fiercely disappoint one another? Can they survive these moments without courage, the virtue that helps us navigate the dark and scary places to which our callings sometimes take us? Courage is an ally to fidelity because courage gives us the fortitude and resolve we need to address the fears and difficulties that are part of living our callings. It steadies us when we are shaken and overwhelmed—and sometimes knocked over—by the slings and arrows of life.

When he was writing about the virtue of courage, Thomas Aquinas said that courage helps us deal with all that opposes us in life.[34] Applied to our callings, the things that thwart us are many. Sometimes the greatest opposition comes from ourselves: doubts and insecurities, lack of self-confidence, fear of being misunderstood by others, or a nagging uncertainty about whether we can succeed at our callings. Each of us struggles with "inner demons" that can gain control of us and convince us there is no use in even trying. As soon as a good opportunity comes our way, we talk ourselves out of it. No matter how many solid reasons there might be for accepting or continuing in a calling, we muster more reasons for turning it down or abandoning it. With courage, we are not ruled by these inner demons, but learn how to resist and overcome them. Other times the opposition comes from people who claim to want the best for us, but are actually intent on undermining us. John Schuster calls them "saboteurs." True saboteurs are skilled at "negating, casting doubt, and destroying your hopes."[35] Often with a smile and a kindly voice, they slyly work against us while rallying others to do the same. Courage is the virtue by which we "take heart," and we surely need to do that in order to expose saboteurs for who they are and to resist being defeated by their malice and their cynicism.

The Two Parts of Courage

There are two parts to courage and both are important in helping us remain faithful to our callings. First, is *daring* or *attack*.[36] With daring our immediate response to difficulties, setbacks, and challenges in living our callings is not to suffer them passively or to be resigned to them as if there is nothing

34. Aquinas, *Summa*, II–II, 123, 2. Quotations in this chapter are from the Ross and Walsh translation.

35. Schuster, *Answering Your Call*, 57.

36. Aquinas, *Summa*, II–II, 123, 3.

we can do, but to confront and try to overcome them. Daring helps us stand up to the saboteurs (whether our self or others) so that we do not succumb to our own fears and anxieties or do not allow ourselves to be deterred or undone by others. Daring enables us to confront people about problems that should not be ignored, for if we continually ignore them we will certainly be hindered in living our callings. Daring gives us the insight, imagination, and determination we need to risk, to be open to new possibilities, and to make difficult but necessary changes in our lives, all of which may be necessary if we are to continue on the journey of our callings.

The second part of courage is *perseverance*. Perseverance helps us "persist to the end of a virtuous undertaking" when doing so is hard.[37] Our callings can rightly be described as "virtuous undertakings" because at the heart of every calling are important goods we want to achieve, goods that give us a sense of identity, meaning, and purpose, and convince us that what we are about is worthwhile, and goods that enable us to give ourselves for the sake of others. It can be the unquestionable good of striving to always treat people with respect, to help them if we can, and to be generous with our talents and our time. It could be resolving to be a person who is trustworthy and loyal and honest; someone who refuses to lie. For spouses, partners, friends or community members, it could be promising to look for what is best in one another, to be patient with one another, and to love in ways that affirm the unique goodness of another's existence. For athletes that worthwhile good may be to do one's best while helping teammates do their best as well. For any student it is persevering through one semester after another in order to graduate.

These are all worthwhile goods and inspiring goals, but none of them can be immediately or easily achieved. With perseverance, we resist the urge to give up, to abandon our callings and commitments at the first signs of difficulty or to forsake them the moment we realize we have invested in something that will be much more challenging than we anticipated. These temptations may be especially strong for young adults if their parents or teachers have shielded them from the setbacks and defeats that can not only help them grow and mature, but that should also be expected if they are to achieve excellence in any area of life. Similarly, someone who gives up quickly because success has always come easily will lack the steadfast endurance that virtually every calling requires. People who achieve excellence in any profession—or in life itself—are not those who always succeed, but those who do not allow occasional failures to deter them. They know that inability to persevere in worthwhile endeavors will rob them of the richest

37. Aquinas, *Summa*, II–II, 137, 1, 2.

and most satisfying goods of life that we receive through our callings. As Aquinas emphasized, perseverance is necessary because "it is more difficult to continue firm in great enterprises," which is certainly a fitting description of our callings.[38]

Conclusion

Callings don't take care of themselves. We cannot take our callings for granted because, unless we become adept at caring for them, we can abandon or lose them when persevering in them is hard. This is where fidelity, justice, and courage can help us. We call them *steadying* or *protecting virtues* because they help us stand fast in our callings when we are faced with setbacks and frustrations, when we are tempted by rival possibilities, when we feel ourselves growing complacent, or simply when we are not sure we have the energy and resolve needed to continue to invest in them. Fidelity stabilizes our relationship with our callings so that we do not walk away from the very things that will, if we let them, give us life. Justice steadies us in our callings by drawing our attention to the obligations and responsibilities we have toward others on account of our callings and by alerting us to the terrible harm they can suffer if we betray our callings. And courage protects us in our callings by helping us battle through the trials and tribulations that are part of any vocational journey.

Our analysis of these virtues again demonstrates the tight connection between living vocationally and the virtues. To embrace a calling is to embark on an immensely blessed and graced adventure, but without virtues such as fidelity, justice, and courage, we will lack the qualities of character necessary to continue the journey when doing so is hard. If that is the case, we will perpetually deny ourselves the most promising possibilities of our lives, being left instead with an endless chronicle of rejected opportunities and heartbreaking regrets. Nobody wants that for a legacy. With fidelity, justice, and courage, we can write a much better story of our lives.

38. Aquinas, *Summa*, II–II, 137, 3, 2.

CHAPTER 9

Virtues for Completing the Journey— Hope and Patience

WHAT COULD IT MEAN to have virtues that help us *complete* our vocational journey? Haven't we already said that we remain on our vocational journeys all of our lives, responding to the call all the way through? So is "completing our journey" simply a tricky way to talk about our deaths?

In fact, we do need virtues to receive our deaths; these will include, obviously, some of those we have already discussed, like courage or fidelity. The virtues we will consider in this final chapter do indeed relate to our deaths, but they are also virtues we need to be fully alive. For they orient us to our futures; they are "timeful" virtues. Sometime in the future our vocational journeys will be complete, and we will move beyond this life. But as we travel today, how do we bring the future that lies ahead of us on our vocational journey into our present place within it—in the right way? How can we live now with the best orientation toward where we are going, and someday will arrive?

The two virtues that most help us do this well are hope and patience. For Christians, hope is one of the three theological virtues, standing between faith and love. We often "hope" for things, but we do not typically think we need to *learn* hope. However, if hope is really a virtue, training will be necessary, for we always need to grow in the virtues, and this requires instruction. Patience sustains us as we hope; it is most directly related to the cardinal virtue of fortitude. It requires waiting, although actively, not simply twiddling our thumbs. Both of these virtues, hope and patience, are demanding, not the least because they are about difficulties that arise in our journey. And both are absolutely essential as we reach out towards what lies ahead.

Getting Real about the Future

From the start, "call" sends us off into some new future. As the disciples receive Jesus' call on the shores of the Sea of Galilee, they leave the patterns and practices of the past and step into a new future. Indeed, when it first arrives, a call is really entirely about our futures. This can be exhilarating—but also daunting. For the future can be a very dangerous place.

As Screwtape, the senior devil in C. S. Lewis's *Screwtape Letters*, explains to his protégé Wormwood, the future is the devil's playground.

> It is far better to make them [the humans] live in the Future. Biological necessity makes all their passions point in that direction already, so the thought about the Future enflames hope and fear. Also, it is unknown to them, so in making them think about it we make them think of unrealities . . . Nearly all the vices are rooted in the future. Gratitude looks to the past and love to the present; fear, avarice, lust and ambition look ahead.[1]

Lust may seem to be about the present, but, if we think about it, we can see it is always on the hunt. It wants sexual pleasure, but even if it finds it, the next minute it is off again grasping after some future conquest. Similarly, "avarice"—another name for greed—is never satisfied with the money or possessions it now has, but always wants more. It goes into the future looking for it. Ambition is like this too, always looking forward to accumulating more status and recognition for higher achievement.

These vices keep us imagining the future as the place where we get what we want. I envision a future where my ship will finally come in, I finally have all the money I ever wanted—and *then* I will be satisfied, or happy, or fulfilled. This way of thinking about the future has some unfortunate corollaries whose fruits can be even worse. Especially if we live in a culture in which dreamy thoughts about the future are encouraged—having everything I always wanted or achieving all of my goals—anxiety about the future will press hard on us, especially on young adults as they look ahead to large and looming choices about marriage, career, and further education. For if I can dreamily imagine some future day when I will have everything I always wanted, in another mood I can suddenly become aware that I might *not* have it. This opens the door to fear and anxiety—which may in fact justify the same grasping behavior in another way. "You never know what might happen! And if it does, I don't know what I'd live on. Could I provide properly for myself? Keep up my lifestyle? So let me accumulate a little bit more."

---

1. Lewis, *Screwtape Letters*, 41.

For religious people who genuinely wish to discern God's call, this second orientation is likely the more dangerous. Thoughts about a future in which I get everything I want—by lust or greed or ambition—are evidently self-focused; even a little reflection about call can warn me that my life is not all about getting things for me. In our modern context, however, anxiety about the future, that something bad will happen, or that I will not realize my hopes and dreams, or even fulfill what I think is my calling, can overtake us in thousands of ways. As we have noticed, talk about being "called" can get tangled up in our modern Western culture of choice and achievement. We want a call so we can be certain about where we are going, and about what we need to do to get there. But this sort of craved certainty is easily undermined when obstacles arise or suddenly it looks like we won't make our goal. In such times, false hopes will crumble, anxieties multiply, and the demon of despair will find an opening.

Anxiety names that state of mind or soul when we constantly turn worried thoughts about the future over and over again in our minds, without any resolution. As we are anxious, our present lives are consumed by the future; we are "living in the future" exactly in the way Screwtape wants us to. And the key reason he wants us there is to keep us from the reality of today. The further the devil can keep us from reality, the better—for we will be able to do nothing in the real present. Anxiety about tomorrow renders us completely ineffective today.

While anxiety is especially strong in our time, it is not new. In fact, Jesus explicitly addressed it: "do not worry about tomorrow," he says (Matt 6:25 NIV). To this St. James later adds in his New Testament letter, "you do not even know what tomorrow will bring." As James's way of putting it implies, tomorrow is unreality. To this he adds one more thing: that we are "a mist that appears for a little while and then vanishes" (Jas 4:14). In this regard, we must admit that our uncertainty about the future must be qualified on one point: in the future we will die; each of us can know this, with utter and complete certainty. Now this may not sound very hopeful, but that is because we have been deceived about hope. If hope is real it must also be real about death.

Here we can turn back to Jesus, who told a powerful and remarkably relevant story about a man who forgot he was going to die. After an excellent harvest, this man decides to pull down his barns and build bigger ones. He is sure that he can coast happily into the future, and makes plans to "relax, eat, drink, be merry." In Jesus' parable God says to him, "You fool! This very night your life is being demanded of you. And the things you have prepared, whose will they be?" To which Jesus adds, "So it is with those who store up treasures for themselves but are not rich toward God" (Luke 12:19–21). This parable warns us about riches, yes, but also about how we can be tempted—by riches, or plans and projects such as building new barns or houses—to live in an unreal future world. And, its evidence is death.

Death will come, this we know. At the same time our call in life is to live. The reminder about our death comes to us during our lives *in order to help us live well.* The rich man's problem is that he forgets, or denies, that he will die—which means any thinking about his death will be left for others to do after he is gone. As such, it can do him no good.[2] He could have thought about it since it was obvious, yet he refused. Oddly enough, he thinks about everything in the "future" except the one future reality he can certainly know will come.

In contrast to this rich man, medieval Christians were urged to think of death every day—and Christians today are commanded to do so at least once in the year, on Ash Wednesday: "Remember that you are dust, and to dust you shall return." If they are to be a thoroughly hopeful people, Christians must truthfully remember that life is circumscribed by death—although they can truthfully add that death does not defeat life. In fact, the remembrance of our certain death is one way to make sure our life is not defined by it.

As many have pointed out, our modern time is one in which death is largely denied. This leads to lifelessness. The best way for our lives to be defeated by death is for us to deny it, acting, like Jesus's rich man, as if it has no bearing whatsoever in our lives of grasping and accumulating and planning big parties. Or, in our anxiety about the certainty of death, we might work feverishly to stack up signs of our self-worth, be they possessions or accolades or marks in the earth. Both approaches amount to almost the same outcome; and both are fueled by denial or anxiety that will surely defeat our callings, because neither can teach us how to live truthfully in the present. As well, both are undergirded by a kind of practical atheism that imagines our lives are entirely our own. But—and here is the ultimate source of our hope—they are not; rather they are God's. This means, first, that they are, past, present, and future, entirely in God's hands. And it means, second, that there is nothing we must do to secure their worth. Which leads us to ask a question that seems never to arise for the rich man in Jesus's story: in this time I have been given, with the many and varied benefits I have received, how might God wish for me to live? More than any other, this question opens a space for rightfully receiving our callings.

2. For a striking account of the various ways human beings avoid serious thought about their own death see Tolstoy, *Death.*

Living for Today

We have tried in various ways in this book to say that the called life is not the easy life. The reminder that our lives are God's and not our own lifts the anxiety that comes with thinking we need to secure our own future, but this does not turn them into a walk in the park. A called life demands great work, effort, striving. But striving in a new way, as Jesus makes clear.

> "Therefore I tell you, do not worry about your life, what you will eat or what you will drink, or about your body, what you will wear. Is not life more than food, and the body more than cloth-ing? . . . Therefore do not worry, saying, 'What will we eat?' or 'What will we drink?' or 'What will we wear?' For it is the Gen-tiles who strive for all these things; and indeed your heavenly Father knows that you need all these things. But strive first for the kingdom of God and his righteousness, and all these things will be given to you as well. So do not worry about tomorrow, for tomorrow will bring worries of its own. Today's trouble is enough for today." (Matt 6: 25, 31–34)

Here Jesus actually encourages striving, for the kingdom of God. No one should believe this kind of striving is easy; for more than a few, it has meant bodily death, accompanied by great suffering. But Jesus takes pains in this passage to distinguish it from the striving of "the Gentiles"—which is ac-companied by worry, and grasping for all those things that Jesus wants his followers to receive as gifts. "The Gentiles" in this context can be taken not simply as non-Jews, but as the standard way most people, those of the "nations," live their lives. It is rightly matched with Jesus's teaching to his disciples, offered just before they reach Jerusalem where he faces suffering and death, about what it means to follow him: "You know that among the Gentiles those whom they recognize as their rulers lord it over them, and their great ones are tyrants over them. But it is not so among you; but who-ever wishes to become great among you must be your servant, and whoever wishes to be first among you must be slave of all" (Mark 10:42–44).

The striving of "the Gentiles," the nations, relates to the vices of the future C. S. Lewis identified: working for more for me, leaving less for you, and using the difference against you. Striving for the kingdom of God is different, not because it is easier, but because, rather than taken or earned or accomplished, it is offered as service. The best work of the called life is always work that is turned over as an offering to God. This is quite different from achieving a goal. The called life, in fact, is an offered life, a gift given back in gratitude to the original giver. And this yields another difference, for we know that the giver knows what we need—which is why our callings, the offerings of our lives, do not need to be withheld today so we can be sure they are still there tomorrow. Rather, we can offer them, confidently, freely, and joyfully—every day. Don't worry about tomorrow. Bring today what you have, and offer it.

One of us travels to Africa where he has had the special privilege of joining frequently in worship with Christians there. Among the many contrasts to worship services in North America is the time and energy African Christians pour into the offertory. The singing is loud and long and joyous. Gifts are frequently danced to the altar. In some cases, an auction of sorts is part of the mayhem, as parishioners with a little money bid on the fruits and vegetables that poorer members have brought forward and that cover the floor, spilling out as far as the first pew. Pineapples and yams, papaya and cassava, are passed from hand to hand and the proceeds come back to the pastoral staff, to be used once again in another way, for feeding the poor and sustaining the life of the church. The cycle of giving and receiving is perpetual; it will stop only as we withhold what has been given us in creation, worried about tomorrow. As is sometimes sung in these exuberant gatherings, "This is the day that the Lord has made. Let us be glad and rejoice in it."

The day-by-day called life that brings forth such offerings of joy is, importantly, not the life we are sometimes counseled to take up in our time, namely that we should "live for the moment." Paraphrased, this advice is to "get the most from this moment, for it might be your last." This assumes a scarcity of gifts; yet Jesus offers his advice in the context of abundance. God has given us all we need to live for today; as he will tomorrow.[3] There is no disparagement of the future in Christ's living for today. Indeed, there cannot be, since the future is in God's gracious hands.

Our calling into the kingdom is for *both* tomorrow and today, in a way that connects them firmly together. For Christians, how we are living (or dying) tomorrow can be in deep continuity with how we are living today—and one way this is indicated is by the calls we have received and are living out. Furthermore, the kingdom is not about what I do myself but rather about what and how I participate in what God is doing. This change of perspective is especially difficult for those us of trained by a culture that sucks everything into the self. The challenge comes in a question: can I begin to imagine the future offered to me in my calling as not so much about where I am headed with my own individual life but rather about the ongoing work of the kingdom of God I am right now being invited to join?

3. For a thorough development of this point see Wells, *Companions*, 18–25 and 192–214.

If we can imagine this, we can readily see how Jesus's "living for today" is fundamentally different from the "living for today" recommended by our self-aggrandizing culture.

In fact, the "live-for-the-moment" approach often recommended in our culture is a life given over to despair. Despair is the opposite of hope, understood as the theological virtue we need to carry our callings from to-day into tomorrow. St. Thomas Aquinas believed despair is the *deadliest* of the sins, not so much because it is the worst but because it is the most dangerous. Greed and ambition cause us to lose the realities of the present into the unrealities of our imagined or projected future. Despair, on the other hand, loses the future altogether and shrinks the present moment into itself. In a way, despair takes us out of time since by it we read the past as a flat desert that gives us nothing of importance worth remembering or continuing to develop in our lives—and so we can imagine no future in which what we once cared about comes to fruition. The deadly outcome is that we no longer think of ourselves as the story of a person living through time; the only thing left is a bundle of little desires, good only for this present moment.

Hope, by contrast, enables us to live today in the light of a future we have not fully seen or grasped, but trust in because we know it is God's future. It is a very hopeful thing that Christians believe there is such a virtue as hope. Screwtape is right that most of the virtues deal with the past or the present. Hope is an exception; it looks for what is to come. Yet genuine hope does not separate the future from the present; rather, it knits the two together in such a way that neither can be understood, or lived well, or its story told, without the other. Patience helps sustain hope, teaching us to watch and wait in the midst of our present sorrows for the coming kingdom, refusing to separate our difficult present from the promised future, for which we hope. Together, hope and patience hold us firmly in our time—the time we have been given. Called into this life as we were on such and such a day, we know we will be called beyond it on such and such another day, when we die. In between, hope and patience help us to keep track of the time, God's real time, while we live firmly within it.

Hope and Call

A call can open up a *new* future, one that is significantly different from our past: call brings change. When they were called by Jesus, the disciples left their nets on the shore and started a new kind of life. Or, Moses's life changed quite radically after he was called at the burning bush to participate in God's plan to rescue the Israelites. Hearing a call often marks a new beginning, setting out a different kind of future than we might have been expecting.

However, while this future can be exciting and different, it cannot be *any* future whatsoever. This is because when we are called we are already someone, someone with a definite past, the child of a certain set of parents, born in a particular time and place. A call does not reinvent us; it rather directs who we already are. And we are this person because others have given it to us. We owe these others a debt of gratitude—which is one reason why our calling cannot be to anything at all. Whatever we do in the future, we must always honor those who have graciously brought us into the present.

Screwtape wants Wormwood to coax his human charge to live in a future that is dreamy and unreal. We are easily tempted to this, mainly because today we are urged so often to "follow our dreams"—which usually means that we must leave our past behind. But this is not the sort of future call opens; whatever it is, call does not involve the abandonment of our past. We are never called to be someone other than the human being we were born as. This does not mean that we are *only* the daughter or son of the particular mother and father who gave us birth, as if we should aspire to be nothing more than that. We are created not just to "be," but to "become." Call opens a journey of discovery of who we are most fully created to be, a journey that includes our full growth into God's life. It is therefore not surprising that sometimes we are called to leave our families, as, for example, Abraham was called to do. "Go from your country and your kindred and your father's house to the land that I will show you," says God to Abram (Gen 12:1). Yet leaving is not dishonoring. Indeed, stories like Abraham's or Moses's, where call seems to disrupt family life, often circle back around, with family reentering on the other side of the initial call. So we hear about Lot, Abraham's nephew, whom he later protects, or of Miriam, Moses's sister, who, after caring for Moses as a baby, pops back into the story decades later to sing about God's rescue of the Israelites from the wrath of Pharaoh. Even Jesus, who warns that "I have come to set a man against his father, and a daughter against her mother" (Matt 10:35), in his last moments on the cross provides for the care of his mother Mary (John 19:27).

The point is this: if we are to be just, any call we answer cannot discard those to whom we are already bound by ties of gratitude, those to whom we owe our lives. Moreover, if we believe that we are God's creatures, born in the particular time and place we were born, we do not need to "overcome" this. Put another way, any call into some new life ahead of us, into the future, cannot destroy our past. If it did, it would deny who we are. As just noted, we are bound to specific people because of what they have given us as children. Further, if we have lived at all we have made promises to friends and family and community that we cannot forget. If we are honest, we know there are times in our lives when we have not kept those promises as well as we should have, and to abandon them entirely would undercut the long human work of constancy, faithfulness, and forgiveness. Our debts of gratitude and our promises hold us in a web of connection that any call must honor—even if honoring it well might be complicated.

Hope steers our lives into a future in which we can sustain the complicated work of stitching our past together with our future, without giving into the temptation to throw this work away, to be done with it all, once and for all. This temptation is to despair. In difficult times, despair gives up. "Striving" for the kingdom of God—which seems to be the way Jesus perceives our callings—implies difficulty; it is the long work of our lives. Jesus never offers us the chance to retire from it; it carries on till we die, and beyond. And this is why we need hope.

The vice of despair directly counters hope, not just for a short while, but altogether. Despair entirely gives up; as it does it severs all those connections just spoken of: what we owe to the families we came from, to friends or others to whom we have made promises, explicit or implicit, and to God who created us all. In this way it cuts us off from a meaningful past—and this will also inevitably remove from us any meaningful future. Like a tiny raft adrift on a vast ocean, by despair we become entirely unmoored. Hope will never allow this. By hope we are sustained as one person through time. In hope we are able to offer our whole lives to God and to others.

As noted, Thomas Aquinas calls despair the most dangerous vice. Why so? The two other theological virtues, faith and love, each have countering vices: unbelief opposes faith and hatred opposes love. Since love is the greatest virtue, one might think hatred is the greatest vice—and it is in one sense. But for Aquinas despair is more dangerous than hatred because of *how* it opposes hope. Hatred and unbelief face off against God directly; despair, however, "consists in a man ceasing to hope for a share of God's goodness."[4] Unbelief or hatred confront something: I don't believe in this, or I hate that. By contrast, despair has no clear target. It gives up on everything. Despair simply lets go; it detaches us and sets us adrift. Rather than opposing truth or love directly, it rather says: whatever the truth is, or whatever the story may be, there is nothing in it for me.

When I give into despair my actions lose their place in any bigger story—and so despair will make sure that I will never see my life as called. The very idea that we are called already includes the idea that some other

---

4. Aquinas, *Summa*, II–II, 30, 3. Quotations in this chapter are from the translation by the Fathers of the English Dominican Province.

bigger story is being told than the little story that is only about me. "Strive first for the kingdom of God and his righteousness," says Jesus, and the rest, the stuff about you, will surely follow. Put another way, if there really is a kingdom of God, and if we can really live our lives for it, and if this is what we are each in our unique and particular ways called to do, then the genuine pursuit of a call will always loosen despair's grip.

Indeed, the called life is by nature already hopeful. It gathers us up and sends us on a way that leads somewhere beyond us. So call opens us to hope; but it must also be sustained, and this is where the theological virtue of hope really does its work. For the called life is difficult, and hope is that virtue that enables us to push on through it. Hope is not about easy things; by definition it reaches out for what is "difficult but possible to attain."[5] Understood initially as a sort of summons from God to strike out a certain path, a call can awaken a hopeful feeling within us. But living the called life through time, especially when things become difficult, must be sustained by the clear-eyed virtue of hope that holds us in our time and place, at the same time that it connects it to what lies ahead—in the kingdom of God. As this hope becomes a habit, as we learn to live by it every day, we become fully equipped to follow our callings.

Tempted by despair, we can turn our attention from our callings, especially the difficult parts, and settle for a life aimed at littler things, small targets, such as making enough money to retire early. This is related to the vice of pusillanimity we discussed earlier: the failure to aspire to great things. But as it deepens, despair can become much more dangerous. For while the pusillanimous person aspires only to small things, he still aspires to *something*. When we lose hope entirely, we turn away from *any* future. As Aquinas notes, "when hope is given up, men rush headlong into sin, and are drawn away from good works."[6] This, indeed, is how despair loses the future: by living for one small, momentary pleasure to another. "Let us eat and drink, for tomorrow we die" (Isa 22:13).

As a theological virtue, hope directs us beyond the small things. It refuses to collapse time into little bits of personal experience, but rather stretches us out, reminding us that our final destination is in God. The name "theological virtues" means that these are the virtues that directly orient us to God. Christians say they must first learn to have faith in God, then to hope in God, and finally to love God. This sequence is actually important, especially as we think about how these virtues grow in us. For instance, Aquinas believes we can have a certain kind of faith in God without yet

---

5. Aquinas, *Summa*, II–II, 17, 1.
6. Aquinas, *Summa*, II–II, 30, 3.

having hope; or, put the other way, we can lose hope but still have a certain kind of faith. This is because faith involves the assent of the intellect ("I believe x is true"), whereas hope involves our own personal willing and desiring to connect to what I have faith in. By hope, we become personally invested and involved: what I believe is not just true for everyone, but even also for *me*! If faith tells a story we believe to be true, hope boosts us up into it. Put differently, we can imagine how some Christian might say: "I belong to a religion in which people are called by God," without reaching the next step: "I am called!"

This makes hope a very personal virtue, as well as a theological one—and this once again connects it with call. In faith we affirm certain eternal truths such as that there is a God who created us all. But if we are to hope in God, this must come directly into our lives emotionally. It does this only as it deals directly and personally with our stories. Hope not only affirms my life's story, the one that is unique to me as the particular person I was born as, but it locates this story within a larger story of the redemption of the world, by the God in whom my hope lies. This bigger story precedes my part in it, and it will carry on beyond the span of my days on the earth. The story of the kingdom of God does not begin when we join it, nor will it end when we die—if it did, how could it be hopeful? But if I am to really learn to hope, this bigger story must come specifically to include mine. By hope, in my daily living I participate in my own unique way in the story of God's redemptive work in the world, bringing it to fruition and wholeness. And this is exactly what it means for a Christian to follow her call.

The Work of Hope

Wendell Berry is a farmer who lives and works the land in Kentucky. He also writes novels and poetry. In one of his poems he tells a story of something he once did to his land. He wanted a pond to water his animals, and the place he thought best to put it was on a wooded hillside. He hired a man with a bulldozer to dig the hole. Soon the hole filled with water. Success! thought Berry. Yet the next winter was a wet one, the soil loosened on the uphill side, and part of the woods slipped into the pond. Berry was forced to come to the realization that he had wounded his place. As he concludes his account of what happened: "The trouble was the familiar one: too much power, too little knowledge. The fault was mine."[7]

Over his long life Berry has learned how important it is that his art—his poems, novels, even his farming—remain tied to his place, the home

7. Berry, *What Are People*, 5.

and farm he keeps near the Kentucky River. He has come to believe that genuine art cannot be a refuge or escape from reality, a reality in which we are responsible for what we do to ourselves and others who dwell with us. As with Berry's pond, even with the best intentions, we often cause damage. Art that remains tied to our place must struggle with this damage. It must remember and learn and ask for forgiveness. Just as "art" might sometimes be thought to offer us escape from such realities, so also we are tempted to think of "hope": as an escape to dreamy thoughts about the future, leaving present realities behind. But this is *not* genuine hope.

If it is real, hope must find a way to address the damage we do in our lives and work. In fact, the work of hope begins only with the truthful acceptance of the trouble we often cause. It must know and remember it, like a scar is the remembrance of a wound. Genuine hope cannot take flight; if we are to live and work in hope we cannot run from the damage. When we run from damage we have caused we pretend either that there is no damage or that we are not the same person who caused it. We may "hope" that everything will fix itself once we are gone—but this is false hope; it creates an unreal future that we put there only for our convenience. Moreover, it cuts us off from the work that real hope is there to help us do. Work done in hope, as Berry says, "accepts the clarification of pain, and concerns itself with healing. It cultivates the scar that is the course of time and nature over damage: landmark and mindmark that is the notion of a limit. To lose the scar of knowledge is to renew the wound."[8]

Berry has animals to feed and water; as a farmer, it is part of his calling to do this. Digging the pond made sense in one way; at the time he did it Berry thought he *should* do it. Our callings give us things to do, things to work on. Even with the best intentions, as we do this work, as we act on considered ideas about what is the right way to respond to our callings, we will sometimes fail. This is what happened to Wendell Berry: he failed. He used too much power, and operated with too little knowledge, specific knowledge of the contours of his own land. Over time nature will work to heal the wound Berry made with the bulldozer, and there is hope in this. But if he is himself to work in hope, he must remember what he did, taking it up into the future. The only way he can do this is to know, remember, learn, and abide with. Hope arises and guides our work not as we run off to some new exciting future, but rather as we remain, as we work with.

Berry goes on in another poem called "Healing" to contrast the work of hope with the "shoddy work of despair" and the "pointless work of pride." Both arise "out of the failure of hope or vision. Despair is the too-little

8. Berry, *What Are People*, 7.

of responsibility, as pride is the too-much."[9] As we have noticed, despair disconnects us from our responsibilities, and so also from those relationships that hold our lives in a meaningful web of connection and embrace. Despair's work is shoddy, for it takes no responsibility. It inevitably does damage, but it doesn't care if it does damage—it is not in it for the long haul. Indeed, it is so uninterested it is not even able to identify the damage it does. If trouble arises—someone notices the damage, or it multiplies and what it was at work on entirely collapses—despair abdicates, usually by rushing on to something new that it imagines will be easier and more fun. It moves quickly and thoughtlessly, skipping hastily along to the next thing, forgetting the previous one.

What Berry calls the work of pride is no better; in fact, the effects can be even more damaging. If despair is the sin that is most dangerous to the person who gets lost in it, pride is perhaps the most dangerous to the world surrounding the prideful one. If despair does as little as possible, and denies any link between what it does and the impact this has on the world, pride imagines it can handle anything, create anything. The "too-much" in its responsibility is that it supposes that it can fashion on its own an ever more perfect world. Invariably, pride takes on more than it can handle, and so damage will come, usually quickly, and on a grand scale.

A part of prideful work that is especially opposed to hope is the false security it is based on. "I will take care of it," says the prideful person. "Trust me, everything will be back to normal tomorrow." But in this attitude the prideful person overestimates his power and underestimates the damage he has caused, or will again cause in his prideful work. Pride never learns anything from the damage it causes; it either denies it, justifies it as necessary in such important work, or imagines that the next prideful thing it does will fix everything.

In St. Thomas's lexicon, hope is opposed not only by despair on the one side but by "presumption" on the other. As a theological virtue, hope reaches towards God, recognizing as it reaches that the work of the human journey is difficult and that we who journey are often naïve and consistently dragged back by sinful habits, despair and pride to name two. Hope acknowledges the need for help from God; as St Thomas says, it "leans on God."[10] Despair gives up on this altogether—or says to itself that even if there is a God, he is not interested in helping me. Presumption, on the other hand, imagines this is all so easy. "Of course God is there for me; we are clearly working for the same thing. Maybe I mess up a little here or there, but God forgives me, and

9. Berry, *What Are People*, 10.
10. Aquinas, *Summa*, II–II, 17, 1.

we carry on." This attitude is "presumptuous"; it is rooted in an "inordinate trust in God's mercy."[11]

Despair is highly dangerous, and we are all susceptible to its shrinking spirit. Yet for those who suppose they are called, the smugness of presumption is likely the more frequent foil. It can easily accompany a self-satisfied religiosity. In fact, the Christian church has not infrequently fallen prey to it, overconfident in its own righteousness, and certain that it knows just the right way to go. One can see it today, as Christians express certainty about how to right a political world gone wrong: "Just let our people in there to straighten things out! God is on our side, after all." As Josef Pieper notes, "[p]resumption has its source in a self-esteem that, while false, is somehow affirmed by the individual's own will: it consists in the will to achieve a certainty that is necessarily invalid . . . [T]his false esteem of oneself is a lack of humility, a denial of one's actual creatureliness and an unnatural claim to being like God . . . Saint Augustine says in his Commentary on the Psalms that only to the humble is it given to hope."[12]

In remembering his mistake with the pond, Wendell Berry comments: "a creature is not a creator, and cannot be. There is only one creation and we are its members." For us creatures, hopeful work consists in doing well what fits us as the specific, God-created human beings that we are. As Berry names this: "to keep oneself fully alive in the creation, to keep the creation fully alive in oneself, to see the creation anew, to welcome one's part in it anew."[13] To be called means to be given a part, a specific part suitable to the specific creature that one is, in God's creation—and to humbly accept this part. It will often be difficult to play out, but we do not do this on our own. For Berry, the hope that will carry us through these difficulties actually comes in a kind of membership; we are in the company of many who have worked before us and have passed on gifts to us, and in the company of many who work beside us. Indeed, the bad work of despair or pride or presumption leads to loneliness. The prideful worker thinks that in his superiority he can produce something entirely new, something so original no one else would ever imagine it. Similarly, the one who works in despair has no interest in learning and following a tradition, so he produces something that is merely novel, that can capture attention today, even if it will be old tomorrow. In pursuing "originality" or "novelty" such work pursues false images of the genuine creativity open to us as we work not as God but rather as God's human creatures. "Pursuing originality, the would-be creator works

11. Aquinas, *Summa*, II–II, 21, 4.

12. Pieper, *Faith, Hope, Love*, 127.

13. Berry, *What Are People*, 9.

alone. In loneliness one assumes a responsibility for oneself that one cannot fulfill . . . For despair there is no forgiveness, and for pride none. One cannot forgive oneself, and who in loneliness can forgive?"[14] Only if we live and work together in the company of others, those with us now and those who have gone before, can we learn where we have failed and for what we need forgiveness—and receive it from them.

The Letter to the Hebrews similarly counsels us to draw hope for the journey from those who have gone before us. After listing a variety of lead-ers from the Old Testament, including Abraham, Moses, and Rahab, the author adds: "Therefore, since we are surrounded by so great a cloud of witnesses, let us also lay aside every weight and the sin that clings so closely, and let us run with perseverance the race that is set before us, looking to Jesus the pioneer and perfecter of our faith, who for the sake of the joy that was set before him endured the cross" (Heb 12:1–2). Hope, which comes to us individually and personally, is gathered from the many who surround us and Jesus, who goes before us, passing through the difficultly of his call. We can lean on him. The many witnesses are not simply everybody, but rather those from whom we learn. In fact, for Berry hope can begin to dawn as we acknowledge our ignorance and look for teachers.

> In ignorance is hope. If we had known the difficulty, we could not have learned even so little. Rely on ignorance.
> It is ignorance the teachers will come to . . .
> The teachings of unsuspected teachers belong to the task, and are its hope.
> The love and the work of friends and lovers belong to the task, and are its health.
> Rest and rejoicing belong to the task and are its grace.
> Let tomorrow come tomorrow. Laugh. Sleep. Not by your will is the house carried through the night.[15]

This last line reminds us of St. Augustine's claim that "only to the hum-ble is it given to hope."[16] It is not by our power or will that tomorrow arrives as a new gift; in so many ways we are not masters but humble recipients of what is daily provided us. This is true all the more of our callings. We are not called to sustain the world, nor to fix all its problems. Rather, we are called on each new day that comes to us as gift to continue faithfully to do what we have been given to do. This is to be called and to work in hope. Genuine hope remembers both its gifts and its limits, rejoicing in both. Its work is

14. Berry, *What Are People*, 9–10.

15. Berry, *What Are People*, 13.

16. Augustine, *Expositions*, Ps 119.

not so much invention as preservation. As Berry says, the work of hope "preserves the given so that it remains a gift."[17] It keeps what it has received, cultivates it and learns from it, then passes it on once again as gift.

Christians have always understood themselves to be people on the way. In fact, this is how they first named themselves: the people of the Way (Acts 9:2). St. Thomas later adds the Latin phrase: a Christian is *homo viator*, a human traveler or wayfarer. Christians are on the way from the earthly city to the city of God. They travel by hope, which moves them onward when the path is difficult. They are called forward, passing even through death as they press on to their final end, their ultimate destination in God. Yet they are also not in a hurry. The callings they have in this life involve ministering to a world in need—a world that is, as God's created order, also filled with beauty and grace. It contains precious things, which we are also called to keep well and pass on to those who follow. As Berry reminds us, and Jesus before him, tomorrow will come tomorrow. Because we hope, we can live in this day, and sleep this night; we can rest and rejoice and learn and love, knowing that the work we are called to do is also not merely our work but God's, who is at work redeeming creation. By call, we are extended the extraordinary privilege of joining in.

Patience, the Protector of Hope

Hope requires that we keep on moving, working, responding to our callings, all the while without hurrying. Yet being in a hurry seems to be a defining characteristic of our time. Everything seems to be moving so quickly, as if we are all in a race to get somewhere, even if we can't say exactly where that is. We have little idea where we are headed, but we certainly are intent on getting there fast! Part of this comes with the quickness and efficiency of our instruments. We can plan a vacation on a Caribbean island, book a flight online, leave our car in EZ-Park by the airport, and, a few hours later, be basking on a wide, white-sand beach in the sub-tropical sun. It all worked—just as we expected. So let's do it again!

Of course, such speed requires money; it is a luxury of the rich. Rich people get used to having their expectations fulfilled, which makes them particularly susceptible to the vice of impatience. It is a spiritual disease of our time. We may not think of ourselves this way, but, in fact, most of us reading (and writing) this book are rich by global standards. So most of us are susceptible to the disease of impatience. Its antidote, of course, is patience. Patience is that virtue that protects against living a hurried, frenzied

17. Berry, *What Are People*, 10.

life; but even more, it protects us against inordinate sorrow, which, ironically enough, hurrying tries to drown out, always unsuccessfully. As a "protective" virtue, patience also preserves hope and so sustains us in our callings.

Impatience can be ironic, even comical. It tricks us into taking unnecessary risks, which can set us far behind wherever we were when we became impatient. Or it causes us to rant and rave furiously against whatever obstacle stands in our way, which usually turns out to be an utterly senseless thing to do, since it only angers others and delays us more. Have you ever stood in an airport behind someone who is shouting at an attendant because his travel plans have been disrupted? He looks positively silly.

Simply put, impatience is stupid. As the medieval philosophers would say, impatience causes us to relinquish "the good of reason," which patience protects. The fact that patience has this protective function makes it a "helping" virtue. Its role is not, like the theological virtues, to find the way to our destination or "our highest good." Rather, it keeps "a check on the things that lead man away from good."[18] So, it is subordinate to hope; on the other hand, we cannot hope rightly unless we are patient. Agreeing with Tertullian, Robert Wilkin notes how patience "becomes the key to the other virtues, including love, which can never be learned, he [Tertullian] says, 'without the exercise of patience.'"[19] Put differently, while patience does not by itself point us toward our destination in God, unless we learn it, this destination can never be reached.

We should not mistake patience for passivity. It does require waiting and watching, but this also prepares us for the right moment when we must move. The memorable scene in the garden of Gethsemane where Jesus will be betrayed into the hands of his killers begins with Jesus saying to his disciples, "'Sit here while I pray.' He took Peter, James, and John along with him, and he began to be deeply distressed and troubled. 'My soul is overwhelmed with sorrow to the point of death. even to death," he said to them. 'Stay here and keep watch.'" As the story continues, Jesus goes off by himself, falls on the ground and prays that the cup that he is about to drink be taken from him. After praying he returns to find his disciples sleeping. He wonders, could they not watch even for one hour? And then he adds: "Watch and pray so that you will not fall into temptation." This happens three times. Finally, after the third time, Jesus wakes his disciples with "The hour has come . . . Rise! Let us go!" (Mark 14:32–42 NIV). And with this begins the cascade of events that lead to Jesus' crucifixion.

18. Aquinas, *Summa*, II–II, 136, 3.

19. Wilken, *Spirit*, 284.

We should not be surprised to see Jesus weeping, sweating, dreading. Deep sorrow rolls over him, justified sorrow. The problem is not the sorrow itself, nor its depth. Sorrow is a passion, or sentiment, that rightly arises in us (and Christ) because the world contains very real evils; when we encounter these we are rightly sad, sometimes deeply so. But we cannot be overcome by them so that, when the right time comes, we are stuck in place, unable to rise and go.

As St. Augustine notes, sorrow can produce in us an "unequal mind," which will "abandon the goods whereby he may advance to better things."[20] In the garden Jesus bears his sorrow, not only by praying fervently, weeping before God, but also by keeping his eyes fixed on the work that lies before him, and, at the right time, proceeding on to do it. He does so by patience. As for the disciples, the text does not mention that they are sorrowful in this scene—perhaps they are avoiding it, as we often do—but their inordinate sleep and their failure to watch and pray indicate that they have been knocked off course, and have acquiesced to the dark fog that surrounds them. Without Christ pressing them into action, they might have slept through the crucifixion and, after that, the resurrection.

In our callings we must work to be whole in both our acting and waiting. For we will be tempted on both sides, either to rush ahead and get the thing done, or, struck by sorrow or disappointment or anger, to hole up, away from it all. "The good of reason" as the medieval theologians understood it, indicates no more nor less than a match between reality and our passions and actions. It is, in short, to have integrity. Patience is the keeper of this integrated correspondence of a human life and action with the world in which it is lived. As Josef Pieper put it, "[p]atience is not the tear-veiled mirror of a 'broken' life, but the radiant embodiment of ultimate integrity."[21] Such an integrated life knows sorrow; it must, if it is truthful. But it also knows great joy. Indeed, patience is that virtue that "accounts for the coincidence of joy and sorrow."[22] For Christians this accounting comes in a story that connects the agony of the cross and the joy of the resurrection, in a calendar that includes Good Friday and Ash Wednesday as well as Christmas and Easter. Consciously living within such a time helps integrate our lives through love. Loving rightly now, in this present world, requires both sorrowing and rejoicing. In a sense, patience is simply knowing what time it is, not by the clock, but by what is really transpiring, and what this calls for from us.

20. Augustine, *On Patience*, #2.
21. Pieper, *Four Cardinal Virtues*, 129.
22. Werpehowski, "Weeping," 178.

Kelly Johnson has pointed out how time became something different in the late middle ages. Earlier, bells in a given European town tolled from the monastery when the monks were called to prayer. "It is time to pray," they announced. Yet as commerce grew, merchants and businesspeople needed a more regular method to divide up the day so that money could be justly and efficiently exchanged for services rendered. This changed how the bells tolled. Previously, the "bells served and preserved a sense of time that was *for* the purposes of seeking holiness and fostering the life of the town. The new bells created ordinary, predictable divisions of everyday life, unrelated to any purpose. This in turn created a sense of time much more akin to our experience of the objective, relentless ticking backdrop of our days."[23]

A vestige of this older kind of time can be found in the game of baseball which, unlike so many other games, runs not by the clock but on its own time. An inning lasts as long as it takes to get six outs; a game as long it takes for one team to be ahead at an inning's end, after the nine minimum. Whether or not we are baseball fans, it is helpful to think of our "called lives" in relation to it—and the patience that we are required to have in order to play. We are called to live our lives like we play baseball: not by the clock, but by the rhythm of the game itself. Patience keeps time not by dividing it into regular, predictable units but by equipping us to know and describe what we are doing each day. For instance, in baseball when an infielder holds up two fingers, he or she is indicating to the rest of the players that there are two outs. The gesture reminds the rest of the players where they are in the progression of their task for that inning. It does not mean: only a few more minutes and we will be finished. Rather it is a sign that indicates and reminds all players how the next batter should be played. Two fingers up in baseball says, in effect, given what we have just come through, here is what we are doing now.

In this way patience "protects the good of reason" not by telling us to hold on for a few more minutes, or hours, or days, or years, for this will all be over soon, but rather by reminding us what we are doing right now in this particular time—which also relates this particular time to how far we have come, and to the end we are aiming at. Put differently, the "now" in our human journey, which is also the journey of our called life, does not relate to how much time has gone by on the clock but rather where we stand in the game. If we are patient, the question "what time is it?" will be answered not by a whistle that indicates "quitting time" but by a bell that says, "it is time to pray," or by a sign that reminds us that, given what we are working

23. Johnson, "Hurry," 12.

towards in this game (or in this life), this is what we must set ourselves to do just now.

Patience keeps us squarely in *this* time by resisting the forces by which sorrow overwhelms joy and stymies hope. If we are patient, we have the power to go forth even if our heart aches, as Jesus went forth in the garden to face his betrayer. Or we have the grace to wait for an errant child to return to the truth, as St. Monica was counseled to do as she worried that her son Augustine was lost among the Manicheans.[24] If we believe that Jesus was called to bear the cross, and that Monica was called to stick by Augustine until he finally came to faith at age thirty-three, then we can see all the more clearly how patience equips us to live out our various callings.

We noticed earlier how hope charts a course between despair and presumption. Despair arises from a sorrow or sloth that sucks the meaning from all our activities. Patience can help keep us from despair by teaching us how to bear our sorrows. Also, especially in our modern time, when we have become so accustomed to the "successes" of our fancy technologies, patience is a hedge against presumption. The stupidity impatience fosters is almost always presumptuous—the presumption, for instance, that "my time is my own," or, another one, that I am the "master of my fate, the captain of my soul."[25]

Any wise ship's captain knows he cannot master the sea; if he believes so it will master him. His life and the life of those on board depend on the movements of the winds and the currents. He must mark these well and work patiently with them. Indeed, the deceptions of impatience, the fog that it brings, can clear only as we recognize our dependent place in a world that we do not own or control. This is a necessary admission if we are to learn patience. As Wendell Berry early helped us see, the natural world, God's creation, is a place to begin to learn patience, even as our failed plans with bulldozers expose our lack of it. This is also the world in which we live out our callings in hope, staying with those we love while wounds heal and what is good is preserved and can grow. Patience assists hope in this work by keeping the time, telling us both when to wait and to act.

St. James illustrates patience this way: "Be patient, therefore, beloved, until the coming of the Lord. The farmer waits for the precious crop from the earth, being patient with it until it receives the early and the late rains. You also must be patient" (Jas 5:7–8). If we grow crops, or gather herbs, or admire flowers or birds, or even notice with joy the changing of the seasons, we will receive training in patience. We will recognize, as does any

24. Augustine, *Confessions* 3, 12.
25. Henley, "Invictus," 435.

good farmer, that we are not the makers of our own destiny, nor can we live without the sustaining help of others. The rhythms of the earth, which bring such variety in its different seasons, teach us to wait on another and receive her or his gifts with gladness. We can learn patience as we learn to live well as we are, creatures that come from and depend on the earth.

Christians affirm that the source for such patience lies beyond us. Sr. Helen Prejean, a tireless advocate for the abolition of the death penalty and spiritual advisor to many death-row inmates, ends her popular memoir *Dead Man Walking* with the story of Lloyd LeBlanc, construction worker, father and husband, whose life took a horrible turn, but who nonetheless moved on beautifully with the help of a God-given patience. Prejean calls LeBlanc the hero of her book.

One quiet night Lloyd and Eula LeBlanc's son David and his girlfriend Loretta Bourques were parked on a country road after a high school football game in St. Martinville, Louisiana. There they were accosted by Patrick Sonnier and his brother Eddie, who brutally murdered them. Patrick was convicted and sentenced to death. In the months prior to his execution by electrocution, Sr. Helen became his spiritual advisor. Her opposition to the death penalty grew as she visited him in prison, and she felt called to speak out on Sonnier's behalf.

On one occasion, after testifying at Sonnier's pardon board hearing, Sr. Helen was greeted by Lloyd LeBlanc, who said pointedly, "Sister, I'm a Catholic. How can you present Elmo Patrick Sonnier's side like this without ever coming to visit me and my wife? . . . How can you spend all your time worrying about Sonnier and not think that maybe we needed you too?"[26] LeBlanc's forthright comments made Sr. Helen aware of what, in her rush, she has failed fully to consider: the deep pain of the murdered victims' families. She later visited the LeBlancs and began to learn from Lloyd of a patience deep enough to emerge whole from the horror of such senseless killing. While Lloyd had spoken up against Sonnier at the hearing, he did so principally to support the Bourques. He did not want Sonnier dead; he simply wished for an apology. At his execution, Sonnier surprisingly offered this to Lloyd. Later, after the execution, Sr. Helen visited Lloyd again, and trust grew between them. He invited her to join him in a chapel in St. Martinsville for the adoration of the Blessed Sacrament where Lloyd prays each Friday from four to five a.m. There Sr. Helen learned how Lloyd prays.

> Lloyd has told me how he prays for "everyone, especially the poor and suffering." He prays for the "repose of the soul" of David and for his wife, Eula. He prays in thanksgiving for his

26. Prejean, *Dead Man Walking*, 64.

daughter Vickie, and her four healthy children. It is the grand-children who have brought Eula back to life—but it has taken a long, long time. For a year after David's murder, Lloyd had frequently taken her to visit David's grave. Unless he took her there, he once told me, "she couldn't carry on, she couldn't pick up the day, she couldn't live."

But this is not all Lloyd prays for.

> Lloyd LeBlanc prays for the Sonniers—for Pat and for Eddie and for Gladys, their mother. "What grief for this mother's heart," he once told me in a letter. Yes, for the Sonniers too, he prays. He knows I visit Eddie, and in his letters he sometimes includes a ten-dollar bill with the note: "For your prison ministry to God's children." And shortly before Gladys Sonnier's death in January 1991, Lloyd LeBlanc went to see her to comfort her.[27]

How can a man who has endured such sorrow pray and comfort like this? Prayer, Josef Pieper notes, "in its original form as a prayer of peti-tion, is nothing other than the voicing of hope. One who despairs cannot petition, because he assumes his petition will not be granted. One who is presumptuous petitions, indeed, but his petition is not genuine because he fully anticipates its fulfillment." As we live out our callings, difficult as they are, we must remain aware of the "never-ceasing necessity of a hope that is humble enough really to pray and, at the same time, magnanimous enough to wait cooperatively for the fulfillment of its prayer."[28] Who can imagine the difficulty of Lloyd LeBlanc's callings—mourning his son, supporting his girlfriend's family, conversing with their killer, forgiving him, upholding his grief-stricken wife—callings that came to him not at all by choice but rather from great tragedy and horror. Yet he teaches us how to pray in hope. And he also teaches us patience, voicing his deep sorrow, but seeing beyond his tears to the reality of a mother's grief for two sons, crushed by their own sins and by a system that responds by crushing them further. At the right time, he visits her, offering comfort. Lloyd's is the hope and patience of Christ.

Conclusion

We cannot expect that our callings will be easy. Among the most difficult of our tasks will be to look forward to, and pray for, what is not yet, and, in its light, to live and act in the present as it really is. As we have tried to

27. Prejean, *Dead Man Walking*, 242–43.
28. Pieper, *Four Cardinal Virtues*, 127.

display in this chapter, hope and patience, the "timeful virtues," equip us to do just this. God may be calling us, and we may hear his call, but we will not be able to see it through to its completion without help from these essential companions.

Yet as we live vocationally we can be confident that so to live is inherently hopeful. As a call comes to us, it invites us to respond, to work and to give our lives as an offering to others and to God. A call plants the seeds of hope. As we learn to live our callings, as we struggle and work and patiently wait, we can also grow in the virtue of hope that can sustain us till the end, till, united in charity, we share fully in God's trinitarian life.

Bibliography

Aquinas, Thomas. *Summa Theologiae*. Translated by Anthony Ross and P. G. Walsh. New York: McGraw-Hill, 1966.

———. *Summa Theologica*. Translated by Fathers of the English Dominican Province. Allen, TX: Christian Classics, 1981.

Augustine. *Confessions*. Translated by Sarah Ruden. New York: Modern Library, 2018.

———. *Expositions on the Psalms*. In *Nicene and Post-Nicene Fathers, First Series 8*, edited by Philip Schaff, translated by J. E. Tweed. Buffalo, NY: Christian Literature, 1888. Revised and edited by Kevin Knight. http://www.newadvent.org/fathers/1801.htm.

———. *On Patience*. In *Nicene and Post-Nicene Fathers, First Series 3*, edited by Philip Schaff, translated by J. E. Tweed. Buffalo, NY: Christian Literature Co., 1887. Revised and edited by Kevin Knight. http://www.newadvent.org/fathers/1315.htm.

Badcock, Gary D. *The Way of Life*. Grand Rapids: Eerdmans, 1998.

Berkson, Mark. "The Cultivation, Calling, and Loss of the Self: Confucian and Daoist Perspectives on Vocation." In *Calling in Today's World: Voices from Eight Faith Perspectives*, edited by Kathleen A. Cahalan and Douglas J. Schuurman, 161–201. Grand Rapids: Eerdmans, 2016.

Berry, Wendell. *The Gift of Good Land*. San Francisco: North Point, 1981.

———. *Hannah Coulter*. Berkeley, CA: Counterpoint, 2004.

———. *Jayber Crow*. Washington, DC: Counterpoint, 2000.

———. *What Are People For?* New York: North Point, 1990.

Bloom, Matt. "Middle Adulthood: The Joys and Paradoxes of Vocation." In *Calling All Years Good: Vocation throughout Life's Seasons*, edited by Kathleen A. Cahalan and Bonnie J. Miller-McLemore, 123–47. Grand Rapids: Eerdmans, 2017.

Bonhoeffer, Dietrich. "The Cost of Discipleship." In *Callings: Twenty Centuries of Christian Wisdom on Vocation*, edited by William C. Placher, 389–99. Grand Rapids: Eerdmans, 2005.

———. *Ethics*. Edited by Eberhard Bethge. New York: Collier, 1986.

Breward, Ian, ed. *The Works of William Perkins*. Abingdon: Courtneny, 1970.

Brooks, David. *The Second Mountain: The Quest for a Moral Life*. New York: Random House, 2019.

Brouwer, Douglas J. *What Am I Supposed to Do with My Life? Asking the Right Questions*. Grand Rapids: Eerdmans, 2006.

Buechner, Frederick. *The Sacred Journey*. New York: HarperCollins, 1982.

————. *Wishful Thinking: A Theological ABC*. New York: Harper and Row, 1973.

Cahalan, Kathleen A. "Called to Follow: Vocation in the Catholic Tradition." In *Calling in Today's World: Voices from Eight Faith Perspectives*, edited by Kathleen A. Cahalan and Douglas J. Schuurman, 26–51. Grand Rapids: Eerdmans, 2016.

————. "Callings Over a Lifetime: In Relationship, through the Body, over Time, and for Community." In *Calling All Years Good: Christian Vocation throughout Life's Seasons*, edited by Kathleen A. Cahalan and Bonnie J. Miller-McLemore, 12–32. Grand Rapids: Eerdmans, 2017.

————. "Finding Life's Purposes in God's Purposes." In *Calling All Years Good: Christian Vocation throughout Life's Seasons*, edited by Kathleen A. Cahalan and Bonnie J. Miller-McLemore, 1–11. Grand Rapids: Eerdmans, 2017.

————. "Late Adulthood: Seeking Vocation Once Again." In *Calling All Years Good: Christian Vocation throughout Life's Seasons*, edited by Kathleen A. Cahalan and Bonnie J. Miller-McLemore, 150–70. Grand Rapids: Eerdmans, 2017.

————. *The Stories We Live: Finding God's Calling All Around Us*. Grand Rapids: Eerdmans, 2017.

Canons of Hippolytus. In *Ante-Nicene Fathers 7*. Edited by Alexander Roberts, James Donaldson, and A. Cleveland Coxe, translated by James Donaldson. Buffalo, NY: Christian Literature, 1886. Revised and edited by Kevin Knight. http://www.newadvent.org/fathers/07158.htm.

Cavanaugh, William T. "Actually, You *Can't* Be Anything You Want (And It's a Good Thing, Too)." In *At This Time and In This Place: Vocation and Higher Education*, edited by David S. Cunningham, 25–46. Oxford: Oxford University Press, 2016.

Clapper, Gregory S. *Living Your Heart's Desire: God's Call and Your Vocation*. Nashville: Upper Room, 2005.

Conyers, A. J. *The Listening Heart: Vocation and the Crisis of Modern Culture*. Dallas: Spence, 2006.

Cunningham, David S. "Hearing and Being Heard: Rethinking Vocation in the Multi-Faith Academy." In *Hearing Vocation Differently: Meaning, Purpose, and Identity in the Multi-Faith Academy*, edited by David S. Cunningham, 1–17. Oxford: Oxford University Press, 2019.

————. "'Who's There?' The Dramatic Role of the 'Caller' in Vocational Discernment." In *At This Time and In This Place: Vocation and Higher Education*, edited by David S. Cunningham, 143–64. Oxford: Oxford University Press, 2016.

Deane-Drummond, Celia. "The Art and Science of Vocation: Wisdom and Conscience as Companions on a Way." In *Vocation Across the Academy: A New Vocabulary for Higher Education*, edited by David S. Cunningham, 156–77. Oxford: Oxford University Press, 2017.

Eilberg, Amy. "*Hineini* (Here I Am): Jewish Reflections on Calling." In *Calling in Today's World: Voices from Eight Faith Perspectives*, edited by Kathleen A. Cahalan and Douglas J. Schuurman, 1–25. Grand Rapids: Eerdmans, 2016.

Epplin, Luke. "You Can Do *Anything*: Must Every Kids' Movie Reinforce the Cult of Self-Esteem?" *Atlantic*, August 13, 2013. https://www.theatlantic.com/entertainment/archive/2013/08/you-can-do-em-anything-em-must-every-kids-movie-reinforce-the-cult-of-self-esteem/278596/.

Farley, Margaret A. *Personal Commitments: Beginning, Keeping, Changing*. San Francisco: Harper & Row, 1986.

Farnham, Suzanne G., et al. *Listening Hearts: Discerning Call in Community*. New York: Morehouse, 1991.

Flannery, Austin, ed. "Declaration on the Relation of the Church to Non-Christian Religions (Nostra Aetate)." In *Vatican Council II: The Basic Sixteen Documents*, 569–74. Northport, NY: Costello, 1996.

———. "Dogmatic Constitution on the Church (Lumen Gentium)." In *Vatican Council II: The Basic Sixteen Documents*, 1–95. Northport, NY: Costello, 1996.

Fong, Bobby. "Theological Exploration of Vocation at Butler University: A Meditation on Calling." Address given at Butler University Center for Faith and Vocation, Indianapolis, April 7, 2011.

Ford, David F. *The Shape of Living: Spiritual Directions for Everyday Life*. Grand Rapids: Baker, 1997.

Fortin, Jack. *The Centered Life: Awakened, Called, Set Free, Nurtured*. Minneapolis: Augsburg Fortress, 2006.

Francis, Pope. "Free to Choose Good." In *The Church of Mercy: A Vision for the Church*, 121–23. Chicago: Loyola, 2014.

———. *On Care for Our Common Home: Laudato Si'*. Washington, DC: United States Conference of Catholic Bishops, 2015.

———. *Rejoice and Be Glad: Gaudete et Exsultate*. Washington, DC: United States Conference of Catholic Bishops, 2018.

Fuller, Millard. "A Life Endured." Speech given on October 23, 2007. https://www.youtube.com/watch?v=jq8_Y4fP6pI

Furey, Robert J. *Called By Name: Discovering Your Unique Purpose in Life*. New York: Crossroad, 2000.

———. *The Road to You: Callings and How to Fulfill Them*. New York: Alba House, 1997.

Gandhi, M. K. *Non-Violent Resistance (Satyagraha)*. Mineola, NY: Dover, 2001.

Garber, Steven. *Visions of Vocation: Common Grace for the Common Good*. Downers Grove, IL: InterVarsity, 2014.

Grisez, Germain, and Russell Shaw. *Personal Vocation: God Calls Everyone By Name*. Huntington, IN: Our Sunday Visitor, 2003.

Guinness, Os. *The Call: Finding and Fulfilling the Central Purpose of Your Life*. Nashville: Word, 1998.

Hahnenberg, Edward P. *Awakening Vocation: A Theology of Christian Call*. Collegeville, MN: Liturgical, 2010.

Hardy, Lee. "Investing Ourselves in the Divine Economy." *Christian Reflection* (2004) 29–35.

Harman, Paul F. "Vocation and the *Spiritual Exercises* of St. Ignatius of Loyola." In *Revisiting the Idea of Vocation: Theological Explorations*, edited by John C. Haughey, 97–118. Washington, DC: Catholic University of America Press, 2004.

Haughey, John C. *Should Anyone Say Forever? On Making, Keeping, and Breaking Commitments*. Chicago: Loyola University Press, 1975.

———. "The Three Conversions Embedded in Personal Calling." In *Revisiting the Idea of Vocation: Theological Explorations*, edited by John C. Haughey, 1–23. Washington, DC: Catholic University of America Press, 2004.

Henley, William Ernest. "Invictus." In *Leading Lives That Matter: What We Should Do and Who We Should Be*, edited by Mark R. Schwehn and Dorothy C. Bass, 434–35. Grand Rapids: Eerdmans, 2006.

Henry, Douglas V. "Vocation and Story: Narrating Self and World." In *At This Time and In This Place: Vocation and Higher Education*, edited by David S. Cunningham, 165–88. Oxford: Oxford University Press, 2016.

Himes, Michael J. *Doing the Truth in Love: Conversations about God, Relationships, and Service*. Mahwah, NJ: Paulist, 1995.

Hollenbach, David. *Claims in Conflict: Retrieving and Renewing the Catholic Human Rights Tradition*. New York: Paulist, 1979.

Infancy Gospel of Thomas. In *Ante-Nicene Fathers 8*, edited by Alexander Roberts, James Donaldson, and A. Cleveland Coxe, translated by Alexander Walker. Buffalo, NY: Christian Literature, 1886. Revised and edited by Kevin Knight. http://www.newadvent.org/fathers/0846.htm.

Ishaq, Ibn. *Sirat Rasoul Allah* (The Life of Muhammad). Translated by A. Guillaume. New York, Oxford University Press, 1955. http://www.archive.olrg/details/SiratlifeOfMuhammadBy-ibnIshaq.

John XXIII, Pope. "Christianity and Social Progress (Mater et Magistra). In *Catholic Social Thought: The Documentary Heritage*, edited by David J. O'Brien and Thomas A. Shannon, 84–128. Maryknoll, NY: Orbis, 1992.

John Paul II, Pope. "Sollicitudo Rei Socialis: On Social Concern." In *Catholic Social Thought: The Documentary Heritage*, edited by David J. O'Brien and Thomas A. Shannon, 393–436. Maryknoll, NY: Orbis, 1992.

Johnson, Kelly S. "Hurry and the Willingness to Be Creatures." *Christian Reflection* (2016) 11–18.

Kalanithi, Lucy. "Epilogue." In *When Breath Becomes Air*, by Paul Kalanithi, 201–25. New York: Random House, 2016.

Kalanithi, Paul. *When Breath Becomes Air*. New York: Random House, 2016.

Kelsay, John. "Divine Summons, Human Submission: The Idea of Calling in Islam." In *Calling in Today's World: Voices from Eight Faith Perspectives*, edited by Kathleen A. Cahalan and Douglas J. Schuurman, 82–106. Grand Rapids: Eerdmans, 2016.

King, Martin Luther, Jr. *I Have a Dream: Writings and Speeches that Changed the World*. Edited by James M. Washington. New York: HarperSanFrancisco, 1992.

Kleinhans, Kathryn A. "Places of Responsibility: Educating for Multiple Callings in Multiple Communities." In *At This Time and In This Place: Vocation and Higher Education*, edited by David S. Cunningham, 99–121. Oxford: Oxford University Press, 2016.

LaReau, Renee M. *Getting a Life: How to Find Your True Vocation*. Maryknoll, NY: Orbis, 2003.

Laurel, Sr. Jane Dominic. "Medicine as a Sacred Vocation." *Baylor University Medical Proceedings* 31 (2018) 126–31. https://www.ncbi.nlm.nih.gov/pmc/articles/PMC5903528/.

Levoy, Gregg. *Callings: Finding and Following an Authentic Life*. New York: Three Rivers, 1997.

Lewis, C. S. *Mere Christianity*. New York: HarperSanFrancisco, 2001.

———. *The Screwtape Letters*. London: Centenary, 2016.

MacIntyre, Alasdair. *Three Rival Versions of Moral Inquiry: Encyclopaedia, Genealogy, and Tradition*. Notre Dame, IN: University of Notre Dame Press, 1990.

Mahn, Jason A. "The Conflicts in Our Callings: The Anguish (and Joy) of Willing Several Things." In *Vocation Across the Academy: A New Vocabulary for Higher*

Education, edited by David S. Cunningham, 44–66. Oxford: Oxford University Press, 2017.

Marcel, Gabriel. *Creative Fidelity*. Translated by Robert Rosthal. New York: Crossroad, 1982.

Martin, James. *Becoming Who You Are: Insights on the True Self from Thomas Merton and Other Saints*. Mahwah, NJ: Paulist, 2006.

McIntosh, Mark A. "Trying to Follow a Call: Vocation and Discernment in Bunyan's *Pilgrim's Progress*." In *Revisiting the Idea of Vocation: Theological Explorations*, edited by John C. Haughey, 119–40. Washington, DC: Catholic University of America Press, 2004.

Mercer, Joyce Ann. "Older Adulthood: Vocation at Life's End." In *Calling All Years Good: Christian Vocation throughout Life's Seasons*, edited by Kathleen A. Cahalan and Bonnie J. Miller-McLemore, 174–97. Grand Rapids: Eerdmans, 2017.

Miller, Arthur. *After the Fall*. New York: Bantam, 1964.

Miller, Keith Graber. *Living Faith: Embracing God's Callings*. Telford: Cascadia, 2012.

Miller-McLemore, Bonnie J. "Childhood: The (Often Hidden yet Lively) Vocational Life of Children." In *Calling All Years Good: Christian Vocation throughout Life's Seasons*, edited by Kathleen A. Cahalan and Bonnie J. Miller-McLemore, 38–62. Grand Rapids: Eerdmans, 2017.

Mohrmann, Margaret E. "Vocation Is Responsibility: Broader Scope, Deeper Discernment." In *Vocation Across the Academy: A New Vocabulary for Higher Education*, edited by David S. Cunningham, 21–43. Oxford: Oxford University Press, 2017.

Murdoch, Iris. "On 'God' and 'Good.'" In *The Sovereignty of Good*, 46–76. London: Routledge & Paul, 1970.

Neafsey, John P. "Psychological Dimensions of the Discernment of Vocation." In *Revisiting the Idea of Vocation: Theological Explorations*, edited by John C. Haughey, 163–95. Washington, DC: Catholic University of America Press, 2004.

———. *A Sacred Voice Is Calling: Personal Vocation and Social Conscience*. Maryknoll, NY: Orbis, 2006.

Newman, Elizabeth. "Called through Relationship." *Christian Reflection* (2004) 20–28.

Newman, John Henry. "Divine Calls." In *Callings: Twenty Centuries of Christian Wisdom on Vocation*, edited by William C. Placher, 343–49. Grand Rapids: Eerdmans, 2005.

Niebuhr, H. Richard. *The Responsible Self: An Essay in Christian Moral Philosophy*. San Francisco: Harper & Row, 1963.

Organ, Jerome M. "Of Doing and Being: Broadening Our Understanding of Vocation." In *Vocation Across the Academy: A New Vocabulary for Higher Education*, edited by David S. Cunningham, 225–43. Oxford: Oxford University Press, 2017.

Palmer, Parker J. *Let Your Life Speak: Listening for the Voice of Vocation*. San Francisco: Josey-Bass, 2000.

Percy, Walker. *Love in the Ruins*. New York: Avon, 1971.

Pieper, Josef. *Faith, Hope, Love*. Translated by Richard and Clara Winston et al. San Francisco: Fortress, 1997.

———. *The Four Cardinal Virtues*. Translated by Richard and Clara Winston et al. Notre Dame, IN: University of Notre Dame Press, 1966.

Pinches, Charles. "Stories of Call: From Dramatic Phenomena to Changed Lives." In *At This Time and In This Place*, edited by David S. Cunningham, 122–42. Oxford: Oxford University Press, 2016.

Placher, William C., ed. *Callings: Twenty Centuries of Christian Wisdom on Vocation*. Grand Rapids: Eerdmans, 2005.

Pohl, Christine D. *Living into Community: Cultivating Practices that Sustain Us*. Grand Rapids: Eerdmans, 2012.

Prejean, Helen. *Dead Man Walking*. New York: Vintage, 1994.

Radcliffe, Timothy. *What is the Point of Being a Christian?* New York: Burns & Oates, 2005.

Rambachan, Anantanand. "Worship, the Public Good, and Self-Fulfillment: Hindu Perspectives on Calling." In *Calling in Today's World: Voices from Eight Faith Perspectives*, edited by Kathleen A. Cahalan and Douglas J. Schuurman, 107–32. Grand Rapids: Eerdmans, 2016.

Ray, Darby Kathleen. "Self, World, and the Space Between: Community Engagement as Vocational Discernment." In *At This Time and In This Place: Vocation and Higher Education*, edited by David S. Cunningham, 301–20. Oxford: Oxford University Press, 2017.

————. *Working*. Minneapolis: Fortress, 2011.

Riswold, Caryn D. "Vocational Discernment: A Pedagogy of Humanization." In *At This Time and In This Place: Vocation and Higher Education*, edited by David S. Cunningham, 72–95. Oxford: Oxford University Press, 2016.

Roberts, Robert C. *Spiritual Emotions: A Psychology of Christian Virtues*. Grand Rapids: Eerdmans, 2007.

Ryan, Robin. "The Foundations and Dynamics of Prayer." In *Catholics on Call: Discerning a Life of Service in the Church*, edited by Robin Ryan, 44–61. Collegeville, MN: Liturgical, 2010.

Schell, Hannah. "Commitment and Community: The Virtue of Loyalty and Vocational Discernment." In *At This Time and In This Place: Vocation and Higher Education*, edited by David S. Cunningham, 235–54. Oxford: Oxford University Press, 2016.

Schultze, Quentin. *Here I Am: Now What on Earth Should I Be Doing?* Grand Rapids: Baker, 2005.

Schuster, John P. *Answering Your Call: A Guide for Living to Deepest Purpose*. San Francisco: Berrett-Koehler, 2003.

Schuurman, Douglas J. "To Follow Christ, to Live in the World: Calling in a Protestant Key." In *Calling in Today's World: Voices from Eight Faith Perspectives*, edited by Kathleen A. Cahalan and Douglas J. Schuurman, 52–81. Grand Rapids: Eerdmans, 2016.

————. *Vocation: Discerning Our Callings in Life*. Grand Rapids: Eerdmans, 2004.

Schwehn, Mark R., and Dorothy C. Bass, eds. *Leading Lives that Matter: What We Should Do and Who We Should Be*. Grand Rapids: Eerdmans, 2006.

"Sheikh Yusuf Al-Qaradawi Condemns Attacks Against Civilians: Forbidden in Islam." September 13, 2001. https://archive.islamonline.net/?p=17698.

Smith, Gordon T. *Courage & Calling: Embracing Your God-Given Potential*. Downers Grove, IL: InterVarsity, 1999.

Taylor, Barbara Brown. *An Altar in the World: A Geography of Faith*. New York: HarperCollins, 2009.

Tolstoy, Leo. *The Death of Ivan Ilyich*. Translated by Lynn Soltaroff. New York: Bantam, 2004.

Turpin, Katherine. "Adolescence: Vocation in Performance, Passion, and Possibility." In *Calling All Years Good: Christian Vocation throughout Life's Seasons*, edited by Kathleen A. Cahalan and Bonnie J. Miller-McLemore, 67–91. Grand Rapids: Eerdmans, 2017.

————. "Younger Adulthood: Exploring Callings in the Midst of Uncertainty." In *Calling All Years Good: Christian Vocation throughout Life's Seasons*, edited by Kathleen A. Cahalan and Bonnie J. Miller-McLemore, 95–118. Grand Rapids: Eerdmans, 2017.

Wadell, Paul J. "The Call Goes On: Discipleship and Aging." *Christian Century* 128 (2011) 11–12.

————. *Happiness and the Christian Moral Life: An Introduction to the Christian Moral Life*. Lanham, MD: Rowman & Littlefield, 2016.

————. "An Itinerary of Hope: Called to a Magnanimous Way of Life." In *At This Time and In This Place: Vocation and Higher Education*, edited by David S. Cunningham, 193–215. Oxford: Oxford University Press, 2016.

Wells, Samuel. *God's Companions: Reimagining Christian Ethics*. Malden, MA: Blackwell, 2006.

Werpehowski, William. "Weeping at the Death of Dido: Sorrow, Virtue, and Augustine's Confessions." *Journal of Religious Ethics* 19 (1991) 175–91

Wilken, Robert. *The Spirit of Early Christian Thought: Seeking the Face of God*. New Haven, CT: Yale University Press.

Williams, Rowan. "Vocation (1)." In *A Ray of Darkness*, 147–53. Cambridge, MA: Cowley, 1995.

Index

Abraham (Abram), 4, 66–67, 205
absolute good, achieving, 192
"accidents of life," 137, 151
achievement, with no effort, 128
adharma, as the oppo-
    site of *dharma*, 58
adolescence, 91–94
adulthood. *See* early adulthood; late
    and older adulthood; middle
    adulthood; young adulthood
adventures, callings as, 87
African Christians, energy of, 203
After the Fall (Miller), 177
age, limiting ability to respond
    to callings, 33
ahimsa (non-violence), 138
alienation, between partners of
    a marriage, 191
An Altar in the World
    (Taylor), 127, 172
alternatives, 22, 116
ambition, 199, 204
American dream, pursuit of, 80
Ananias, 81
Andrew, 51, 52
angels, saying "do not
    be afraid," 74–75
anxiety, 102, 129, 199, 200
apostle, every Christian as, 51
"apostolate of the laity," 51
Aquinas, Thomas
    on courage, 195
    on despair, 204, 206

on faith in God
    without hope, 207–8
on fear, 75
on happiness, 17
on hope, 207
on magnanimity, 30
on perseverance, 197
on pusillanimity, 32
Aristotle, 17
arrhythmia, Lucy identifying, 145–46
Ash Wednesday, 201
atheism, 201
attention. *See also* paying attention
    benefits of, 164
    changing us for the good, 158
    cultivating the virtue of, 162–64
    enabling self-transcendence, 158
    virtue of, 157–64
    to where we are on our voca-
        tional journey, 104–6
attentiveness, 157–64, 166, 170. *See
    also* paying attention
St. Augustine
    on being humble, 211, 212
    Monica called to stick by, 217
    Paul Kalanithi called by, 144
    on sorrow producing an "un-
        equal mind," 215
    on those who died unbaptized, 41
authentic "being," 55
authentic self, 21–22, 53
"avarice," never satisfied, 199
Awakening Vocation (Hahnenberg), 55

bad habits, addressing, 156
Badcock, Gary D., 45, 109
baptism
    becoming a member of the priest-
        hood of Christ through, 50
    change in the practice of, 41
    consecrating one as a priest, 42
    as the foundational calling, 38
    responding to God's offer of salva-
        tion in Christ, 37
baptismal calling, faithfulness to, 114
Barth, Karl, 48–49, 51, 169–70
baseball, running on its own time, 216
becoming ourselves, by moving out-
    side ourselves, 20
Becoming Who You Are (Martin), 19
being
    preceding doing, 52
    who we are meant to be, 14–17
being anything we want to be, as
    not possible, 128
"Being anything you want," freeing us
    from constraints, 129
being "in Christ," by vir-
    tue of baptism, 42
being quiet, as a discipline, 119
bells, tracking time, 216
benevolent human being, as ultimate
    for Confucians, 59
Berkson, Mark, 59–60
Berry, Wendell
    on being members of creation, 211
    on hope, 209, 212
    on the natural world, 217
    on not knowing our places, 117–18
    on remaining tied to place, 208–9
betrayals, 183, 189
Bible, pattern of call in, 62
biblical calls, 67, 78, 83
biblical tradition, of call, 63–68
Bloom, Matt, 95
blueprint
    call as, 134
    for our lives, 109
blueprint model, of callings, 110–11
Bonhoeffer, Dietrich, 47, 48, 132, 133
Bourques, Loretta, 218
breakdowns in love and justice, 26

broken promises, 177–78
brokenness of our world, 26
Brooks, David, 136–37
Bruges, Jean-Louis, 166
Buechner, Frederick, 23, 124
burdens, callings as, 155–56
busyness, 162

Cady (Paul Kalanithi's daughter), 150
Cahalan, Kathleen A.,
    97, 110, 113, 116
call(s)
    always wanting some-
        thing from us, 134
    biblical tradition of, 63–68
    bringing profound
        change, 65, 78, 132
    cannot destroy our past, 205
    choosing as a way of handing our-
        selves over, 131
    coming from Jesus, 132
    to conversion coming from "real-
        ity itself," 53–54
    to discipleship, 51–52
    of God, 49, 56, 73
    importance of the notion of, 83
    of Isaiah as exceedingly difficult, 78
    of justice, 26
    limits and, 138–43
    loosening despair's grip, 207
    to medicine, 151
    as not the same as a choice, 131
    opening up a new future, 204–5
    planting seeds of hope, 220
    as "reflexive," 132
    refusing, 133
    to responsibility, 93
    rich young man refusing, 135
    sending us off into some
        new future, 199
    starting things, 139
    stories of, 7, 62–83
    struggle and, 131–38
    understanding by
        committing to, 100
    to work for a more just and
        humane world, 55
call stories, 7, 67, 75, 83

called life
  bringing forth offerings of joy, 203
  Christians having
    no corner on, 139
  demanding great work, ef-
    fort, striving, 202
  finding ourselves through, 24
  as hopeful, 207
  invitation to, 13–35
  joy of, 14
  learning from anyone
    the meaning of, 4
  living, 128–51, 216
  Moses not wanting to live, 71
  not an easy life, 143, 151
  setting limits on us, 143
  struggle accompanying, 135
calling(s). *See also* vocation(s)
  accepting, 178
  already committed to, priority over
    later callings, 33
  applying to everyone in
    the church, 38–39
  as attentive and responsive to the
    needs of our neighbors, 43
  being released from, 190–92
  as blueprints, 109–10
  challenges in living, 33–34
  in circumstances that are
    less than ideal, 93
  coming from outside us, 125
  coming to an end with death, 99
  comprehending only by liv-
    ing into them, 100
  contributing to Jesus' cen-
    tral mission, 28
  contributing to something larger
    than ourselves, 60–61
  contributing to the narrative
    of our lives, 2
  dangers of no limits for, 143
  demanding commitment, 120
  determined by our gifts, 46
  difficulty of Lloyd LeBlanc's, 219
  discerning our, 108–27
  discovered over time through
    trial and error, 92
  discovering worthy within reach, 28

  distinguishing among various as we
    discern, 112–13
  doing justice to all, 33
  drawing us out of ourselves, 24
  as dynamic and evolv-
    ing, 99–101, 110
  embracing, 1–2
  emerging, 49, 103, 115
  essential aspects for ear-
    ly Christians, 38
  experimenting with several
    possibilities, 115
  extending far beyond our jobs
    or our careers, 2
  feeling the tug of a variety of, 25
  fidelity safeguarding, 181–87
  finding, 1
  for the first Christians, 37
  as the focus of our lives, 25
  full meaning of always
    ahead of us, 178–79
  giving "a vision of something
    to live for," 23
  growing from a promise
    made to others, 177
  growing from yearnings and
    attractions, 120
  having a beginning, a mid-
    dle, and an end, 3
  for Hindus, 58
  identifying and telling the full
    significance of, 81
  imagining for three days, 126
  implying movement to-
    wards something, 95
  importance of different, 177
  increasing goodness, 2
  intertwined with and dependent
    upon the callings of others, 7
  as journeys, 3, 87, 101
  language of belonging be-
    yond childhood, 89
  language pertinent at any
    stage of life, 88
  left behind as new
    callings emerge, 88
  living on generosity, 169
  living our, 174

called life *(continued)*
    loving our neighbors, 43
    making demands on us, 125
    making possible for all, 193
    ministering to a world in need, 213
    as much harder than imagined, 169
    multiple in middle adulthood, 94
    not being able to pursue every, 33
    not taking care of themselves, 175
    not ultimately about us as
        individuals, 124
    opening us to risks
        and surprises, 32
    opposition to, 195
    ordering and prioritizing, 182
    in particular times and places, 3
    process for discerning, 115–27
    providing a plot or story line
        for our lives, 29
    relinquishing some, 34
    requiring self-denial and
        self-sacrifice, 44
    requiring virtues to flourish, 157
    responding to a more urgent, 88
    revealing our most im-
        portant goals, 3–4
    saving us from ourselves, 2
    secondary to the call of
        discipleship, 38
    as synonymous with one's career
        or profession, 47
    tensions among, 34
    threats to, 179
    thrusting themselves
        with urgency, 103
    trying to discern, 161–62
    turning away from, 88, 180
    understanding retrospectively, 100
    unexpected in late adulthood, 97
    uniqueness of, 111
    as worthy of our lives, 25–27
Calling All Years Good, 88
Calvin, John, 45–47
"capaciousness" of call, 138
capacity, to follow a call, 78
capitalist culture, 24–25
capitalist economy, 48
care, receiving as a calling, 99

career, 3, 20, 70
Catholic Church, understanding
    of vocation, 50
Catholics, calling to the religious life
    or priesthood, 42
Cavanaugh, William, 66, 128, 130
celibacy and virginity, 41
certainty, in vocational
    discernment, 115
challenges, in living callings, 33–34
changing for the better, as al-
    ways possible, 168
"channels," of our lives be-
    coming jammed, 161
character, 59, 156
characters, in vocational narratives, 4
chemotherapy, on Paul Kalanithi, 150
childhood, 89–91, 93
children of God, 16, 163–64
choice, 95–96, 129, 130–31
"choosing whatever we want," as the
    go-to good, 148
Christ
    call to imitate, 98
    calling us all through our life, 136
    following, 114, 141
    ministry of to his disciples, 4
    priesthood of, 42, 50
    putting on, 38
    salvation in, 37
Christian life, as the primary voca-
    tion for Barth, 48
Christian theology of voca-
    tion, 14, 28, 29, 35
Christians. *See also* early Christians
    called by God, 60
    called continually, 13
    calling giving distinctive identity
        and purpose to, 36
    classes of, 40
    equality and unity among all, 50
    growing in holiness, 43, 50
    having no monopoly on
        vocation, 4, 60
    open engagement with others, 4
    open to narratives of others, 5
    pursuing holiness in monasteries
        and convents, 41

putting on Christ, 38
righting a political world
    gone wrong, 211
rulers and decision-makers after
    legalization, 39
church
    accommodating the needs of the
        Roman empire, 39
    helping me be the person God is
        calling me to be, 114
    members helping one another, 38
    monasticism brought a re-
        newed health to, 40
    people having different roles in, 42
classes, of Christians, 40
cleansing, received by Isaiah, 77
college experience, 105
college students, gaining a sense of
    who they are, 117
commandments, of God calling
    Jewish people, 57
commitment(s)
    as an appeal to God to help us, 187
    being faithful to, 178
    callings demanding, 120
    to causes, 21, 22
    closing off options and limiting
        possibilities, 22
    discovering who we are
        called to be, 21
    emerging as callings, 94
    fidelity reminding us of, 182
    leading to new possibilities, 100
    limiting self-process, 22
    no longer binding, 192
    not having to be permanent, 22
    taking risks in, 22–23
    weakening to callings, 180
committed lives, becoming
    observers of, 180
common good, 26, 46, 193–94
"common vocation," caring for
    flourishing, 55
communion, as the center of a
    grateful life, 171
community, human beings
    created for, 26
community engagement

of adolescents, 91
    growing in the virtue of atten-
        tion through, 164
community organizing, left
    Parker Palmer burned out
    and exhausted, 15
companions, on our vocation-
    al journeys, 107
"companions in discern-
    ment," need for, 122
comparing ourselves to others, as a
    waste of time, 18
compassion, adolescents begin-
    ning to learn, 91
competitiveness, society
    celebrating, 165
conformity, society encouraging, 19
confrontation, Saul's call as, 79
Confucianism, 59
"consolation," feelings of, 127
constancy, as a deficient form of
    fidelity, 184–85
Emperor Constantine, 39
consumer society, borrowing as-
    sumptions from, 135
consumerism, 171
conversion
    baptism as a sacrament of, 37
    moving out of ourselves, 54
Conyers, A. J., 47, 53, 158, 160
core calling, of being ourselves, 16
corporate ladder, as unre-
    al for Martin, 20
Council of Independent
    Colleges (CIC), 6
courage
    as an ally to fidelity, 195
    protecting us, 176, 197
    serving fidelity, 176
    two parts of, 195–97
    virtue of, 194–97
    vocational discern-
        ment demanding, 116
Courage & Calling (Smith), 16
"coworkers" with God, becoming, 45
creative act, vocation as, 112
creative fidelity, 184, 185–86

crises, making vocational reflec-
    tion more urgent, 6
cultural gospel, not seeming
    like good news, 17
culture
    denying the limitations of every
        person's life, 117
    influence of, 80
    making an idol out of busyness, 162
    not encouraging magnanimity, 32
Cunningham, David, 138, 139

damage, 209, 210
dance of life, joining, 134
daring, as an immediate
    response, 195–96
darkness, responding to with light, 24
daughter, birth of Paul Kalanithi's, 150
David, left his job as an engineer, 1
Dead Man Walking (Prejean), 218
death, 200, 201
deathbed, looking back at life on, 126
"decision," meaning to cut or
    to separate, 180
decisions, imagining making, 126–27
"deep gladness," calling bringing, 125
"deep listening," attentive-
    ness enabling, 159
deepest self, being held to
    the word of, 179
desert, men and women fled to, 39–40
desires, 119–20, 121, 136
"desolation," feelings of, 127
despair
    disconnecting from responsibilities
        and relationships, 210
    giving up on everything, 206
    losing the future, 204, 207
    as more dangerous than hatred, 206
    as the opposite of hope, 204, 206
    shoddy work of, 209–10
"detours," caused by other
    callings, 87–88
devil's playground, future as, 199
dharma, living according to, 58
dialogue, between Moses and God, 69
disappointments, middle adults
    living with, 96

discernment, of callings, 108–27
disciples, 67, 132, 215
discipleship
    call to, 38, 48, 51, 52, 132
    disassociated from the more com-
        mon human activities, 41
discoveries, being open to new, 104
discovering, by committing, 20–23
discovery, of gifts and
    circumstances, 131
disillusionment, moments of, 175
distractions, feeding inat-
    tentiveness, 160
divine call to be a Christian, 48–49
divine origin, of call, 140
"Doctrine of the Two Ways," 40, 42, 47
drama, of call stories, 67, 75, 83
dreams, following, 205
dying well, as a calling, 99

early adulthood, commitments in, 22
early Christians, 36–37, 169. *See
    also* Christians
easy life, 62, 202
education, purpose in
    Confucianism, 59
efficiency, replaced self-
    sufficiency, 130
ego, seeking to follow its own way, 25
"ego-centered" desires and
    inclinations, 121
Eilberg, Amy, 56
ekklesia, meaning of, 36
elderly, dependence and growing
    frailty of, 98–99
Emma, Paul Kalanithi's doctor, 148
empathy, adolescents begin-
    ning to learn, 91
entitlement, society en-
    couraging, 170–71
environment, knowing, 118
envying others, refusing to, 167
Epplin, Luke, 128
Eucharist, 171
Evangelical Christians, call as a way
    out of confusion, 134
everyday life, meaning to ordinary
    activities of, 44

evidence, as bad for promises, 177
Examen prayer, of St. Ignatius of
    Loyola, 118–19, 172
excellence, achieving, 196–97
exclusion, patterns of making callings
    impossible, 193
"external calling," as one's "particu-
    lar calling," 43

failures, dealing with wise-
    ly and well, 168
faith, 149, 187, 206, 207–8
faithful friends, as a sturdy shelter, 107
faithfulness, 182–83, 187
falling, as not always pleasant, 133
false esteem, as a lack of humility, 211
false hope, 209
false self, cultivating, 19
the familiar, leaving for
    the unknown, 104
families, being called to leave, 205
Farley, Margaret A.
    on commitments, 22, 100, 188–89
    on fidelity, 179, 183
    on promises, 189
    on sacrificing every-
        thing we are, 191
fear, 74, 75, 76, 77
feelings, 120, 127
fidelity
    Christian understanding of, 186–87
    consequences of not having, 180
    as crucial, 9
    depending on those to whom we
        have committed ourselves, 190
    as essential, 175, 178
    extending beyond relationships
        created by promises, 188
    giving control over time, 186
    justice extending responsi-
        bilities of, 192–94
    maintaining the relationship be-
        tween callings and ourselves, 176
    in a marriage, 176
    as a matter of justice, 188–90
    meaning of, 176
    as mutual and reciprocal, 190
    need for, 177–81

never associated with rigidity or
    immutability, 184
protecting us, 175, 179
for the rest of one's life, 186
safeguarding callings, 181–87
shaping the future in favor of
    our callings, 186
stabilizing our relationship with
    our callings, 177, 179, 197
teaching us how to deal with chal-
    lenges of callings, 175
virtue of, 176–87
finding ourselves, by forgetting
    ourselves, 24–25
"finding your vocation," as a nervous
    guessing game, 136
finite creatures, restricted by
    space and time, 33
first job, as rarely a perfect fit, 102
flourishing
    magnanimity necessary for, 30
    Shalom resulting in, 27
    virtues leading to, 156
    of the world, 55
following a call, not making
    our lives easy, 62
forks in the road, on our vocation-
    al journeys, 104
Fortin, Jack, 117
fortitude, related to patience, 198
forward-looking feature, of
    vocation, 104–5
foundational virtue, loyalty as, 21
framework, for vocational dis-
    cernment, 109–14
Pope Francis, 31, 50–51, 118
St. Francis of Assisi, 24
freedom, of the dominated tak-
    ing priority, 194
friends, 66, 100, 107, 121
friendship, as a calling, 34
Fuller, Millard, 80
fullness of life, as possible, 16
fundamental calling, 34, 35. *See also*
    primary callings
fundamental vocation, of all Chris-
    tians for Luther, 42
future, 101–2, 186, 199–201, 203–4

future orientation, of call, 82

Gandhi, Mahatma, 68, 138
Garber, Steven, 55, 157, 192
Gaudete et Exsultate ("Rejoice
    and Be Glad"), 50
"general calling," 42–43, 141, 142
generosity, 169
"the Gentiles," striving of, 202
*Getting A Life: How to Find Your True
    Vocation* (LaReau), 172
gifts
    callings as, 109–12, 155
    coming to us from God,
        46, 111, 123–24
    discovering after being called, 123
    honest assessment of our, 122
    knowing as truly humble, 165
    shared with others, 150
    using to do good, 14
    vocations as, 139
giving, thinking more
    about than taking, 2
giving and receiving, celebrated by
    African Christians, 203
giving thanks. *See* gratitude
God
    accompanying those he calls, 70
    activity in the world, 68
    appearing in a burning
        bush to Moses, 69
    as the caller, 63
    calling each of us to be ourselves,
        14–17, 20, 49, 66, 116
    calling everyone, 4, 64, 68
    commanded that the Sabbath
        be kept holy, 163
    concerned with the direction
        of our lives, 111
    continuing to create us by
        calling us, 129
    creating us with capacity for
        vocations, 111–12
    depending on us, 28
    as the great civil engineer
        in the sky, 134
    inviting us into his redeem-
        ing work, 66, 72

joining in his perfect life, 138
loving us and want-
    ing our good, 127
meeting every one of Moses's
    objections, 70–71
presence of, 119
punishment of, 76
sending prophets
    for Muslims, 57–58
summoning us through
    our callings, 13
voice of as the echo of our indi-
    vidual voice, 143
wanting everyone who is willing
    to be called, 64
wanting our good, 109
working with our abilities
    and aptitudes, 123
God-Doctor, saving us
    from death, 147
a good life, 99
good news, receiving a call as, 62
good of others, devoting
    ourselves to, 23
"the good of reason," 214, 215, 216
good shepherd, Gospel story of, 136
good things, 172, 183
good way to live, discovering, 14
goodness, acts of contributing to
    God's mission, 29
goods, 65, 180, 192, 196
grace, praying for, 118
grammar of call, 56, 77
gratitude, 157, 169–72, 205, 206
great enterprises, callings as, 197
greed, 199, 204
Grisez, Germain, 28
growth, resistance to genuine, 136
gun violence, tragedies of, 103

Habitat for Humanity, founder of, 80
Hahnenberg, Edward P.,
    5, 41, 43, 49, 55
happiness, 17, 24, 125–26
Hardy, Lee, 28, 46
hatred, opposing love, 206
Hauerwas, Stanley, 9–10
Haughey, John C., 53–54, 124

healing, hope concerning
   itself with, 209
"hearing," as selective, 161
hearts, listening to our, 119
Hebrews (Book of), on drawing
   hope from those who have
   gone before, 212
heroic savior, vision of
   the doctor as, 147
heroism, call tempting us to, 151
"hierarchy of holiness," 40
higher education, growing interest
   in vocation, 5–6
Himes, Michael J., 120
Hinduism, 58–59
Hippocratic oath, 142
holiness
   different ways to pursue, 50
   as exclusive to monks, nuns,
      and priests, 40
   focus on, 51
   of life, 56–57
   link with the religious and
      priestly life, 41
Hollenbach, David, 194
Holy Spirit, 75, 123
honesty
   about ourselves, 116
   in assessing our gifts, 122
   having, 156
   of patients, 149
   of prayer, 121
hope
   call and, 204–8
   keeping us focused, 9
   as one of the three theologi-
      cal virtues, 198
   patience as the protector of, 213–19
   work of, 208–13
human beings
   all can receive the gift of call, 139
   made to journey and grow, 21
   responsible, 159
   as social beings, 193
   "wired to serve," 23
human need, for something meaningful and promising, 6

human traveler or wayfarer, a
   Christian as, 213
humble people, 166–67, 168
humility, 164–68, 211
humor, 168
hurrying, trying to drown
   out sorrow, 214
hurt, reluctance about getting, 132

identity, 19, 22, 82, 163
identity issues, of Moses, 69
St. Ignatius of Loyola,
   118–19, 126, 127
ignorance, acknowledging, 212
image of God (*imago
   Dei*), 17–20, 35, 53
impatience, 213, 214
inattentiveness, 160, 161
inauthenticity, society encouraging, 19
independence, claiming
   from parents, 93
industrial revolution, outcome of, 130
Infancy Gospel of Thomas, 90
infants, baptism of, 41
infants and young children, cannot
   understand being called, 89
infidelity, terrible cost of, 189
ingenuity, 182
ingratitude, 170, 171
"inner demons," struggling with, 195
integrated life, knowing sorrow and joy, 215
integrity, 21, 33, 215
intellectual conversion, 54
"interdependent character of
   life," for Hindus, 58
interruptions, as callings we
   should embrace, 103–4
intimacy, with God, 65
invitation, of a call, 83
Isaiah, fear turned to
   confidence, 73–78
Islam, 57

St. James, 51, 52, 217
James and John, calling Jesus aside, 25
Jayber Crow, 88, 102
Jayber Crow, Wendell Berry's novel, 87

Jeff (Paul Kalanithi's friend), reaction
    to a "difficult complication," 147
Jeremiah
    "appointed" as a prophet before he
        was born, 63, 89
    becoming friends with God, 63–64
    not some superhuman creature, 90
    as one of a kind, 67
    pushing back against God's call, 74
Jesus
    addressed anxiety, 200
    "calling" to grow and
        to learn, 90–91
    calling us into a relationship, 134
    as an example of humility, 166
    in the garden of Gethsemane, 214
    as "the great physician," 141
    introduction of himself to Saul, 79
    keeping his eyes fixed on
        his work, 203, 215
    providing for the care of his
        mother Mary, 205
    on servant leadership, 202
    story about a man who forgot he
        was going to die, 200
    transgressed established
        boundaries, 4–5
    went to Jerusalem to suf-
        fer and die, 24
Jethro (also called Reuel), 64, 69
Jewish ancestors, of Christians
    called by God, 37
Jewish people, called to repen-
    tance for sins, 57
job market, demands of, 130
jobs, 34, 92–93
John, call of discipleship to, 51, 52
Pope John Paul II, on
    solidarity, 193–94
John the Baptist, as harbinger, 73
Pope John XXIII, on solidarity, 193
Johnson, Kelly, 216
Jonah, 121–22
Jordan, Clarence, 80, 81
journey. *See also* vocational journey(s)
    calling as, 87
    describing living vocationally, 3

as a fitting metaphor for
    living, 7–8, 88
not understanding until
    we walk it, 100
stages of, 88–99
virtues for beginning, 155–73
journeyers, formed by the jour-
    ney itself, 105–6
joy
    called life bringing forth, 14, 203
    calling bringing the sense of, 125
    coming from a calling as
        we live it, 126
    filled a dying man's days, 150
    patience resisting forces
        overwhelming, 217
    of the resurrection, 215
    "The Servant Song" on sharing
        with sorrow, 150
    in step six in vocational dis-
        cernment, 125–27
Judaism, 56, 57
just persons, living with oth-
    ers in mind, 187
justice
    allowing the pursuit of life-
        giving callings, 176
    answering the call of, 27–28
    closely linked to fidelity, 175
    innate hunger and thirst for, 26
    steadying us in our callings, 197
    virtue of, 187–94

Kalanithi, Paul, 8, 143–51
Kant, Immanuel, 120
"keeping the Sabbath holy," 163
keeping things the way things are, 132
Khadija, comforting Muhammad, 76
King, Martin Luther, Jr., 73, 94
kingdom of God, 202, 203–4, 206, 208
Koinonia Farms, founder of, 80

laity, 40, 51
LaReau, Renee
    on discovery of one's vocation, 106
    on God inviting along our voca-
        tional journeys, 111
    on humility, 165, 167, 168

on the inner conviction of
doing good, 126
on jotting down things for which
we are grateful, 172
on silence unclutter-
ing our minds, 163
Last Judgment, parable of, 194
late and older adulthood, 96–99
learning, as a struggle, 135
LeBlanc, David, 218, 219
LeBlanc, Eula, 218, 219
LeBlanc, Lloyd, patience of, 218–19
LeBlanc, Vickie, 219
lesser callings, as worthy, 27–29
Let Your Life Speak (Palmer), 14, 119
Levoy, Gregg, 120
Lewis, C. S., 134, 199, 202
lies, 16, 74, 122
life. *See* lives
life transitions, 8
lifelong process, vocational discernment as, 106
lifestyle, putting first as
not a calling, 145
Lilly Endowment Inc., 5
limitations, 117, 140, 142, 151, 168
listening, 119, 121, 122, 159
Listening Hearts, on discernment, 115
"live-for-the-moment" approach, 204
lives
doing something worth-
while with, 23–24
as gifts that bless the world, 35
keeping on course with fidelity, 182
leading magnanimous, 16
living deeply divided, 15
living for today, 202–4
locating in relation to certain
possibilities, 181
"from the outside in, not the
inside out," 15
responding to mundane parts of, 31
as a sacrifice to others
and to God, 126
without creative fidelity, 186
"living for the moment," assuming scarcity, 203

"living for today," as ad-
vised by Jesus, 204
"living in the future," as
Screwtape wants, 200
living magnanimously, 29–33
living responsibly, call to, 54
living vocationally
blessings and benefits from, 14
bringing challenges, setbacks,
doubts, hardships, and
heartbreaks, 35
freeing us to imagine, 14
giving freedom to
be who we are, 19
impact of, 2
leading to magnanimity, 31
making life better for others, 13
managing challenges and
frustrations, 174
as more than a career or a lifelong
commitment, 157–58
pertaining to all of life, 2
requiring multiple callings, 33
seizing opportuni-
ties to do good, 28
testifying that call-
ings are dynamic, 3
through the later stages of life, 98
virtues going hand in hand, 173
as a way out of emotional and
spiritual malaise, 6
loneliness, 211
Lonergan, Bernard, 53–54
longings of our hearts, coming
as a calling, 27
Lord's Supper, as the center of a
grateful life, 171
losses, in older and late
adulthood, 97, 98
love
acts of as spiritually significant, 44
callings deepening our
capacity to, 192
casting out fear, 77
of God and one's neighbor, 42
of Lucy for Paul Kalanithi in his
final months, 150

love *(continued)*
  requiring both sorrowing
    and rejoicing, 215
  requiring paying attention, 160
  transcending ourselves in, 2, 6
  vulnerability required to
    experience, 189
  wedding ring as an endur-
    ing sign of, 176
  world crying out for, 27
Love in the Ruins (Percy),
  scene from, 161
loyalty, 21
Lucy, 146, 147–48, 150
Lumen Gentium, 50
lust, 199
Luther, Martin, 42, 43, 45, 141

MacIntyre, Alasdair, 65
Mackin, Theodore, 191
magnanimity, 30, 31–32, 34
magnanimous life, living, 29–33
making a life, more important than
  making a living, 3
Marcel, Gabriel, 182, 183, 184, 185
marginalized groups, tak-
  ing priority, 194
"market," forced subsistence farmers
  into cities, 130
marriage
  beyond repair, 191
  celibacy as better than, 41
  fidelity in, 176
  giving meaning through mu-
    tual promise, 189
  of Lucy and Paul Kalanithi, 149
  partners called to support and love
    one another, 33
  in which each spouse devel-
    ops virtues, 156
Martin, James, 19, 119
McIntosh, Mark A., 53
meaning and purpose, in middle adulthood, 95
meaningful past, cutting off, 206
medicine as a profession,
  141–42, 144, 145

medieval Christians, thinking of
  death every day, 201
King Melchizedek,
  blessing Abraham, 64
memory, fear marking, 74
Mercer, Joyce Ann, 99
middle adulthood, living vocationally in, 94–96
milestones, in callings, 179
Miller, Arthur, 177
Miller, Keith Graber, 40, 114
minor callings, 177
Miriam, Moses's sister, 205
misfortunes, grateful people more
  responsive to, 170
mistakes, 102, 103, 168
Mohrmann, Margaret E., 54, 123
monastic Christianity, as a protest
  against the world, 48
monastic vocation, Bonhoeffer on, 48
monasticism, 40, 41, 43
St. Monica, worried about her
  son Augustine, 217
moral clarity, needed to practice medicine, 145
moral conversion, responding to
  the call to, 54
mortality, 97, 151
Moses, 68–73, 74, 205
Muhammad, 68, 75
Murdoch, Iris, 25
Muslims, at complete
  service to God, 57
mysteries, vocations as, 111

narrative pattern, stories of call
  fitting into, 65
need(s)
  to be brave, 194–95
  for a call, 62
  of the poor taking priority, 194
  of the world, 124
NetVUE (Network for Voca-
  tion in Undergraduate
  Education), 5–6, 9
neurosurgeons, as masters of
  many fields, 147

neurosurgery, as a calling and
    sacred thing, 149
New Testament, on gratitude, 169
Newman, John Henry, 133, 136, 137
Niebuhr, H. Richard, 54
Nostra Aetate, on religious
    traditions, 139
"novelty," pursuing false images of
    creativity, 211–12
the "now," 216–17

objections, raised by Moses, 71
obligations, 34, 120, 159, 188
occasion of a call, as a significant
    turning point, 67
offered life, called life as, 202–3
older adulthood. *See* late and
    older adulthood
ongoing growth and conver-
    sion, calling to, 53
openness, to call, 131
opposition, to callings, 195
option for the poor, illumining an
    understanding of fidelity, 194
ordinary Christians. *See* laity
Organ, Jerome M., 52, 101, 102, 113
original sin, baptism cleansing, 41–42
"originality," pursuing false images of
    creativity, 211–12
others
    being intertwined with and
        dependent upon, 7
    calling(s) drawing us
        to respond to, 24
    calling(s) from prom-
        ises made to, 177
    Christians growing open to
        narratives of, 5
    Christians open engagement with, 4
    comparing ourselves to as a
        waste of time, 18
    devoting ourselves to
        the good of, 23
    gifts shared with, 150
    goods enabling us to give
        ourselves for, 196
    having unreasonable
        expectations, 167

just persons having in mind, 187
listening to, 122
lives as sacrifice to, 126
living vocationally making
    life better for, 13
making things better for, 2, 13
not separating our well-being
    from that of, 192
presence of on our vocation-
    al journeys, 107
self, exchanging for one more
    pleasing to, 19
self-forgetfulness binding us to, 22
serving, 20
vocational discernment opening
    our eyes to, 124–25
ourselves, discovering by
    committing, 20–23

pain, bearing continually as
    a physician, 146
Palmer, Parker J., 14–15, 52–53, 119
"paralysis of analysis," suf-
    fering from, 116
parenthood, calling of, 149
parents, 33–34, 93, 99–100, 168
"particular calling," of a Christian, 141
passions, 120
passivity, patience compared to, 214
past, telling us about how we might
    be called, 118–19
pastoral role, of a physician, 146
path to life, unfolding before us, 18
paths, 62, 101
patience
    as an ally to hope, 9
    protecting hope, 213–19
    sustaining hope, 198, 204
patients, facing both
    life and death, 149
pattern of call, in the Bible's stories, 62
patterns, suggesting pos-
    sible callings, 118
St. Paul, 81–82, 123, 150
paying attention. *See also* attentiveness
    as a virtue, 157–64
"people of God," Christians as, 37
people of the Way, Christians as, 213

pep talk, distinguishing from a call, 77
Percy, Walker, 161
"the perfect choice," not making, 102
perfection, as the endgame for any-
     one God calls, 133
Perkins, William, 141
perseverance, 185, 196, 197
person we want to become, focus-
     ing first on, 113
Peter, call of discipleship to, 51, 52
Pieper, Josef, 211, 215, 219
"places of responsibility,"
     for callings, 49
plan, 80, 134, 148
"plan" idea of call, 135
Pohl, Christine D., 170, 171, 172
the poor, 193, 194
possibilities, 13, 104, 180–81
pouches, Native American for need-
     ing "to be brave," 194
prayer
     attentiveness as, 158
     avoiding, 121
     deepening dispositions to
          gratitude, 171–72
     importance to Muslims, 57
     as indispensable to discern-
          ing callings, 121
     keeping us honest, 121
     of Lloyd LeBlanc, 218–19
     of St. Francis, 24
     of St. Ignatius of
          Loyola, 118–19, 172
     as the voicing of hope, 219
Prejean, Helen, Sr., 125, 218
presence, as characteristic of cre-
     ative fidelity, 190
the present, living truthfully in, 201
present reality, connecting to future
     fulfillment, 186
present time, capacity to live in, 105
preservation, as the work of hope, 213
presumption, 210–11, 217
pride, 167, 209–10
the priesthood, language of calling or
     vocation associated with, 41
priesthood of Christ, 42, 50
primary callings, 112, 113, 114

primary vocation
     of every Christian, 114
     of the Jewish people, 57
prodigal son, choosing badly, 129
professional conduct, codes of, 142
professions, 141, 142–43, 151. *See also*
     medicine as a profession
Programs for the Theological Explora-
     tion of Vocation (PTEV), 5
"promise," of the image of God, 53
promises
     callings making our lives a
          tapestry of, 188
     changing the moral meaning of a
          relationship, 189
     connecting us with life, 178
     creating obligations and responsi-
          bilities, 175, 188
     forgetting when something more
          alluring comes along, 179
     holding us in a web of
          connection, 206
     renunciations at the
          heart of every, 181
     ruling out other possibilities, 180
"Protestant work ethic," 47
Protestantism, saved vocation
     from captivity, 47
providential care, of God
     through callings, 45
prudence, compared to at-
     tentiveness, 157
pusillanimity, 32, 207
pusillanimous person, 32–33

Quentin, on broken promises, 177
quiet, learning to be, 119
quiet time, by ourselves
     as necessary, 162

Radcliffe, Timothy, 166
radical disruption, in biblical calls, 67
Rambachan, Ananta-
     nand, on *dharma*, 58
Ray, Darby Kathleen, 41, 125, 161
"real world," entering, 105
reality
     awakening within us, 158

basing vocational dis-
  cernment on, 117
being authentic by living in, 54
devil keeping us from, 200
perceiving accurately, 159
that life and relationships all
  require work, 156
rebirth, of Christians, 37
reconstruction, need for, 137
redemption, vocational
  narratives of, 103
reflexive feature, in call, 134
"reflexivity," of all God's callings, 133
refugees, vocational paths redirected to help, 103
regret, from refusing certain callings, 33
reign of God, becoming a
  "citizen" in, 38
relationships, 58, 60, 188
relative goods, helping achieve absolute good, 192
relaxation and leisure, setting
  aside time for, 163
religious communities, 140, 151
religious conversion, achieving, 54
religious life, language of calling or
  vocation associated with, 41
religious traditions. *See also* tradition
  carrying a history of a
    God who calls, 64
  carrying a vision, 65
  Christian, 81
  interpreting calls, 140
  turning our attention to the
    transcendent, 139
  vocation in other, 55–60
religious vows, of poverty, chastity,
  and obedience, 40
reluctance, to be changed, 133–34
"repair of the world" (*tikkun olam*),
  committing to, 57
rescue, 66, 71–72
response to a call, on a subsequent iteration, 136
responsibility
  to all members of the glob-
    al community, 193

as the center of what we do, 54–55
coming with committed relationships, 94–95
expanding our sense of, 13
greater for young adults, 91
needs evoking a sense of, 125
taking for the future
  with fidelity, 186
too-little and too-much of, 209–10
weight of, 146
woven through every calling
  of our lives, 159
rest and leisure, regular
  practices of, 163
resuscitation, of the concept of vocation, 5
retirement, as a call, 96–97
rhythms of the earth, teaching patience, 218
rich people, having expectations fulfilled, 213
rich young man, 133, 135
riches, being tempted by, 201
right choices, worrying too much
  about making, 101
"right in front" of us, discovering a
  calling that is, 117
"right relationship" with others, justice as all about, 187
Riswold, Caryn, 55
rites of passage, 91, 105
roadmap, call as, 134
Roberts, Robert, 165
routines, days comprised of, 29
Royce, Josiah, 21
ruled-out possibilities, awakened by
  the appeal of, 181

Sabbath, keeping holy, 163
saboteurs, 195, 196
sacred trust, vision of
  medicine as, 147
sacredness, of the call to
  protect life, 146
"salvation history," as the story of God
  and God's dealings, 4
Saul, placed on a new road, 78–83
Schell, Hannah, 21

Schuster, John P., 195
Schuurman, Douglas J.,
    44, 49, 130, 140
Screwtape, 199, 204, 205
Screwtape Letters (Lewis), 199
seasons, to living callings, 155
"second mountain people," 136–37
Second Vatican Council, on not
    having to flee the world
    to find God, 51
secondary callings, 113, 114
secular Protestant vocation,
    Bonhoeffer on, 48
security, humility giving us, 166
seeing ourselves as called, giving deep
    meaning to ordinary details, 29
self
    development of for Confucians, 59
    inseparable from the im-
        age of God, 17–18
    making an appraisal of, 18–19
    making an idol of, 17
    as a mystery unfolding through-
        out our lives, 21
    no such thing as a truly separate
        and autonomous for Confu-
        cians or Hindus, 60
    shaken by disappointments in
        middle adulthood, 95
    true, 16–17
    vocation exclusively or primarily
        focused on, 192
self-centered ways of living, tradition-
    ally known as sin, 121
self-confidence, 76–77, 166
self-deception, 121–22
self-discovery, coming through self-
    forgetfulness, 22
self-enclosed existence,
    breaking out of, 54
self-esteem, as an essential char-
    acter trait, 165
self-forgetfulness, 22, 24, 25
self-interest, life of not requiring
    magnanimity, 32
self-worth, young adult
    questions about, 92
sense of joy, calling bringing, 125

sense of limits, humility giving us, 168
"The Servant Song," on sharing joy
    and sorrow, 150
servants, those following the call
    becoming, 72–73
service, Moses called into, 68–73
Shalom, restoration of, 27
shaping our callings, as a continu-
    ous process, 101
Shaw, Russell, 28
"signs," giving us a sense of
    our callings, 118
silence, activities during
    times of, 162–63
sin, of Isaiah blotted out, 74
sinners, in need of redemption, 76
"situating virtues," 8, 157
Smith, Gordon T., 16,
    18–19, 93, 97, 167
social and political vision, preventing
    "calling" from merging with, 141
social beings, human beings as, 59–60
social institutions, bringing into line
    with vocations, 46–47
social justice, 193
social mobility, encour-
    aged by Calvin, 47
society, understood in an
    organic way, 44
solidarity, 194
Sonnier, Eddie, 218
Sonnier, Gladys, 219
Sonnier, Patrick, 218
Sonniers, Lloyd LeBlanc
    praying for, 219
sorrow, 146, 215
"spark" of the divine, 18
speed, as a luxury of the rich, 213
"spiritual elitism," cri-
    tiqued by Luther, 42
Spiritual Exercises, of Igna-
    tius of Loyola, 126
"spiritual" martyrdom, offering whole
    lives to God, 40
spouses, called every day, 33
stages, of the journey, 88–99
"station," Calvin avoided strong
    emphasis on, 46

"station" or "standing," every
    person having, 44
"stations," turning into callings, 141
steadying or protecting virtues, 197
step back and step back in, calling in
    later adulthood as, 97
stories
    of call, 7, 62–83
    callings as, 3
    vocational, 102–3
story of God, as the framing narrative
    for Christians, 4
straight line, living life as, 87
striving, for the kingdom
    of God, 202, 206
struggle, 135, 137–38
Strydom, Barend, 140
students
    callings of, 34
    as journeyers, 105–6
    keeping lives centered
        and balanced, 182
    not doing well on every exam, 168
stupidity, of impatience, 214
substantial callings, connect-
    ed with vows, 177
successful life, as a relentless-
    ly busy one, 162
suffering, 55, 78, 137, 149

Tarceva, as the best course of
    treatment for Paul Kalani-
    thi's cancer, 148–49
Taylor, Barbara Brown
    on being lost, 104
    on her process of vocational
        discernment, 127
    on learning you are worth more
        than what you can produce, 163
    on people wanting to do something
        that matters, 172–73
    on prayer, 158–59
    on recognizing where we
        actually are, 105
    on successful people as very
        busy people, 162
teachers, looking for, 212
teaching, requiring attentiveness, 160

technical skill, high demands of, 142
technology, 160–61, 213
temporary callings, 177
temptations, 183, 196, 206
St. Teresa of Avila, on prayer, 121
Tertullian, on patience, 214
thanks, becoming ex-
    perts in saying, 172
"theological virtues," directly orient-
    ing us to God, 207
"thread," a calling as like, 100
threats, callings as, 155
"threshold of impossibility," 191
time, 186, 204, 215, 216
"timeful virtues," 198, 220
today, living for, 202–4
tradition. *See also* biblical tradition;
    religious traditions
    carrying a set of shared goods
        and judgments, 65
transcending ourselves, in love
    and service to people
    and projects, 2, 6
transition, from one's career
    into retirement, 96
transitional time, for young adults, 92
treasures, storing up, 200
"trial and error," discern-
    ment including, 115
true fidelity, 185
true self, discovering, 16–17
trust, between doctor and patient, 146
truth of ourselves, continually
    growing into, 53

unbelief, opposing faith, 206
uncertainty, 101, 115
unchosen possibilities, revisiting, 181
unclean lips, meaning false
    speech, lies, 74
unemployment, as the
    greatest vice, 47
unfinished business, late adult-
    hood addressing, 96
unique individual, every hu-
    man being as, 49
"The Universal Call to Holiness,"
    chapter in *Lumen Gentium*, 50

"universal community," callings contributing to, 59
unlimited choice, 129, 130
unreality, tomorrow as, 200
unworthiness, felt by Isaiah, 76

vices, 199, 202
virtues
    becoming persons formed by, 8
    beginning the journey, 155–73
    completing the journey, 198–220
    connection between living vocationally and, 197
    for continuing the journey, 174–97
    defined, 156
    endowing us to excel in life, 173
    magnanimity as one, 30
    practicing to become a self, 17
virtuous person, having
    fewer choices, 182
"virtuous undertakings,"
    callings as, 196
vision
    to guide and inspire our lives, 23
    of Isaiah seeing God in
        the temple, 74, 77
Visions of Vocation (Garber), 192
vocation(s). *See also* calling(s)
    as about all of life, 13
    as about who we are
        and what we do, 55
    as both a call from outside
        the self and a discovery of
        our true self, 66
    capacity for, 111–12
    Catholics talking about a
        "shortage" of, 42
    Christian theology of, 4, 7
    of Christians, 37
    combining our passions
        with our gifts, 126
    connecting to ordinary life, 43
    connection with magnanimity, 31
    of creatures to exist
        as themselves, 18
    disastrous misunderstandings of, 48
    discovery of as a process, 106

of every child to come more
    fully to life, 91
exploring the traditions, 36–61
finding, 1
first Christians and, 36–39
historical broadening, 42–51
historical narrowing of, 39–42
meaning of, 36
mistaken understandings of, 8
as mysteries of God's love
    and goodness, 111
not all about me and what is
    good for me, 192
not exclusively about careers, 96
other approaches to, 51–55
in other religious traditions, 55–60
permeating every aspect
    of our lives, 13
personal character of, 52
scheming for ways to escape, 175
spanning the whole of our lives, 88
timely moment for, 5–6
vocational detours, as unavoidable, 103–4
vocational discernment
    demanding the courage to
        be patient, 116
    framework for, 8, 109–14
    as inherently provisional, 106
    as a lifelong process, 106
    needing to open our eyes
        to others, 124–25
    no perfect method for, 115
    as a regular practice
        of our lives, 113
    step one, 116–18
    step two, 118–19
    step three, 119–22
    step four, 122–24
    step five, 124–25
    step six, 125–27
    stress and anxiety associated with, 102
vocational journey(s), 87–107.
    See also journey
    appreciating and enjoying, 105
    conclusions drawn from, 99–106

dangers and warnings
    along our, 128–51
friends and companions on, 167
marked with more zigzags than
    straight lines, 88
moving in circles, 102
not taking alone, 107
preparing for, 7
virtues for completing, 198–220
virtues for continuing, 174–97
vocational question, deepest
    as "Who am I?" 15
vocational stories, 102–3
"vocational vision," of
    Confucianism, 60
vulnerability, required to expe-
    rience love, 189

wants and choices, being
    saved from, 129
"The Way of Life," busyness as, 162
The Way of Life (Badcock), 109
the way things are, as the way God
    wills them to be, 45
Weber, Max, 47
wedding ring, as a sign, 176
Weil, Simone, 157
well-being, not separating ours from
    that of others, 192
what are we hearing, as step three in
    vocational discernment, 119–22
what brings us joy, as step six in voca-
    tional discernment, 125–27
what do we do well, as step four in
    vocational discernment, 122–24
When Breath Becomes Air
    (Kalanithi), 144
where are we needed, as step five in
    vocational discernment, 124–25
where we are, God calling us, 117
who and where are we, as step one in
    vocational discernment, 116–18

who we are, understanding
    and accepting, 116
who we are meant to be,
    becoming, 14–17
who we will be, as the funda-
    mental issue of vocational
    discernment, 113
Wilkin, Robert, 214
Williams, Rowan, 18
words, as the surgeon's only tool to
    develop trust, 146
work
    all as essentially equal, 44
    done in hope accepting the clarifi-
        cation of pain, 209
    of hope, 208–13
    providing focus, order,
        and stability, 46
    of Saul interrupted on the road
        from Jerusalem to Damascus, 79
    should not overly de-
        fine our lives, 163
world
    continually needing to be
        transformed, 49
    stepping outside of our usual, 164
worldly structures, 47–48

young adulthood, as "vocational
    territory," 91–94
young adults
    constant shifting experienced by, 92
    experiencing setbacks
        and defeats, 196
    future opening the door to fear
        and anxiety, 199
    seeking callings, 93–94
    separating from their parents, 93
    told to choose their best life, 129
young people, making lifelong com-
    mitments, 22

Made in the USA
Coppell, TX
09 July 2021

58702023R00152